27

Jacques Pépin
LA TECHNIQUE

Also by Jacques Pépin

The Other Half of the Egg with Helen McCully
The Great Cooks Cookbook, James Beard et al.
A French Chef Cooks at Home

Jacques Pépin
LA TECHNIQUE

The Fundamental Techniques of Cooking: An Illustrated Guide

Photographs by Léon Perer

NYT 𝕿𝖎𝖒𝖊𝖘 BOOKS

 For information, address: Times Books, a division of Quadrangle/The New York Times Book Co., Inc., Three Park Avenue, New York, New York 10016. Manufactured in the United States of America. Published simultaneously in Canada by Optimum Publishing Company Limited, Montreal.

10 9 8 7 6 5

Book design: Paul Hanson

Library of Congress Cataloging in Publication Data

Pépin, Jacques.
La technique.

Includes index.
1. Cookery. I. Title.
TX651.P4 1976 641.5 76-9733
ISBN 0-8129-0610-1

To the chefs
who sweat to create friendliness
and cordiality among men

Contents

Introduction

I HAVE OFTEN NOTICED when speaking with people, or teaching a cooking class, that the greatest drawback to a good performance in the kitchen is an inadequate knowledge of basic techniques. You may be extraordinarily creative and imaginative in the kitchen, but you cannot take advantage of these qualities if you do not know the basics. Solid background is essential, and must precede inventiveness. An artistic mind can create a stunning decoration for a cold glazed salmon, but the dish will be triumphant only if the salmon is first properly cleaned and poached, and the aspic rich and crystal clear. This requires hard work and love.

When professionals work with ease and rapidity, their performance relies heavily on long years of practice and discipline. To talk of the "tricks," as they are often referred to by people amazed at the dexterity of a master chef, is delusive and pejorative to the experts. There are no secrets or tricks, only *tours de main* (feats of skill), that can be acquired with prolonged effort.

This is not a book of recipes, per se, although many are featured to exemplify a point. With the help of pictures—is not a picture worth a thousand words?—it intends to acquaint you with the base of cooking. The techniques go into the core, the center, the heart of the profession. They teach what makes things work the way they work.

We do not pretend to have explicated the whole spectrum of cooking skills; in fact, we may have taken for granted very simple, ordinary chores such as peeling a potato, or melting butter. Even with the help of pictures, some of the techniques, like turning mushrooms, will be difficult to perform, and will require patience and perseverance. Others, like peeling and seeding a tomato, or making a rabbit out of an olive, should be mastered instantly. You will discover that there is something quite satisfying about conquering dishes that may have frustrated you in the kitchen before. As a reward, knowledge of the basics will allow you to assert ideas positively in the kitchen, to remedy otherwise catastrophic miscalculations, and to tackle any kind of recipe because you will comprehend the chemistry of food.

Start with simple techniques and work gradually toward more involved and complicated skills which may have to be performed several times before being completely assimilated. Remember, you are not learning new recipes, you are acquiring a new way of cooking; you are going into apprenticeship.

The Basics

1. Position du Couteau *(Holding the Knife)*

A<small>N</small> <small>APPRENTICE CHEF</small> cannot "graduate to the stove" until he has mastered the basic techniques for correctly chopping, dicing, mincing and slicing vegetables, fruits or meat. Perfectly prepared vegetables not only have an attractive texture, but add a good "bite" and taste to the finished dish. Practice, obviously, is of the very essence, and good knives are just as important. Knives should be sharpened professionally at least once every year or two. In the interim, keep a good edge with either a steel or carborundum sharpener.

1. Handling your knife properly is your first concern. Hold the item to be cut with fingertips tucked under, the blade "rests" and slides directly against the middle section of your fingers. The knife follows, in fact, "glued" to the fingers and slides up and down the fingers at the same rate all the time. The speed at which the fingers move back determines the thickness of the slices.

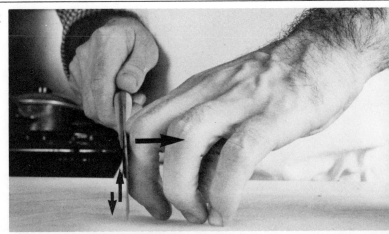

2. To mince an onion, peel it and cut into halves through the root. Place one of the halves flat side down and, holding your fingers and knife properly,

3. cut vertical slices from one end to the other, up to, but not through, the root end. The knife does not go in a straight down motion while cutting, but rather in a down and back motion at the same time.

4. Holding the knife flat, cut 3 or 4 horizontal slices from top to bottom, up to the root end.

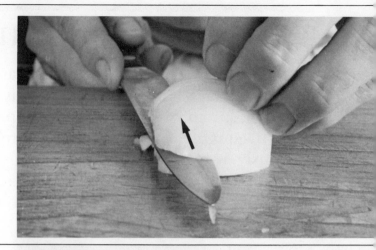

5. Finally, cut across the onion, again up to the root end. (If the dice is not fine enough, chop some more with a large knife.)

6. To slice a potato, place it on its flattest side so that it does not roll under your fingers. If the potato is not stable, cut a slice off so the potato can sit firmly on the cut end. Slice to desired thickness by controlling the progress of the fingers that hold the potato in place.

7. To chop parsley, use a bigger knife. Place the blade horizontally on the chopping block and gather the washed parsley top into a tight ball. Slice the bunch across.

8. Slice, going down and forward, or down and backward, sliding the knife along the fingers.

9. Holding the handle firmly in one hand, the other hand relaxed on top of the blade (this hand does not apply much pressure on the blade, but rather directs it), bring the front of the blade down first, then the back. Repeat in a staccato and rapid up and down motion until the parsley is finely chopped. Draw the pieces together in a heap as you go along.

10. To dice an eggplant, hold the eggplant firmly with the tips of your fingers and cut lengthwise in equal slices.

11. Stack 2 or 3 slices on top of each other. Using the same technique, cut into square sticks.

12. Cut the sticks across to form little cubes. Very small cubes or dices of vegetables are called *brunoise*.

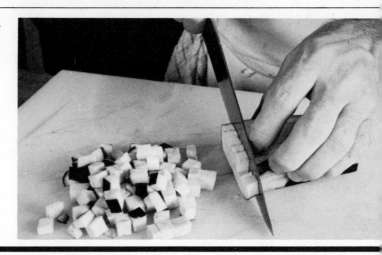

2. Ail *(Garlic)*

THERE ARE MANY TYPES of garlic readily available, the best of which is the smaller "red garlic," so-called because of the reddish color of the skin. Garlic affects foods in different ways depending on how it is cut and used. You can roast a chicken with 3 full heads (about 40 unpeeled cloves) of garlic and serve them with the chicken. Guests can pick up the cloves and suck the tender insides out of the peel. Prepared this way, it is astounding how mild and sweet garlic is. The scent and taste are barely noticeable. However, the smell of one clove of garlic, peeled, crushed, chopped fine and added at the last minute to sautéed potatoes or string beans, or to a salad, can permeate a whole room and remain on your breath for hours. The same crushed chopped garlic—when cooked slowly for a long time, as in a stew—loses most of its pungency and harmonizes, quite modestly, with the other herbs and ingredients. Crushing the garlic releases more essential oil and gives more flavor than slicing it or leaving it whole. Raw garlic chopped to a purée, is the most powerful. Mixed with olive oil, it becomes the garlic-loaded mayonnaise of Provence (*aioli* or *ailloli*), known as *beurre de Provence* (the butter of Provence).

One important point: When making scampi, escargots, sautéed potatoes, zucchini or any dish where the garlic is added at the end and slightly cooked, be careful not to burn it. Burned garlic hopelessly ruins a dish.

1. Holding the "head" on a bias, crush with the heel of your hand to separate the cloves.

2. Using the flat side of a heavy knife, smack the clove just enough to crack the shell open.

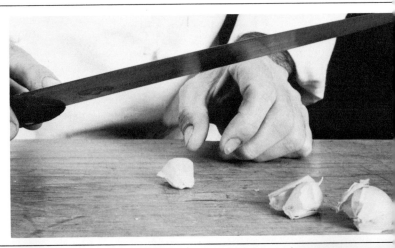

3. Remove the clove from the shell and cut off the root end.

4. Place the blade flat on the clove and smack it down and forward to crush the clove to a pulp.

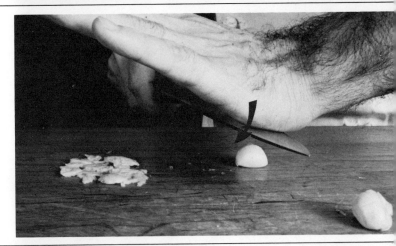

5. Chop to a puree.

3. Poireaux *(Leeks)*

L EEKS, CALLED THE ASPARAGUS OF THE POOR in France, are greatly underrated in the United States. This hardy winter vegetable is unbeatable for soups. It is said that Nero ate leek soup every day to clarify his voice. Leek is great cooked in water and served with a vinaigrette sauce and excellent in stews and quiches.

1. Leek has to be cleaned properly because the center is usually full of sand. Trim off the greener part of the leaves. Keep it for clarifying consommé, technique 38.

2. Remove the roots.

3. Remove the dried and yellowish skin around the leek, if any.

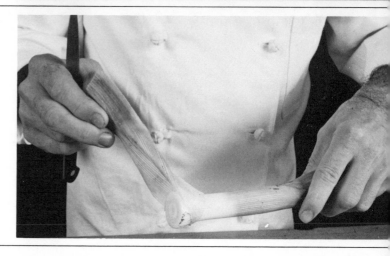

4. Holding the leek, leafy side down, insert your knife through the white part approximately 2 inches down from the root, and cut through the entire length of the leek.

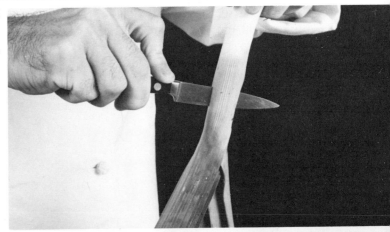

5. Repeat 2 or 3 times to split the leek open. Wash thoroughly under cold water.

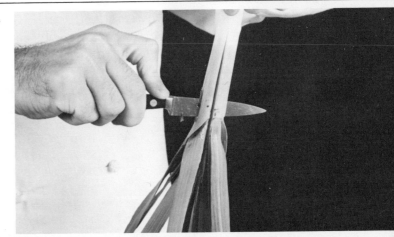

4. Préparation de la Salade *(Cleaning Salad)*

L ETTUCE, PROBABLY THE BEST-KNOWN SALAD GREEN the world over, is also one of the most delicate and delectable. Bibb, oak leaf or Boston lettuce go well with a light oil and vinegar or a cream dressing because they are very tender and mild. Escarole, curly endive and the like can support a stronger, garlicky dressing.

1. Holding the lettuce upside down, cut around the center to remove the core and get the leaves loose. Remove the spoiled leaves.

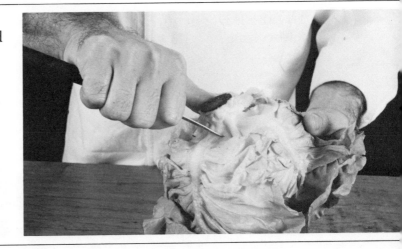

2. The larger, tougher outside leaves should have the top and center rib removed. Only the tender pieces on both sides of the rib are used.

3. With the larger leaves removed, cut through the center rib to separate each leaf into halves.

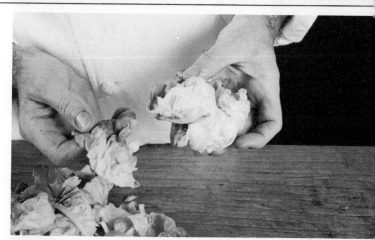

4. Separate the small leaves of the heart and leave them whole. Wash the lettuce in a lot of cold water. Lift up from the water and place on a towel.

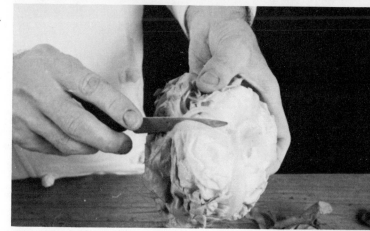

5. Dry the leaves gently, a few at a time, to avoid bruising.

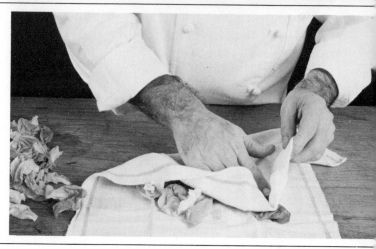

6. Or, place in a salad dryer and

7. spin a few times to extract as much water as possible from the salad.

8. It should be dry and fluffy. Remember that the best dressing will be ruined if watered down by a salad not sufficiently dried. Keep refrigerated in a towel until serving time. A tender lettuce, such as Boston, is never tossed with dressing ahead of time because it becomes wilted very fast.

5. Tomates *(Tomatoes)*

PEELED AND SEEDED TOMATOES are a requisite ingredient in many recipes. They are used to make *boules de tomates*—a perfect garnish for roasts, chicken and the like—and *fondue de tomates,* which is a fresh tomato sauce that's both easy to make and very good.

TOMATES ÉMONDÉES *(Peeling and Seeding Tomatoes)*

1. Remove the stem from the tomato using the point of a knife. Dip the tomatoes in boiling water—they should be fully immersed—and let sit for approximately 20 seconds if well ripened. If the tomatoes are green, it will take a little longer for the skin to come loose.

2. Transfer the tomatoes to a basin of cold water. When cold enough to handle, remove and peel. The skin should slip off easily.

3. Cut the tomato into halves widthwise—not through the stem.

4. Press gently to extrude all the seeds. You now have pure tomato flesh or pulp. The seeds and skin can be used in a stock or long-simmered sauce. (An alternate method is to impale the tomato on a fork and, holding it by the fork handle, roll it over an open flame. "Roast" it for 15 to 20 seconds; the skin should slide off easily.)

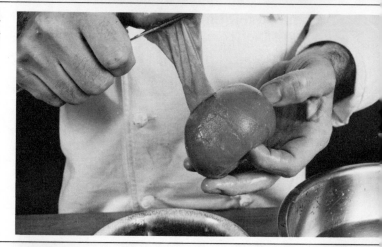

BOULES DE TOMATES *(Tomato Balls for Garnish)*

1. Peel and seed the tomato. Cut each half in two.

2. Place a tomato quarter in a strong kitchen towel, the outside against the towel.

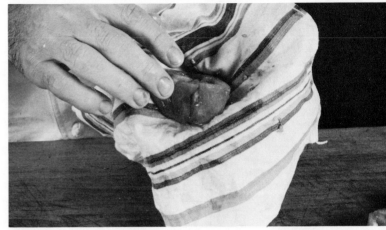

3. Squeeze the tomato pulp to form a nice small fleshy ball.

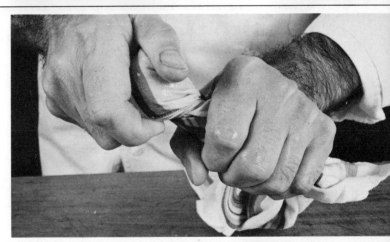

4. Sprinkle with salt and a dash of ground pepper. Moisten with melted butter and heat in a hot oven for a few minutes before serving.

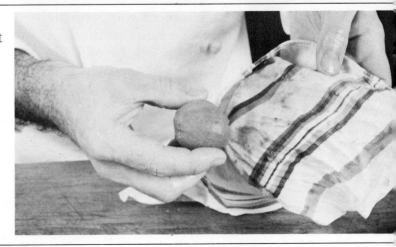

FONDUE DE TOMATES (*Tomato Sauce*)

1. Peel and seed the tomatoes and cut coarsely into 1-inch cubes (*Tomates concassées* in French). Prepare 3 cups of cubed tomatoes and proceed with the recipe below.

1 *tablespoon good olive oil*
1 *tablespoon chopped onion*
3 *cups cubed tomatoes*
Salt and freshly ground black pepper
1 *clove garlic, crushed and chopped very fine*
1 *tablespoon tomato paste, optional*
½ *teaspoon chopped hot serrano pepper,*
    optional

Heat the oil in a saucepan. When it is hot, add the chopped onion and sauté for 1 minute. Add the tomatoes and the salt and pepper to taste. Cook on a high heat for 5 to 6 minutes to evaporate some of the liquid. Add the garlic, and the tomato paste if the tomatoes are too watery or too pale in color. Cook 3 to 4 minutes and taste for seasoning. Add more salt and pepper, if necessary, and some serrano pepper if you like your sauce hot.

6. Oignons Glacés (*Glazed Onions*)

G LAZED ONIONS ARE EXTENSIVELY USED as a garnish in French cooking for *coq au vin, boeuf bourguignon,* veal chop *grandmère,* chicken *Boivin* and the like.

1. Use tiny, white onions (unfortunately hard to get at certain times of the year) the size of a jumbo olive. Peel the onion by removing a small slice at the stem and one at the root end.

2. For 24 onions, you need 1 tablespoon butter, ¼ teaspoon salt and 1 teaspoon sugar. Place the onions in a saucepan in one layer. They should not overlap. Add enough water to barely cover the top of the onions. Add the butter, salt and sugar. Place on high heat and boil until all the water is evaporated (about 18 to 20 minutes). Reduce the heat to medium and shake the saucepan or turn the onions to brown them on all sides.

3. The boiling of the water is necessary because it cooks the onions. When the water has evaporated, what is left is butter and sugar. The onions will glaze in that mixture in a few minutes. If they do not glaze properly on direct heat, place for a few minutes under the broiler. Transfer the glazed onions to a plate until needed.

7. Dégraissage des Sauces *(Skimming Fat)*

WHEN SAUCES ARE COOKING, the fat or scum comes up to the surface of the liquid and has to be skimmed off.

1. With the sauce simmering gently, push the top layer of fat or scum to one side of the pan.

2. With the spoon flat, scoop the fat from the side when it is accumulated.

3. Be sure to scoop only the fat. Repeat every 10 or 15 minutes, as needed, while the sauce is simmering.

8. Décoration en Beurre *(Butter Decoration)*

1. To make hollow butter shells, you need a special tool with small teeth and a curved blade. The success depends entirely on the consistency of the butter. If the butter is too hard, the "peel" will not curl up, and you will be scraping shavings off the stick. If the butter is too soft, the blade will dig into it and make a mush. It is a trial and error procedure. Place each *coquille* (shell) in iced water.

2. For an attractive butter piece to put on a cheese tray, cut a stick of butter in half. Decorate each half, top and sides, with the tines of a fork.

3. The most difficult and the fanciest way of serving butter is to make flowers. The temperature, hence, the consistency, of the butter is the key. (See step 1.) Using the point of a small paring knife, scrape the top of the butter several times to build up a long bank of butter on top of the blade.

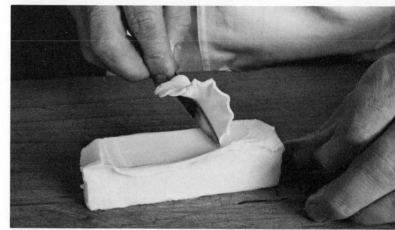

4. Curl the butter on the tip of the knife—jagged surface inside the "flower"—into one large corolla.

5. Curl another strip tighter and

6. place the curled strip in the center of the first corolla

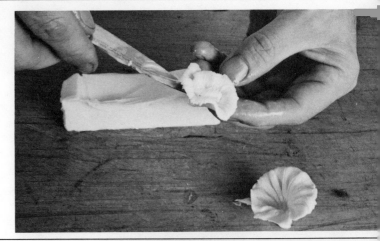

7. to form the heart of the flower.

8. Different butter decorations.

9. Rose en Pomme de Terre *(Potato Rose)*

OFTEN RESTAURANTS GARNISH with flowers sculpted from potatoes, carrots or white turnips. To avoid discoloration, the potatoes, after being carved, should be blanched in boiling water for 1 minute and cooled off under cold water. Then they can be soaked in a mixture of red food coloring and water to obtain a nice pink color. Carve a whole "bouquet" of these flowers and stand each one on a toothpick in a carved orange or grapefruit basket, technique 16. Surround with curly parsley.

1. Using a small sharp knife, cut a pointed shape from a peeled potato. Trim the shape to make it look like a child's toy top.

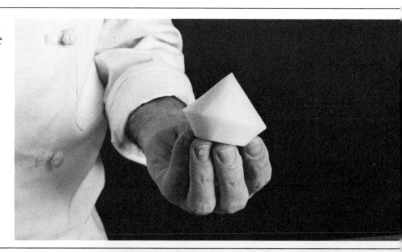

2. Make slits all around the base to simulate petals.

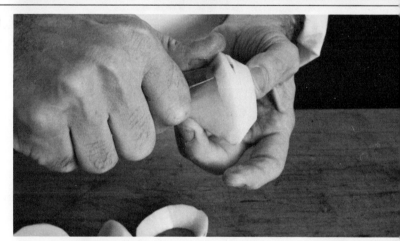

3. Using the tip of the knife, trim the edge all around above the petals.

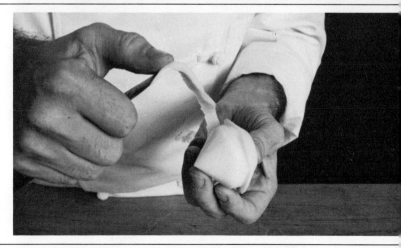

4. Pull out the strip of potato, exposing the bottom layer of petals.

5. Keep cutting layers of slits, alternating the petals to get the right effect.

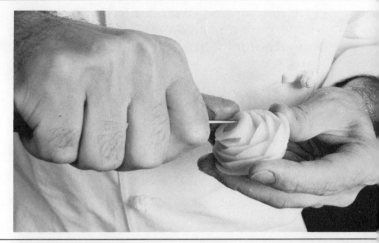

6. Cut the top of the rose, which will be too pointed, and blanch as indicated above.

10. Fleurs en Truffes *(Black Truffle Flowers)*

B LACK TRUFFLES are subterranean mushrooms that grow in the seedlings of "contaminated" trees, mainly oak and birch. They are available canned in this country and, because of their exorbitant price, are used primarily for decoration. With 1 truffle sliced very thin, one can do a lot of decoration. The rugged skin is peeled off and usually chopped and used in sauces, stuffing or pâté. A decoration made with real truffles is sober and elegant and particularly nice for a pâté or mousse like the one used to illustrate this technique.

1. Slice 1 truffle with a truffle slicer or a knife; it should be very thin. Cut little patterns and triangular pieces and make a decorative border on top of the mousse.

2. Use your imagination and make one or two central flowers with the pieces of truffle. Make an aspic. If you are making the mousse pictured here, mix 1 envelope of plain gelatin with the poaching liquid. Beat 1 egg white lightly until foamy and add to the mixture. Bring to a boil, stirring constantly to avoid scorching. As soon as the liquid boils—a crust will be forming on top of the liquid—turn off the heat. Let the mixture settle for 5 to 10 minutes. Strain through a sieve lined with a paper towel.

3. You should have about ¾ cup of aspic. Cool the aspic on top of ice, mixing with a spoon. As soon as the mixture becomes "oily," pour on top of the decorated mousse. If you are making another mousse or pâté, see the directions for aspic in technique 39.

4. Cool at least 2 hours in the refrigerator. Serve by scooping the mousse with a spoon. Serve with thin toast as a first course for an elegant dinner.

MOUSSE DE FOIES DE VOLAILLE
(Poultry Liver Mousse)

1 *pound chicken, squab, goose, turkey or duck*
    livers, trimmed of nerves
1 *cup good chicken stock*
½ *cup sliced white or yellow onion*
¼ *teaspoon salt (omit if stock is salty)*
4 *sticks (1 pound) sweet butter, at room*
    temperature, cut into 1-inch pieces
1½ *teaspoons salt*
¾ *teaspoon freshly ground white pepper*
½ *tablespoon good cognac*

Place the livers, chicken stock, onion and salt in a saucepan. Bring to a boil, reduce heat and simmer 12 minutes. Strain (reserving the poaching liquid) and place the solids in the container of a food processor or blender. Add the remaining ingredients and blend until the entire mixture is well homogenized.

Transfer to a clean bowl. Place in the refrigerator and mix with a spatula every 10 minutes for 1 hour, or until the mixture gets heavy. Place in a nice terrine, cover with plastic wrap and refrigerate.

This mousse will serve 12.

11. Rose en Tomate et Autres Fleurs en Légumes *(Tomato Rose and Other Vegetable Flowers)*

Y OU DO NOT HAVE TO BE a professional to excel in decoration. The spectrum of color that you can choose from is enormous: truffles, black or green olives, tomatoes, scallions, leeks, carrots and so on. Only eatables should be used and they should be "tasteless." Raw orange or lemon peel on top of a mousse or a poached fish might impart some bitterness to the dish. Beets discolor after a while. You may or may not want the effect.

1. To make a tomato rose, start by cutting a "base" from a tomato. Do not sever from the tomato.

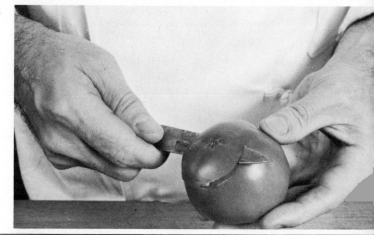

2. Continue cutting a narrow strip about ¾ inch wide, tapering it into a point. Use your knife in a jigsaw, up and down motion to give a natural edge to the petals of the flower. The strip should not be too thick.

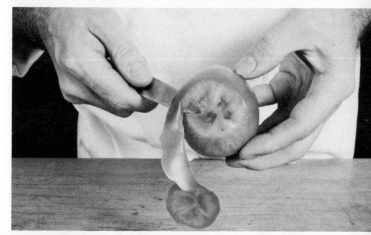

3. Cut another straight strip as long as the first one.

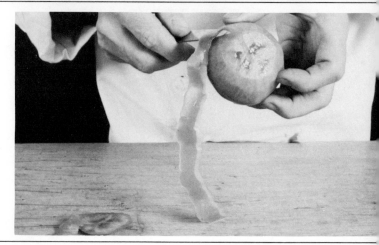

4. Curl the first strip of skin onto its base with the flesh side on the inside of the flower.

5. Roll the second strip into a tight scroll and

6. place it in the middle to make the heart of the rose.

7. To make stems and leaves, blanch the green part of a leek or scallion by plunging it into boiling water for about 30 seconds and cooling it immediately under cold water. The boiling water makes it greener and soft, and the cold water stops the cooking and keeps it green. Dry and lay the green flat, and, on the table, cut long strips following the grain of the leek. To make leaves, cut a wider strip with a pointed end.

8. Cut lozenges of green and arrange around the stems to make small leaves. Use pieces of black from olives, the red of a tomato and

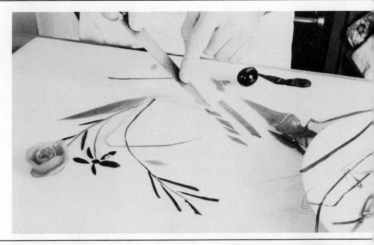

9. the yellow of a hard-boiled egg. Let your imagination help your fingers.

10. Create a nice bouquet to decorate a salad, a cold fish, a ham or a chicken.

12. Champignons en Tomate

(Egg and Tomato Mushrooms)

A**N EASY AND EFFECTIVE WAY** to decorate a cold dish, such as chicken or fish, is to garnish it with egg and tomato mushrooms.

1. Begin by cutting thick wedges from a nice, ripe tomato.

2. Squeeze the seeds out and "push" the flesh in to make a hollow cavity. Cut 1 hard-boiled egg diagonally, one piece bigger than the other. Place the tomato "caps" on top of the egg pieces.

3. Fill up a paper cornet, technique 33, with soft butter or mayonnaise and decorate the top of the mushrooms with little dots so it resembles the cap of a speckled mushroom such as *amanita muscaria.*

13. Champignons Tournés *(Fluted Mushrooms)*

To "TURN" OR FLUTE a mushroom means, in cooking vocabulary, to cut out strips from the cap of the mushroom in an elegant, spiral pattern. It is a difficult technique to master, and it may cost you a few hours of frustration before you get any results. You need a small, sharply pointed paring knife. Use firm, white, fresh mushroom caps. There are several methods or positions of the knife to turn mushrooms. Here is the method I use.

1. Hold the blade of the knife loosely in your fingers on a bias, cutting edge out. Place the side of your thumb behind the blade, on top of the mushroom.

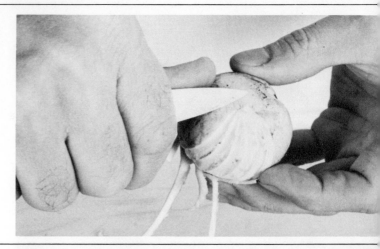

2. Using your thumb as a pivot, push the blade forward and down in a smooth motion by twisting your wrist. The slanted cutting edge should carve a strip out of the mushroom cap. The rotation should be smooth and regular.

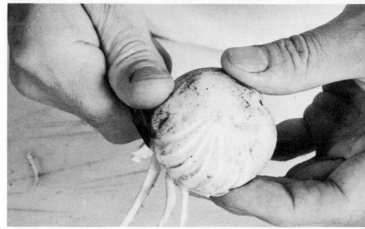

3. If the center is not perfectly formed, make a star by pushing with the point of the knife into the center of the cap. Separate the carved cap from the stem with the knife.

4. Making a relief from a mushroom cap is much easier than fluting. Slice off the crown of the mushroom. "Draw," in this case a little fish, with the point of your knife. Cut about ¼ inch deep into the flesh.

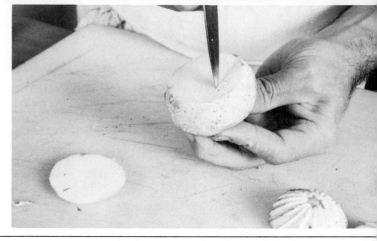

5. Cut the flesh around the outline so that the little fish comes out in relief. Mark the head, eyes and scales with the point of the knife.

6. Trim the cap around the fish and

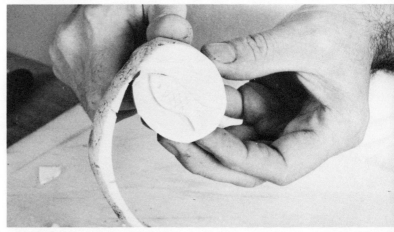

7. slice underneath to make a nice "coin" shape with the relief on top.

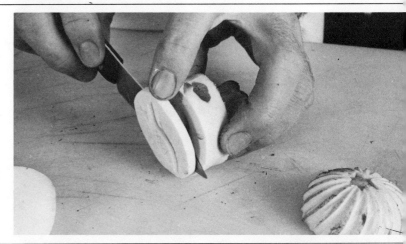

8. Different carved shapes. To stay white, the fluted and carved mushrooms should be cooked in water with a few drops of lemon juice, salt and butter. Three minutes of high boiling is sufficient to cook them. Mushrooms cooked in this manner are usually used to decorate fish dishes and cold dishes such as salads.

14. Lapins en Olive *(Olive Rabbits)*

A N AMUSING WAY TO TRANSFORM OLIVES into a decoration is to make little rabbits out of them. Choose extra large black or green olives with the pits in.

1. Cut a slice lengthwise from one side of the olive. Carve a small triangle from the slice.

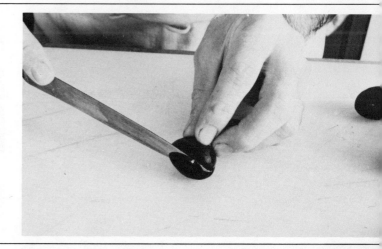

2. Place the olive cut side down. With a small knife, make an incision halfway down, close to the pointed side of the olive.

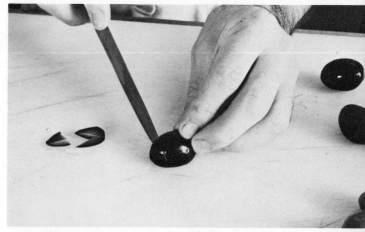

3. Twist the blade to open the cut. Insert the slice so that the pointed ears stand in the air.

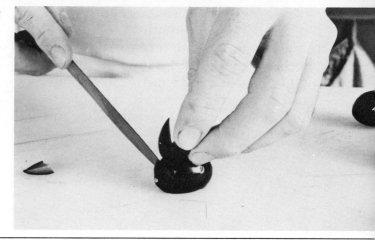

4. Three little rabbits.

15. Quartiers et Tranches d'Oranges ou de Pamplemousses
(Cutting Citrus Fruits)

SECTIONS

1. Taking an orange as an example (always use seedless), hold the fruit flat in one hand. With a thin, sharp paring knife, cut a slice from the top to expose the flesh. Remove the skin in a strip, cutting deep enough to go right down to the flesh.

2. When the orange is "nude," remove each section by cutting with the knife right down to the core, as close to the membrane as you can. Arrange the sections as you go along.

3. Squeeze the membrane over the orange sections to extract all remaining juices.

SLICES

1. Cut the top of the orange to expose the flesh. Place the cut top upside down at the other end of the orange and secure with a fork. This becomes a guard, preventing the knife from sliding and cutting your fingers.

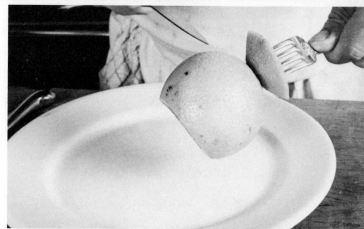

2. Cut the skin down to the flesh in strips, turning the orange as you go along.

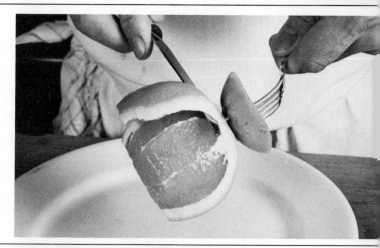

3. Place the peeled orange on the plate and cut into slices. Arrange the slices in a pattern as you go along. This method is principally used in the dining room.

16. Paniers d'Oranges *(Orange Baskets)*

ORANGE BASKETS MAKE a delightful garnish for compatible cold dishes, or for classic dishes such as duck *à l'Orange.* Baskets can be made with whole large navel oranges, or with halves. For large baskets, it is essential to have a stripper to strip the peel off the orange.

WHOLE ORANGE BASKET

1. Cut a thin slice off the blossom end to make a flat sitting surface. Using a stripper, start at the top and cut strips all around the orange, almost down to the flat surface. The strips should fly free, remaining attached to the orange.

2. Cut away wedges on both sides so you are left with a "handle" in the middle of the basket.

3. Carefully cut away the flesh from the handle.

4. Fold the strips over and onto themselves to make loops all around the orange. Fill the area underneath the handle with watercress or parsley to simulate a basket.

HALF ORANGE BASKET

1. Cut a thin slice off both ends of the orange to make a flat sitting surface. Using a round object as a guide, outline half-moons with a knife all around the orange. Cut with a knife, following the outline. Be sure to penetrate deep enough to the center of the orange. Pull apart and you will have two different orange baskets.

2. Cut a strip of skin just below and following the outline of the curve. Empty by scraping the inside of the basket with a spoon.

3. Fill up with orange sections, technique 15.

17. Pelures d'Oranges *(Orange Rind)*

THE THIN OUTER LAYER of the orange skin contains most of the fruit's essential oil and flavor and is very potent in cold Grand Marnier soufflés, orange butter creams, orange *génoise* and the like.

When a recipe calls for grated orange or lemon rind, be sure to grate only the bright orange or yellow part of the skin. The white part underneath is bitter and should not be used. Remove the grated rind from the grater by banging the grater on the table or use a dry brush to pry out the rind.

18. Julienne de Peau d'Orange

(Orange Peel Julienne)

ANY VEGETABLE, MEAT OR FRUIT cut into thin, strawlike strips is called a julienne. The julienne of lemon or orange peel decorates dishes such as duck *à l'Orange* and galantine. The peel can also be cooked in sugar and the candied strips used in cakes, cold soufflés or as a garnish for fruit desserts.

1. Use a vegetable peeler to remove only the orange part of the rind. The white skin between the peel and the flesh is bitter.

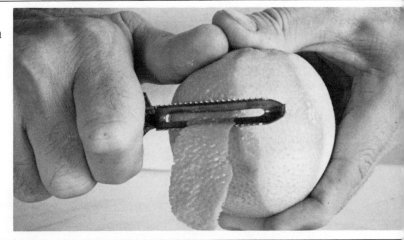

2. Stack a few peels together; fold the stack in half and cut into very thin strips. Whether used as a garnish or candied, the julienne should be blanched at least twice to remove the bitterness. Plunge the julienne in boiling water. Return to a boil and let cook for 1 to 2 minutes. Pour into a strainer and rinse under cold water. Repeat this process once more. Keep in cold water until ready to use.

19. Citron *(Lemon)*

THERE ARE INNUMERABLE WAYS of cutting a lemon, from the simple lemon wedge or slice to one of the more sophisticated ways shown below. Lemon is served with fish, shellfish, oysters, meat (veal or chicken), vegetables (such as asparagus, string beans), dessert (fruit salad), yogurt and cheese to name a few. Hence, it is well worthwhile to vary its preparation.

LEMON PIG

1. Choose a lemon with a nice pointed "nose." With the point of a knife, make one hole on each side of the nose and fill it with a black peppercorn or a piece of parsley or olive.

2. Cut a little wedge in the middle of the nose without separating the piece from the lemon to imitate the tongue. Cut both "ears" on each side of the lemon. Curl up a little piece of parsley to imitate the tail and place toothpicks underneath for the legs.

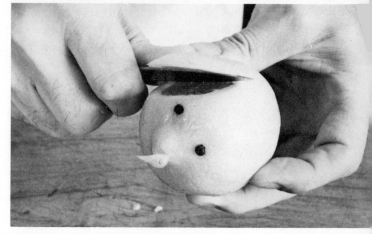

OTHER DECORATIONS

1. Cut a thin slice off both ends of the lemon to make a flat sitting surface. Cut the lemon into halves. Cut two strips of peel of equal size from the sharp edge of the half lemon.

2. Fold each strip around and make a knot to secure. Be careful not to break the strips.

3. Alternatively, cut one long strip of peel from the edge of the half lemon and make a knot with a loop. Place a piece of parsley in the loop.

4. For another treatment, cut both ends of the lemon. With a sharp-pointed paring knife (stainless steel is better with lemon), cut "lion teeth" all around the lemon. Cut deep enough to go to the core of the lemon.

5. For a slightly different look, repeat the same technique as described in step 4, but cut the teeth on a bias.

6. Decorate the different lemons with curly parsley.

LEMON SLICES FOR FISH

1. Trim the lemon, removing the yellow and most of the white skin underneath. Slice into ¼-inch slices, removing the seeds as you go along.

2. Fold each slice and dip into chopped parsley. By folding the slice, only the center gets covered with parsley. You can cover whole slices, half slices, and so on to vary your decoration. For an example, see technique 64, step 10.

20. Décoration d'une Pastèque

(Carving Watermelon)

A SIMPLE DESSERT, such as fruit salad, can become glorious when served in a carved watermelon. Choose a watermelon as dark green as possible and without too many variations of color so that the markings stand out.

METHOD 1

1. Fold a piece of wax paper in half.

2. Fold it in half again and cut with scissors to make a pattern for the handle of the basket.

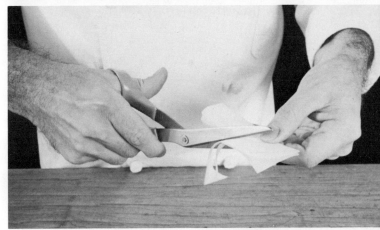

3. Pattern for the handle of the basket.

4. Place the pattern on top of the watermelon and outline it with the point of a knife. Sketch the shape of a lid on both sides of the handle with the knife.

5. Cut a decorative strip under the outline of each lid.

6. Remove the strip to expose the flesh of the melon.

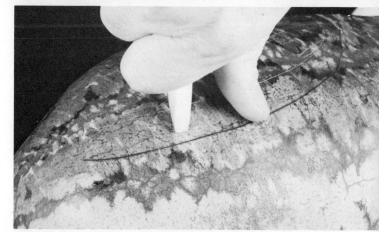

7. Carve little petals with the point of a sharp paring knife.

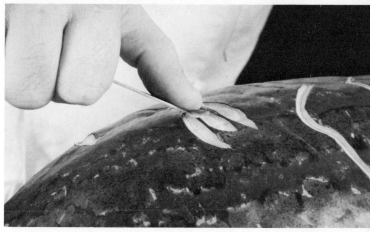

8. Cut out stems for flowers and leaves on the top and all around the melon.

9. Carve a butterfly, or any other object you fancy, on top of the lid. Following the outline of the lid, cut through the top of the melon with the paring knife.

10. Remove both lids and clean the insides with a spoon and a small knife.

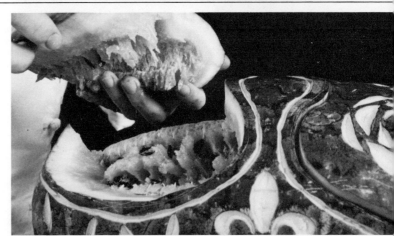

11. Cut the flesh away from the skin all around.

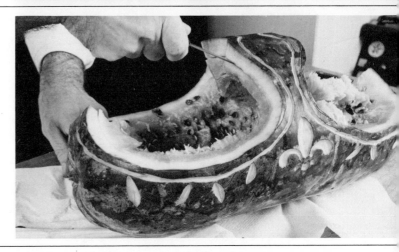

12. With a spoon, scoop the flesh out and pour into a bowl.

13. Replace the carved lids on top of the melon.

14. Watermelon ready to be filled with fruit salad.

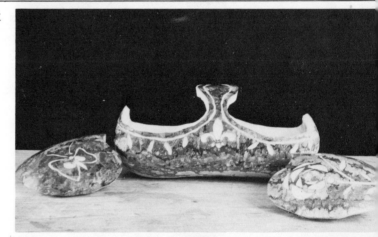

METHOD 2

1. Trim the melon on both ends. Trace waves around the melon using a glass or a small bowl as a guide.

2. Following the contour, separate the melon into halves. Carve a freehand decoration around the melon. You can use small objects (round, square, triangular) as guides to outline a geometric design. Once the pattern is outlined, cut out strips of skin to delineate the design.

3. Scoop out the inside flesh. You may use some of it in the fruit salad.

4. Carved and uncarved halves of melon. Once the melon is carved, cover well with plastic wrap to keep the sculpture relief fresh and vivid looking. It will keep at least one week in the refrigerator. When you are ready to use your masterpiece, empty the melon of any liquid and fill up with fruit salad, using different colored fruits to give an artistic effect. It may also be used to serve a cold punch or ice cream.

21. Beurre *(Butter)*

SWEET FRESH BUTTER, one of the main ingredients in French cooking, is widely used in the professional kitchen for everything from hors d'oeuvre to desserts. And rightly so, because there is no substitute. Buy sweet butter, rather than salted, because salt is added only to act as a preservative, and salted butter may not always be fresh. Sweet butter, on the other hand, gives away its age by turning rancid faster than salted butter.

Clarified butter is nothing more than ordinary butter that has been heated until it melts, and the milky residue (milk solids) has sunk to the bottom of the pan. The clear, yellow liquid that sits on top is clarified butter. Classically, it is used to make hollandaise, *béarnaise* and *choron* sauces, among others, and it is often called for in sautéeing because it does not burn as readily as unclarified butter. However, I personally think clarified butter loses the sweet taste of fresh butter.

Butter is so versatile it often is used for three different purposes in the same sauce: to thicken it with either a "roux" or a *beurre manié,* to enrich it by adding little "nuts" of butter and to coat the surface of the sauce to prevent a skin from forming.

A roux is a mixture of butter and flour in equal proportions which is cooked before it is combined with a liquid. A roux *blanc* (white) should be cooked slowly for 1 minute, stirring. It should not be allowed to brown. A roux *brun* (brown) is cooked until it turns a rich, nut brown. A *beurre manié* is a mixture of soft butter and flour in equal proportions that has been kneaded until smooth.

Béchamel is one of the mother sauces in French cooking. It is made with a *beurre manié.* With the addition of cream it becomes a *sauce crème.*

SAUCE BÉCHAMEL *(White Sauce)*

1. Place soft butter and flour in equal proportions in a bowl.

2. Mix with a spoon until smooth. This is a *beurre manié.*

3. Bring milk to a boil. With a wire whisk, scoop the *beurre manié* and whisk into the milk *vigorously* to avoid any lumps. The kneaded butter should incorporate easily without forming any lumps.

4. Bring the sauce to a boil and cook at low heat for 4 to 5 minutes, mixing with the whisk to avoid scalding. Season to taste with salt, pepper and nutmeg. A thin sauce will take approximately 1½ tablespoons each of flour and butter per cup of milk. A thick, heavy sauce (for soufflés) will take twice the amount of flour and butter.

5. When the sauce is cooked, cut a little bit of butter and put it on top.

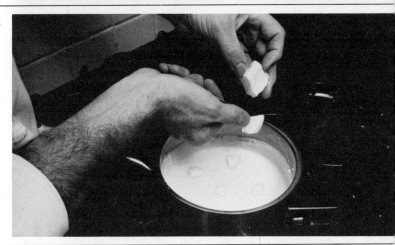

6. As the butter melts, smear it onto the whole surface of the sauce with the point of a fork. This will form a coating of fat on the surface of the sauce and will prevent a skin from forming. At serving time, stir in the butter which is on top.

BEURRE MAÎTRE D'HÔTEL (*Lemon-Parsley Butter*)

1. The *maître d'hôtel* butter is the most frequently used of the many compound butters. It is sliced and used on broiled steak, chops, liver, or on boiled potatoes, cauliflower or even poached fish. To 2 sticks (½ pound) of softened sweet butter, add the juice of ½ lemon, 2 tablespoons chopped parsley, 1 teaspoon salt and 1 teaspoon ground white pepper.

2. Mix thoroughly until all the ingredients are well blended. Spread into a strip on the width of a piece of wax paper.

3. Roll the butter back and forth to make it smooth and equal all over.

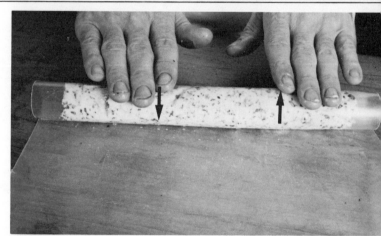

4. Close both ends of the butter tube and place in the refrigerator. Cut into slices as needed. The same method is used to make *béarnaise* butter, *Colbert, anchovy* and so on.

22. Mayonnaise

MAYONNAISE IS, PERHAPS, the most useful cold sauce in the world. The word may come from the medieval French word *mayeu,* meaning egg yolk, or, according to Grimod-de-la-Reynière, from the verb *manier,* meaning to knead. Mayonnaise lends itself to an infinite number of variations.

Mayonnaise is usually served with cold foods such as hard-boiled eggs, cut vegetables, salad, cold fish, shellfish, cold meat and pâté. (Its sister, hollandaise, made with egg yolk and butter, is served warm with fish, eggs and vegetables such as asparagus, broccoli and the like.) In French cooking, when the ingredients of a particular salad are bound with mayonnaise, it becomes: mayonnaise *de volaille* (chicken salad), mayonnaise *de homard* (lobster salad) and so on. Though according to classic French recipe books, mayonnaise is not made with mustard, I have rarely seen it made without. Mayonnaise made in the food processor or blender will keep longer when refrigerated than the handmade counterpart because the elements are more finely bound together.

Mayonnaise can become sauce *verte,* a green sauce made with mayonnaise, watercress, tarragon, parsley and spinach; sauce *gribiche,* mayonnaise with hard-cooked eggs, French sour gherkins, capers and shallots; sauce *tartare,* mayonnaise with parsley, chives, chervil and sour pickles; sauce *La Varenne,* mayonnaise with a purée of fresh mushrooms; sauce *russe,* mayonnaise with fresh caviar; and, of course, the well-known *aïoli,* known as the butter of Provence and made with a very substantial amount of pounded garlic and olive oil. Of course, mayonnaise can be done with olive oil (the best is a virgin oil), or peanut oil, or a mixture of both; it is just a question of personal taste. Buy vinegar of the best possible quality, such as *vinaigre d'Orléans.* Use good mustard. The quality of the ingredients is sine qua non to the end result. Be sure that the ingredients are at room temperature. If the oil is too cool, the mayonnaise will definitely break down. If kept refrigerated, the mayonnaise must come to room temperature slowly before it is stirred or it will break down. This recipe yields about 2½ cups of mayonnaise.

2 egg yolks
1½ teaspoons Dijon mustard
1 tablespoon tarragon or wine vinegar
Dash of salt
Dash of freshly ground white pepper
2 cups oil (peanut, olive, walnut or a mixture)

1. Place all ingredients except the oil in a bowl and stir with a wire whisk. Add the oil slowly, whisking at the same time.

2. Keep mixing, adding the oil a little faster as the mayonnaise starts to take shape.

3. Consistency of the correct mayonnaise.

4. To serve, scoop the mayonnaise into a clean bowl, being careful not to smear the sides of the bowl. (Place the mayonnaise in the middle of the bowl.)

5. Smooth the top with a spatula by turning the spatula in one direction and the bowl in the other direction.

6. When the top is smooth, move the spatula in the same circular and reverse motion, going up and down to make a design on top of the smooth surface.

7. With your finger, push out the mayonnaise left on the blade of the spatula in the center of the decoration.

8. Mayonnaise ready to serve.

9. When the oil is added too fast, or when the ingredients are too cold, the mixture breaks down. It looks like a broken-down custard. Mayonnaise can be put back together with egg yolk, mustard, vinegar, or a small amount of hot water. Place 1 teaspoon of vinegar, if vinegar is used, in a clean vessel. Add 1 teaspoon of the broken sauce and whisk thoroughly. When smooth, add another teaspoon, then another, and when the mayonnaise starts to hold together, you may add the broken sauce at a faster pace.

10. For another method, place the vinegar or hot water directly into the broken mayonnaise in one place along edge of the bowl. Using the tip of your whisk, without getting too deep into the mayonnaise, mix the liquid with the top layer of the broken sauce until you see that it is getting together. Keep mixing, pushing your whisk deeper and deeper into the mayonnaise. Then, whisk larger and larger circles until all of the sauce is back together.

23. Lardons et Bardes *(Larding: Strips and Leaves)*

T HERE ARE BASICALLY TWO KINDS of larding needles: the large grooved needle *(lardoire)* for pot roast and other large pieces of meat and the small butterflied needle *(aiguille à piquer)* used for small cuts, such as filet mignon or rack of hare. The process of larding smaller cuts with fat was once common but it is rarely done nowadays. In our lighter and healthier contemporary cooking, one tries to reduce rather than increase the intake of fat. *Piquage* of meat is not necessary and I do not recommend it. It is shown only as part of a known technique.

Because meat is always cut against the grain, larding is done with the grain of meat. Otherwise, one might cut through whole strips of fat while carving.

Lard leaves *(bardes)* are used to line terrines and pâtés, or to wrap dry meat or game such as partridge or woodcock, and give moisture and enrich the meat during cooking.

LARDING A SMALL CUT OF MEAT

1. The fat used is fat back *(lard dur)* because it is firm and white and is not inclined to disintegrate as easily as fat from other parts of the pig. It is the layer of fat closest to the skin. Keep the piece refrigerated so it can be easily cut into strips. Flatten the piece with a large cleaver.

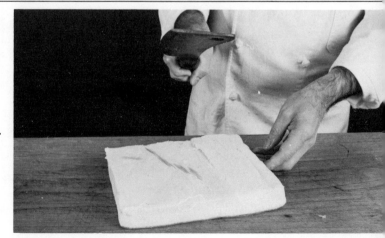

2. Turn upside down and, with a long, thin knife, start cutting the rind off.

3. With one hand pressing tight on top of the fat back, cut the rind off by keeping your blade flat, moving in a jigsaw fashion.

4. Cut the fat in long strips about ½ inch wide for the pot roast. Place in iced water to keep the fat firm.

5. Cut in small strips to lard the small cuts. Keep in iced water.

6. Place the fat strips inside the split end of the *aiguille à piquer* as far as it will go.

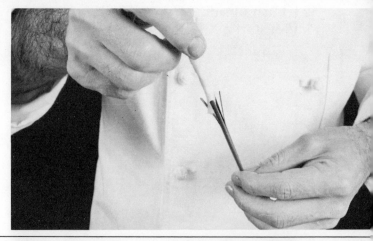

7. With one hand, keep the split end closed on the fat and insert the needle through the meat.

8. Pull with the other hand, leaving a small strip dangling on each side. The meat is larded on a bias in that case.

LARDING A LARGE CUT OF MEAT

1. Cut ½-inch slices of fat back.

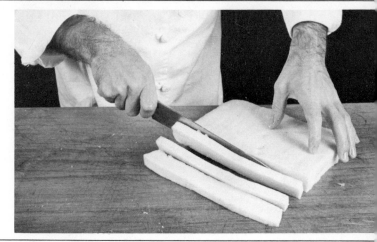

2. Cut the slices into long strips and keep refrigerated, or in iced water to firm up.

3. This is a plain grooved larding needle. Before placing the fat in it, push the needle through the meat to make an opening. Remove the needle, place the fat into the opening, and insert it into the premade hole, twisting as you push the needle in. Lift the end of the fat, and hold with your finger as you withdraw the needle, or the entire strip may come out.

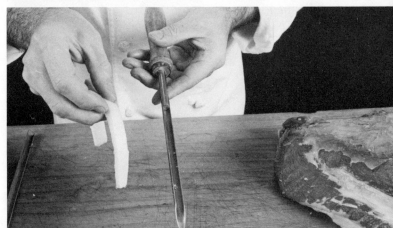

4. This is another type of larding needle. It is easier to use because of its hinged tip.

5. With this needle, you place the fat into the groove and close the tip on top of it.

6. Insert the needle, twisting it through the meat (go with the grain of the meat). Lift up the tip and,

7. holding it between your fingers, pull off the removable handle.

8. Holding the end of the fat with your thumb, pull the needle through in the same direction it went in.

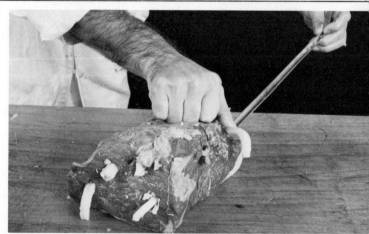

9. Repeat until the entire piece of meat is larded every 1½ to 2 inches.

LARD LEAVES FOR TERRINES AND PÂTÉS

1. To make *bardes* or lard leaves, flatten the fat back with a cleaver. Place skin side down on the table. Stick one or two pointed knives through the rind to keep the fat back from sliding during cutting.

2. Using a long, thin knife, cut "leaves" as thin as you can, holding your blade horizontally.

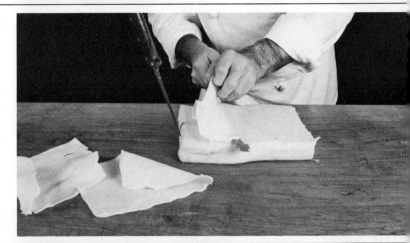

3. This technique requires a certain amount of practice. You could ask your butcher to cut the leaves with his electric ham slicer.

24. Cornets *(Cornucopia Molds)*

Cornets are pastries, ham or salmon slices, or other foods shaped in the form of a horn. A tinned cornucopia mold is used to shape the food. The cornets can be stuffed with a variety of fillings. The stuffed cornets can be served on a *macédoine de légumes,* a vegetable salad, the recipe for which appears below.

CORNETS DE JAMBON *(Ham Cornets)*

1. Roll a square slice of ham so that one end is pointed. (Roll as you would a paper cornet, technique 33.)

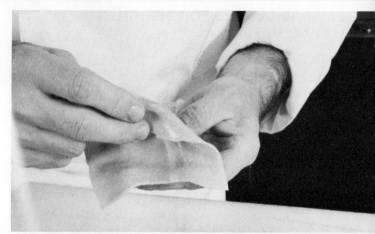

2. Slip into a cornucopia mold. Prepare your favorite stuffing or the one that follows. For 4 horns: 1½ tablespoons butter; ¾ cup chopped, cooked spinach; 1 hard-boiled egg, coarsely chopped; ⅓ cup chopped ham; salt, pepper and nutmeg. Melt the butter in a skillet until black and foaming. Add the spinach and cook, stirring for 1 minute. Remove from heat and add remaining ingredients. Let cool.

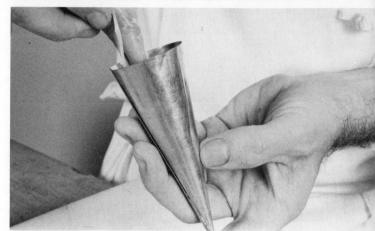

3. When cool, stuff the mixture into the ham cornet.

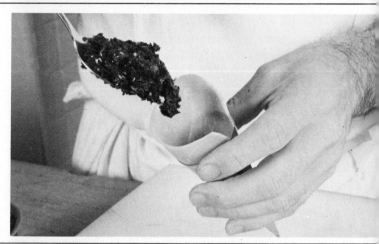

4. Trim the ham at the level of the stuffing.

5. Remove from the mold; the cornet should slide out easily. Trim the ham for a neat, pointed cornucopia.

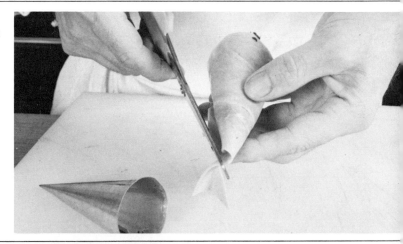

CORNETS DE SAUMON (Salmon Cornets)

1. Using slices of smoked salmon or *gravlax*, technique 56, twist the slices and fit them into the mold.

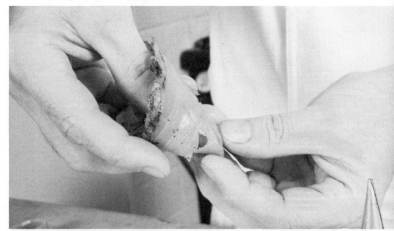

2. You may have to overlap slices to have the mold well lined. Stuff with a mixture of finely chopped hard-boiled eggs mixed with soft butter or mayonnaise and seasoned with salt and pepper.

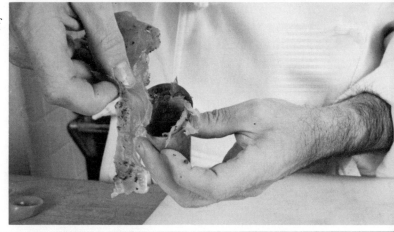

MACÉDOINE DE LÉGUMES
(Vegetable Salad)

½ cup cooked peas
½ cup diced cooked carrots (¼-inch cubes)
2 cups diced cooked potatoes (½-inch cubes)
3 tablespoons finely chopped onion
¾ cup mayonnaise (preferably freshly made, technique 22)
½ tablespoon wine vinegar
Salt and pepper to taste

Mix together all the ingredients and arrange on a platter with the ham or salmon cornets on top and a tomato rose, technique 11, in the middle.

This recipe yields about 4 cups of *macédoine*.

CORNETS À LA CRÈME (*Dessert Cornets*)

1. Dessert cornets are shaped on the outside of the mold. Cut strips of puff paste, technique 153, ⅛ inch thick by about 1 inch wide and 18 inches long. Wet the strips with cold water on one side.

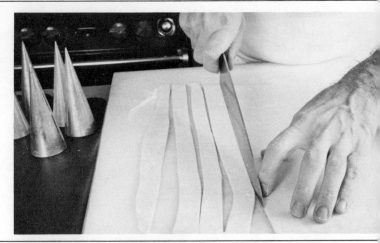

2. Squeeze the dough at the tip of the mold to secure it.

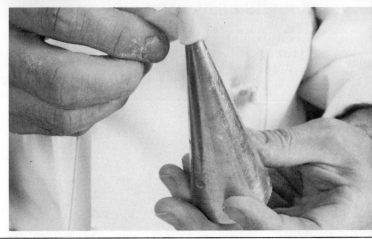

3. Wrap the strip around the mold, overlapping slightly, the wet side of the dough touching the mold.

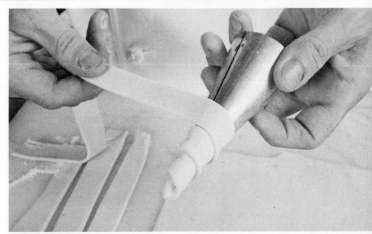

4. Trim the extra dough on the edge of the base of the mold.

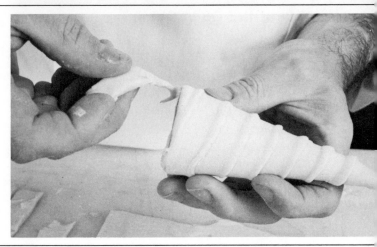

5. Holding the horn with your fingers inside, brush beaten egg over the dough.

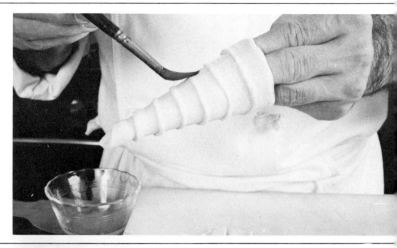

6. Place standing up on a cookie sheet and bake in a 400-degree preheated oven for 15 to 18 minutes. Let cool slightly before unmolding. You may have to run a knife between the dough and the mold to get the pastry loose, making it easier to slide off. Fill with sweetened whipped cream.

25. Croûtons Ronds, Carrés et en Coeur *(Round, Square and Heart-Shaped Croutons)*

B READ IS USED EXTENSIVELY as a garnish and in the presentation of food. When it is cut into a variety of shapes and fried, it is called a crouton. Round croutons are used as a base for fillet, steak, poached eggs and other dishes.

Small crouton cubes are used as a garnish for hot and cold soups and in stuffings and meat loaf. They may be fried or toasted in the oven. Heart-shaped croutons are served as a decorative garnish for *coq au vin,* puree of spinach and beef or veal stews. Trimmings are used to make bread crumbs.

1. Cut slices approximately ¾ inch thick.

2. For round croutons, use a glass or round crouton cutter to cut out circles. Fry in a saucepan in a mixture of butter and oil.

3. For square croutons, stack 2 or 3 slices of bread together and trim the edges. Cut into strips.

4. Cut the strips across to make cubes. Fry in butter and oil or dry in the oven.

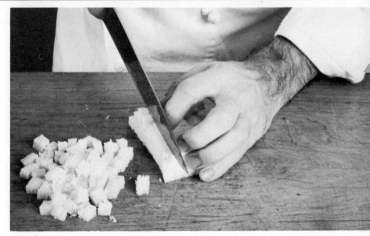

5. For heart-shaped croutons, cut slices of bread into halves diagonally.

6. Trim each half to obtain a more pointed triangle.

7. Trim each piece into the shape of a heart.

8. Fry in a mixture of butter and oil. Dip the tip of each crouton in the sauce of the dish it is to be served with and then into a small bowl of chopped parsley. The parsley, which adheres to the bread because of the wet tip, forms a decorative point.

26. Croûte en Pain de Mie *(Bread Baskets)*

THE CROÛTE IS USED as a receptacle. It is usually fried in oil and butter and filled with chicken hash, a poached egg and a sauce, or even with a small roasted bird such as quail or woodcock.

1. Cut a slice about 1½ to 2 inches thick.

2. Trim and, using the point of a small knife, cut halfway down the outline of the inside.

3. Cut pieces and scrape to hollow the *croûte*. Deep fry in oil, drain and spoon in a filling of your choice.

27. Toasts Melba *(Melba Toast)*

E SCOFFIER CREATED this super-thin toast for the cantatrice Melba. Though melba toast can be bought ready-made, you should try the real McCoy; it is easy to make and quite good.

1. Toast regular slices of bread under the broiler. Trim on 4 sides.

2. Keeping the slice flat, and using a thin knife, cut through the soft middle to split the slice into halves. It is relatively easy because both sides are crusty and will separate easily.

3. Place the slice, soft side up, under the broiler until dry and brown.

4. Slice the thin toast into halves.

28. Socle en Pain *(Bread Socle)*

T HE SOCLE IS USED PRINCIPALLY in classic cuisine as a stand for many garnishes, and as a decorative component around a dish.

1. Cut a thick piece from a loaf of bread and, using a long knife, cut off the crust.

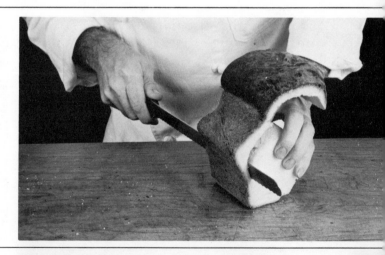

2. Carve the central cylinder according to your own fancy. It is fried in oil before being used. The socle as a decorative piece is not eaten.

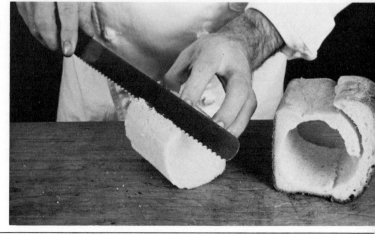

3. In back, from left to right: diced croutons, *croûte*, socle, round croutons and heart-shaped croutons. In the front, melba toast.

29. Canapés

Canapés are small appetizers made from plain and toasted bread, spread or covered with meat, cheese, caviar, anchovies and the like. They can be shaped and varied almost indefinitely, according to your own taste.

1. Make an incision straight down, close to the crust, on one side of a loaf of bread. This becomes a "guard" to protect your hands from the knife.

2. Cut wide slices about ⅓ inch thick.

3. You can use plain white bread as it is or you can toast it. Egg salad, tomato and the like, being moist, are better off on toast than on fresh bread which has a tendency to become soggy. Spread a thin layer of butter on the slices.

4. Cover the slices with ham, salami, prosciutto and so on.

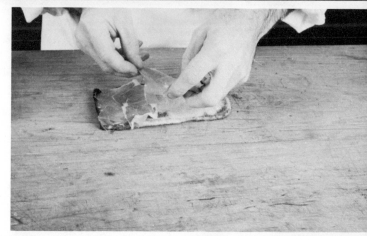

5. To make lozenges, trim the slice all around and cut in half lengthwise.

6. Position the two strips side by side but stagger them slightly.

7. Cut into lozenges.

8. Cover another slice of buttered bread with smoked salmon, trim all around and cut into neat triangles. Cut square pieces of toasted and buttered bread and cover with caviar.

9. Fill a paper cornet with soft butter, technique 33. Cut a straight opening and pipe out a "G clef" on each of the salmon canapés. Decorate the prosciutto canapés with another butter design.

10. Cut the tip of the cornet on both sides to make open pointed lips, technique 33, steps 12 and 13. Pipe out small leaves or petals, three per canapé.

11. With the point of a knife, deposit a little dash of red paprika in the middle to simulate the pistil of the flower.

12. Arrange your canapés attractively on a platter and decorate with small pieces of curly parsley.

30. Garniture en Papier *(Lining Cake Pans)*

BEFORE BAKING PARCHMENT and wax paper were so widely available, cooks used brown wrapping paper to line cake pans. This served the purpose, but the modern papers which come on rolls are easier to work with. Not all cakes call for lined pans, but when they do, they are essential if the cake is to drop out of its cake pan intact.

ROUND CAKE

1. Cut a square piece of wax paper as wide as the diameter of the pan used, and fold in half. Fold the obtained rectangle in half to get a square. Fold the square diagonally, with the uncut corner as the point of the triangle. Fold the triangle onto itself in the same manner several times to obtain a thin, long triangle.

2. For a *savarin* mold, place the thin triangle point at the center of the mold and cut it off at the interior edge of the mold.

3. Cut it off at the other edge and

4. unroll. It should fit exactly.

5. For a round cake pan, fold the paper in the same manner as in step 1, measuring the radius of the pan and centering the point of the triangle at the center of the pan.

RECTANGULAR CAKE

1. Fold a long piece of wax paper in half the long way.

2. Turn the cake pan upside down. Place the folded paper so that the fold is at the center of the pan.

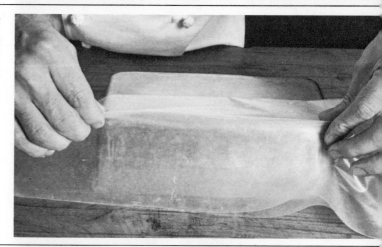

3. Crimp the paper on the lengthwise edge of the pan and

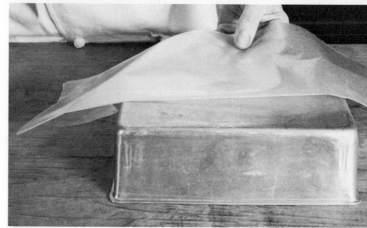

4. then at both ends to score the size of the cake.

5. With a pair of scissors, cut the paper on both sides of the pan extending the fold shown in step 3.

6. Paper cut and ready to be folded.

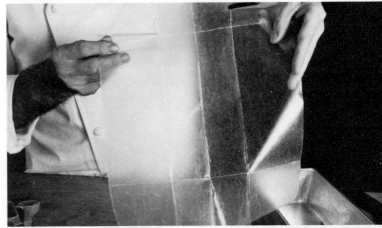

7. Bring the end and outside cut behind the center strip of paper on both sides.

8. The lining should fit perfectly in your cake pan.

31. Cuisson en Papillote *(Paper Casing)*

WHEN YOU SEE "PAPILLOTE" on a menu in a French restaurant, you can safely assume that it describes a dish served in an envelope of parchment paper, usually a veal chop or a filleted or whole fish. The paper is cut in the shape of a heart. The meat or fish is partially pre-cooked, then placed in the center and baked in the oven. When the papillote is folded correctly (it is sealed so that none of the aroma and steam can escape) it browns nicely, inflates, and the dish inside bakes in its own juices. The papillote is served directly on the serving plate and the guest opens it himself.

1. To cook en papillote, start by cutting a large rectangular piece of parchment paper. (In the olden times, cooks used brown paper bags.) Fold the rectangle in half.

2. Using scissors or a knife, start cutting from the folded side, following an imaginary line that resembles a question mark.

3. Open the heart shape and place the food on the bottom. The food should be partially cooked and all seasonings and flavorings added. Fold the top paper over the food.

4. Starting at the fold, fold the edge, overlapping the fold as you go along.

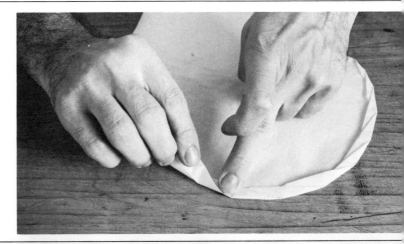

5. Fold the tip of the papillote several times to secure the closing.

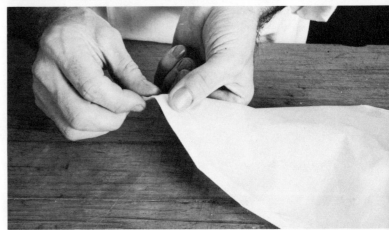

6. Papillote ready to bake.

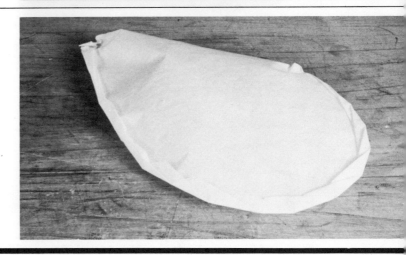

32. Papillote *(Paper Frill)*

IN ADDITION TO THE PAPER RECEPTACLE described in the preceding technique, the word papillote describes a frill—a delicate paper lace rolled into a "hat" and used to adorn the bone of a lamb chop or a ham. Its raison d'être is strictly aesthetic. A papillote is also a Christmas bonbon rolled in a piece of paper decorated with a drawing and a motto, then wrapped in colorful paper with frills at both ends. Another papillote, neither aesthetic nor edible, is a little piece of paper used by women to set their hair.

1. Cut a long rectangle of parchment or wax paper approximately 25 inches long by 5 inches wide. Fold lengthwise twice. Open the last fold. You now have a rectangle folded in half and scored down the center by the second fold. Using scissors, cut strips ¼ inch apart down the length of the paper. (Cut through the folded side to the score line.)

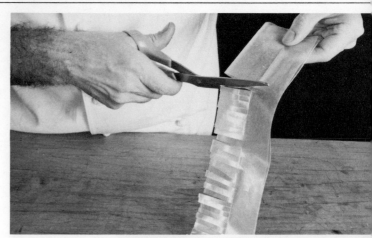

2. Open the rectangle completely and fold in half inside out to give the frills a nice roundness.

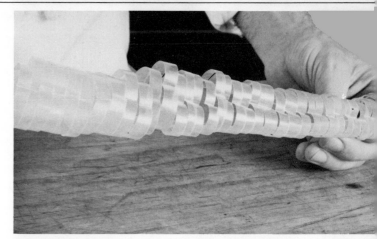

3. Secure with staples or plastic tape.

4. Roll the frill on your finger, or on a pencil if you are making small frills for lamb chops.

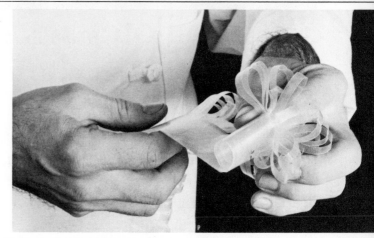

5. Secure the bottom part with a paper clip or a piece of tape.

33. Cornet en Papier *(Paper Cone)*

A PAPER CONE OR HORN is an invaluable tool for fine and elegant piping. It gives a real professional touch to your decoration. Making cornets is not an easy technique to acquire, but it is well worth spending the time to master. They should be made with parchment, sulfurized paper or the best quality wax paper you can find.

1. Cut a triangle of strong paper with a pair of scissors.

2. Grab both ends with your thumbs and forefingers and twist onto itself to make a cone. Do not worry if the cone is not very pointed.

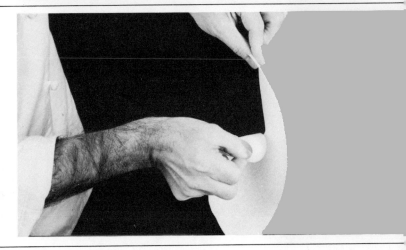

3. Holding the cone at the seam with both hands (thumbs inside and forefingers outside the cone), move the thumbs down and the fingers up to bring up and tighten the cornet making it needle sharp.

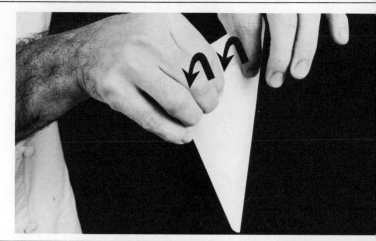

4. Hold the cone tight so that the paper does not unroll.

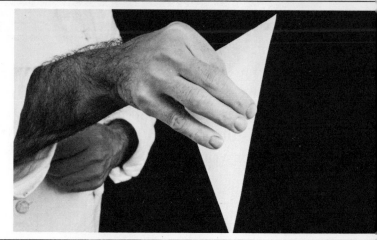

5. Fold the ends inside the cone to secure it and avoid uncoiling.

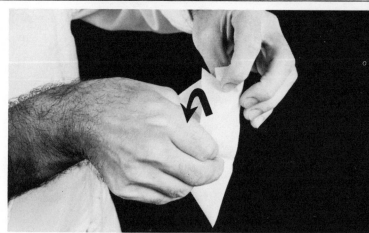

6. The cone is ready to be filled.

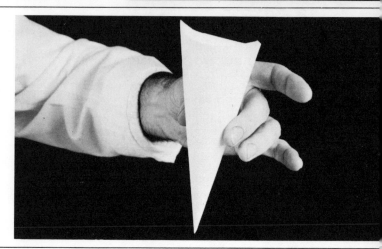

7. Place some filling in the cone, being careful not to soil the edges. Do not fill up more than ⅓ full.

8. Flatten the cone above the filling and fold one side.

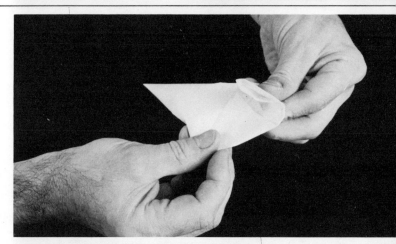

9. Fold the other side.

10. Then fold the center onto itself twice to secure the filling inside.

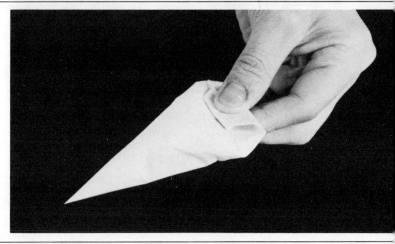

11. For a plain line, cut off the tip of the cone with a pair of scissors. The smaller the opening, the finer the decoration.

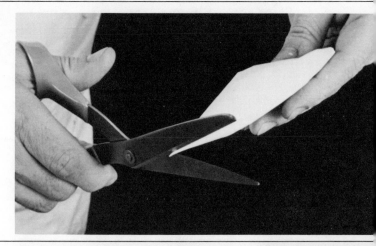

12. To make leaves, cut off a larger piece of the tip on a slant.

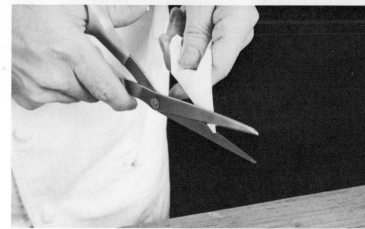

13. Then repeat on the other side so that the tip is open on two sides. For more about leaves, see technique 137.

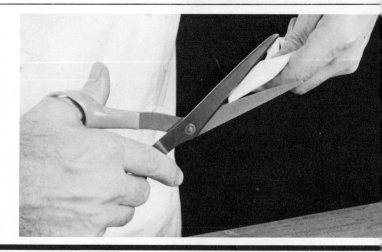

34. Faux Col pour Soufflé *(Collar for Soufflé)*

W HEN SERVED A FROZEN SOUFFLÉ, you may have wondered how it rose to such magnificent heights, sometimes 2 to 3 inches above the mold, without having been baked. It is very simple. Frozen soufflés are, of course, nothing more than whipped cream, a liqueur, egg yolks and sugar mixed together and then frozen. The "rising" of the soufflé is accomplished by the simple device of tying strong parchment paper around the mold and filling the mold up to the "collar." Collars are also used for hot soufflés to keep them from splitting and falling out during baking.

1. Cut a wide piece of strong baking parchment long enough to go completely around the mold and overlap slightly. Then fold the paper two or three times, depending on the width of the paper and on how high you want your soufflé to rise above the mold.

2. Apply your strip of paper to the outside of the mold, pulling the paper together securely and tightly so that the soufflé mixture cannot run down between the paper and the mold.

3. Secure the paper collar with a piece of string, tying it very tightly. For a frozen soufflé, fill the mold up only to the top edge. Place both the filled mold and the remaining mixture in the freezer for 15 minutes. By that time the surplus mixture will have become firmer and will not run. Add the mixture to the mold, filling the collar. Smooth the top surface. Return to the freezer and freeze until firm. At serving time, sprinkle some cocoa over the top to simulate browning in the oven. And don't forget to remove the paper!

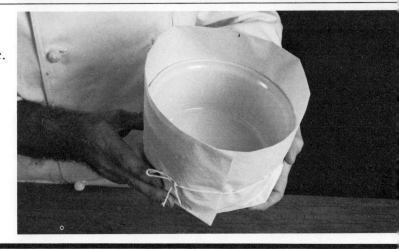

35. Pliage des Serviettes *(Folding Napkins)*

THERE ARE AN INFINITE NUMBER of ways to fold napkins, whether they are used as a liner for food, or placed next to the dinner plate for a guest. The napkins should be large, square, of good quality linen, ironed, and possibly lightly starched. When the napkins are used as liners in the kitchen or dining room, technique 36, they can be folded very fancifully. Next to my plate, I like a napkin which has not been "handled" too much. It is fine simply folded in half or quarters.

1. Using a napkin already folded into a square, fold the opened corner three-quarters of the way up toward the pointed side.

2. Grab the opposite corners with both hands and fold underneath. The napkin can be used just the way it is.

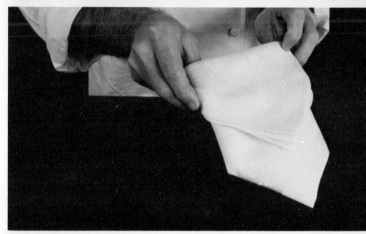

3. Or the opened corners can be folded back onto themselves.

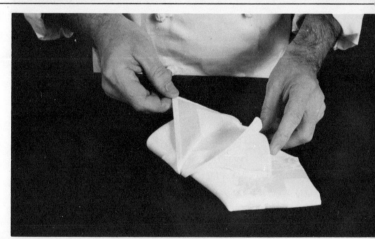

36. Serviettes en Tulipe, Artichaut et Gondole *(Flower, Artichoke and Gondola Napkins)*

FLOWER

1. This is the most commonly used napkin in food presentation. Start with a napkin that is perfectly square. Bring both corners of the same side toward the center.

2. Then bring the two opposite corners to the center.

3. Holding the four corners in place, turn the napkin on the other side. Repeat the above operation by bringing the four corners toward the center.

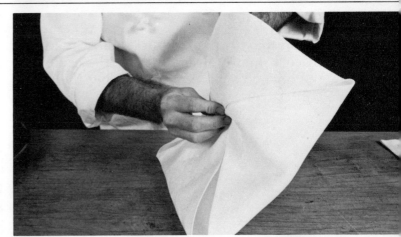

4. Turn the napkin on the other side and "unfold" the four centered corners onto themselves.

5. Folded napkin ready to use. Be sure to hold one hand underneath when transferring the napkin to a platter, or it will unfold.

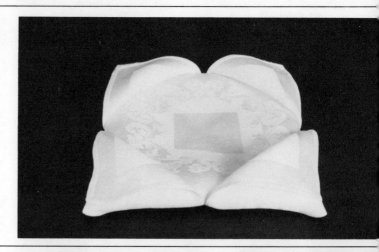

6. To make an eight-petaled flower, fold another napkin in the same manner, but give it one more turn and place it on top of the first one.

ARTICHOKE

1. To make a napkin into an artichoke, place a square piece of foil in the center of the opened square napkin. Bring the four corners toward the center.

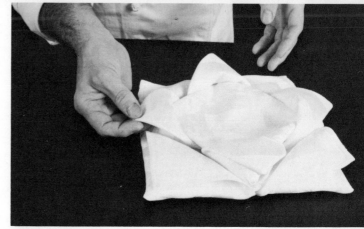

2. Bring the four new corners toward the center.

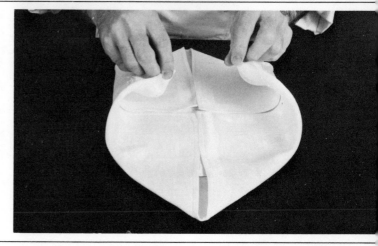

3. Repeat once more without turning the napkin (a total of three times).

4. Turn the napkin on the other side and fold the four corners toward the center.

5. Holding the four corners on the center, turn the napkin over a tall glass and press the napkin on the glass to round it slightly.

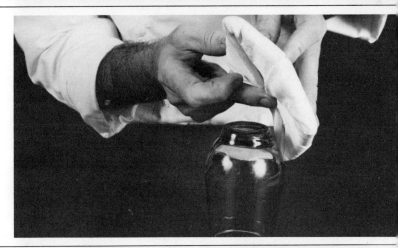

6. Pull the pointed pieces out, as if you were pulling off leaves of an artichoke.

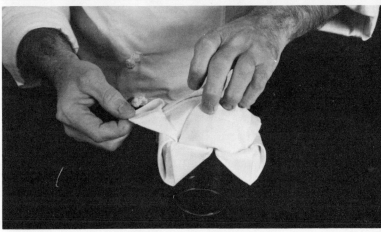

7. Keep pulling the leaves until the last layer, where the aluminum foil is, is exposed.

8. Turn the artichoke down on the middle of a folded flower napkin. Fill with *pommes soufflés,* technique 83, or *gaufrettes,* technique 81.

GONDOLA

1. To make a gondola, place a square piece of aluminum foil in the center of a square napkin (see step 1, artichoke). Fold in half to obtain a long rectangle. Fold one side into the center of the rectangle,

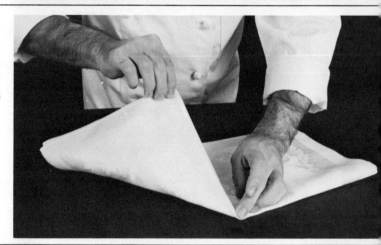

2. then the other side to form a triangular "hat."

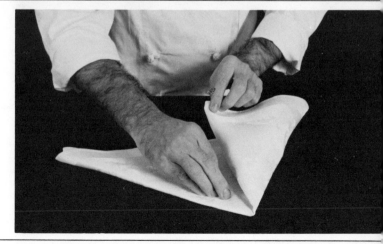

3. Fold in the same manner, making the triangle thinner.

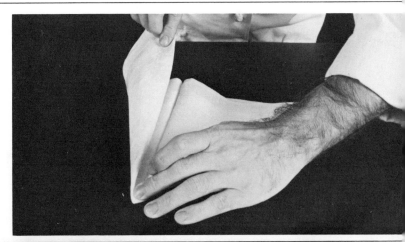

4. Fold a third time, making a long, narrow and sharply pointed triangle.

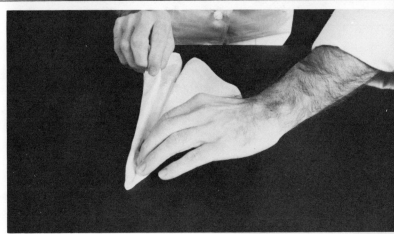

5. Then bring both sides together at the last fold.

6. Keeping the napkin in place with one hand, fold the point inward so it resembles the curved tip of a gondola. Fold a second napkin in the same manner.

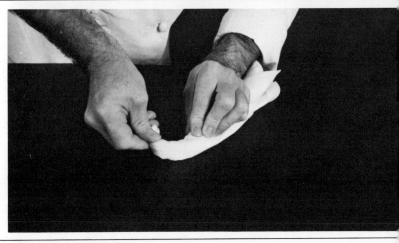

7. Open each gondola and arrange on a platter so that the curved side is on the outside of the platter. Cover the center with a square napkin. Use to present *coulibiac* of salmon, hot pâté in crust, cold fish or even asparagus or artichokes.

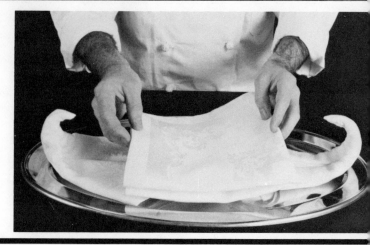

37. Vodka Glacée *(Iced Vodka Bottle)*

Spirits such as vodka, aquavit and pear or raspberry *alcools blancs* are often served ice cold and syrupy. The iced vodka is a must with fresh caviar. An unusual and attractive presentation is to serve the bottle imbedded in ice.

1. Place the bottle in a large empty can or a half-gallon milk carton. Fill with cold water and freeze.

2. Run the container under water and pull out the block of ice with the bottle.

3. Serve it as is, or sculpt the ice with a pointed knife giving it some ridges and roughness, getting rid of the "molded look." Keep frozen.

4. At serving time, fold a napkin,

5. wrap it around the bottle, and secure with a knot.

6. Fold the cover down to dress up the bottle. Keep in the freezer and refill the bottle as needed.

38. Consommé *(Strong, Clarified Stock)*

CONSOMMÉ IS THE BEEF OR CHICKEN concoction that, when perfectly made, is a beautifully clear and sparkling soup. It can be eaten as is or used as a base for other soups, for sauces or for aspic, technique 39. It has all the proteins of meat and none of the fat. There are two steps in making consommé. The first is to make the stock and the second is to clarify it. Clarification is the simple process that gives consommé its crystal-clear appearance.

A very strong consommé *(consommé double)* is made by adding meat to the clarification and cooking it for 1 hour, thus concentrating flavor in the liquid. A cold *consommé double* should be gelatinous without being too firm. With the addition of tomato, it becomes the celebrated *madrilène consommé*.

THE STOCK

1 *unpeeled onion, halved*
4 *pounds beef bones (or a mixture of beef and chicken bones)*
1 *bay leaf*
1 *teaspoon black peppercorns*
1 *medium-sized onion, peeled and stuck with 3 cloves*
2 *teaspoons salt*

Place the split onion, cut sides down, in an iron skillet and place on medium heat. Let cook until the onion is burned and very black. It is essential that the onion is burnt on the cut side. It will cook with the bones for hours, and will give the amber color a consommé should have.

Place all ingredients in a large kettle and cover with cold water. Bring to a boil, skimming any scum that forms at the surface. When boiling, lower the heat and simmer slowly for 6 hours. Strain.

During cooking, add water if there is too much evaporation. You should have 12 cups of liquid left. Let cool and remove fat from top.

THE CONSOMMÉ *(Clarified Stock)*

1 *cup cold water*
1 *pound very lean ground beef*
6 *egg whites*
½ *cup diced celery leaves*
¾ *cup diced tomato*
2 *cups sliced green of leek (or 1 cup green of scallions)*
½ *cup coarsely cut parsley and tarragon mixed*
¾ *cup sliced carrots*
½ *teaspoon black peppercorns*
2 *bay leaves*
½ *teaspoon thyme leaves*
Salt, *if needed*
12 *cups stock*

1. In a large kettle, combine all the ingredients except the stock.

2. Add the stock and bring to a boil over high heat, stirring constantly to avoid sticking. Do not worry if the stock becomes very cloudy and a white foam forms. The albumin in the egg whites and the meat is solidifying, and this is the process that will clarify the stock. When the mixture comes to a boil, STOP STIRRING and reduce the heat to a simmer. As the mixture simmers, you will notice that the ingredients form a "crust" on the surface of the liquid with one or two holes, through which the liquid boils slightly.

3. Allow the consommé to simmer gently for 1 hour without disturbing the little "geysers" in any way. Turn off the heat and let the consommé settle for 15 minutes.

4. Strain the consommé through a sieve lined with a paper napkin, taking care not to disturb the crust.

5. Tilt the pan on one side to get all the liquid out.

6. After the consommé has rested 1 hour, check to see if there is any fat on the surface. If so, remove it by blotting the top with paper towels. The consommé can be served hot or cold. With different garnishes it takes on different names like *célestine* with shredded crêpes, or *royale* with cubes of meat-flavored custard. The crust is usually discarded, but with the addition of whole eggs, bread crumbs and seasonings, it can be turned into a satisfying meat loaf. Be careful to remove the peppercorns for this use.

39. Gelée *(Aspic)*

THE WORD ASPIC refers to any gelatinous liquid which congeals and sets when cold. With a lot of reduction, a natural stock will set. However, it will rarely become firm enough to be used for a mold unless natural aspic in the form of pig's feet, pork rind or the like is added. Also, it is not always desirable to reduce a stock to such a degree as the flavor may become too strong. For these reasons, aspic is usually made with a liquid and unflavored gelatin. The liquid is a stock which can be made from chicken, beef, game, fish, shellfish and the like.

Aspic can be used in a number of ways: it can be used to bind foods in a mold (for examples, see *oeufs en gelée,* technique 45, and *aspic de saumon,* technique 58). It can be used to glaze cold dishes, such as ham (see color plate 1). It can be used to fill the cavity inside a pâté baked in a crust (see technique 114). It can be chopped into a dice and used as a garnish as described in the photographs below.

Because aspic should be transparent, it is important to use a stock that is crystal clear. The process of clearing a stock, clarification, is described in the preceding technique. The stock should be fat free and the equipment immaculate.

To make an aspic from a beef or chicken stock, follow the recipe for consommé in the preceding technique, adding 12 ¼-ounce envelopes of unflavored gelatin to the kettle in step 1. Refrigerate until firm for use as a garnish.

A few words about gelatin: one ¼-ounce envelope will congeal up to 3 cups of liquid if the gelatin is stirred into the hot liquid and no further cooking takes place. In our recipe making aspic from consommé, the gelatin cooks for an hour and therefore loses much of its strength. This is the reason such a large quantity is needed.

GARNISHING WITH ASPIC

1. Unmold a solid piece of aspic. Cut it into slices. Then cut the slices into strips and,

2. finally into dice. Each piece shines like a little jewel. Using a spoon, arrange around the cold dish.

You may also "twist" your knife left to right while cutting the aspic. This makes "ridges" on the sides of the slices and dices, giving even more relief and glitter to the little jewels. (Though some cooks recommend chopping up the aspic and piping it with a pastry bag, it is nonsensical to have gone through the trouble of making a crystal-clear aspic just to chop it into a mush and smear it in the pastry bag.)

40. Plaque Beurrée et Farinée
(Coating a Cookie Sheet)

THERE ARE COUNTLESS RECIPES asking the cook to coat a cookie sheet, a soufflé mold, a tin cake pan and so on. The reason is primarily to avoid sticking and also to give whatever is cooking a nice golden crust and a buttery taste. In the case of a soufflé, it is even more important; it helps the soufflé slide up during cooking. There are basically three ways to coat a dish. Butter is first rubbed on the surface of the dish; then sugar is added for a sweet dessert, cheese for a cheese soufflé or flour for an all-purpose coating.

1. Rub soft butter all over the cookie sheet.

2. Add flour to the sheet and shake it thoroughly in all directions so that all the butter is coated with the flour. Pour the flour onto the second pan and repeat the operation. Give a bang to the back of the cookie sheet to get rid of any excess flour. The coating should be light and uniform.

41. Poche et Douille *(Pastry Bag and Tube)*

WHEN A COOK WANTS TO GIVE a professional look to his desserts, he uses a pastry bag. It simplifies the work and makes the decoration faster, cleaner and more uniform. Buy a plastic-lined pastry bag which is easy to use and to wash. A 14- or 16-inch bag is the all-purpose size most commonly used. Buy your pastry bag with a narrow opening at the point. If it is too small for your tube, you can always cut a piece off the tip to enlarge the opening.

1. Place the fluted or plain tube in the bag and push it so that it fits snugly and some of it shows through the opening.

2. If your batter is soft enough to fall through the opening by itself, it is a good idea to twist the bag above the tube

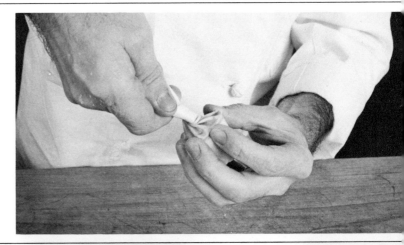

3. and push it inside the tube. This prevents the batter from leaking through.

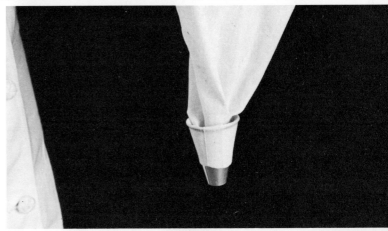

4. Fold the top of the bag approximately 2½ to 3½ inches down on the outside to avoid smearing the sides when filling the bag.

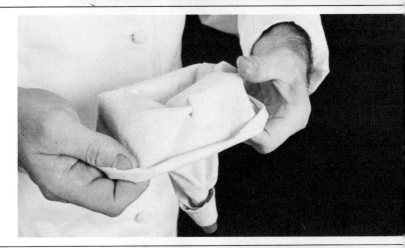

5. Place one hand under the fold to hold the bag and spoon some of the mixture into the bag, "squeezing" the mixture from the spoon with the hand under the fold. Do not fill the bag more than halfway.

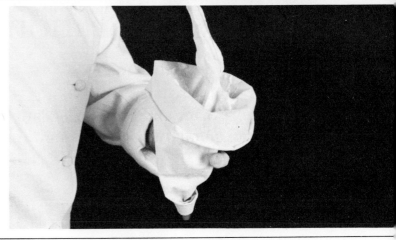

6. Unfold the pastry bag and fold the top in an orderly fashion.

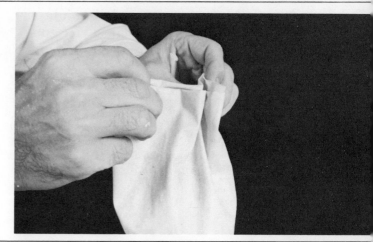

7. Twist the top of the bag and "pull" it through the opening between your thumb and forefinger until your hand is against the mixture. The thumb and forefinger position is important and should keep the top of the bag tightly closed. If you open your fingers while pressing the mixture out, it will come up instead of going down through the tube.

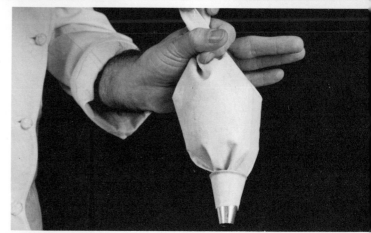

8. Pull the tip of the tube down and use your bag, "squishing" the mixture out by pressing with the palm of one hand and the tips of the fingers. The other hand can be used to control the direction of the bag if you are decorating, or to hold the cornet or other item being filled.

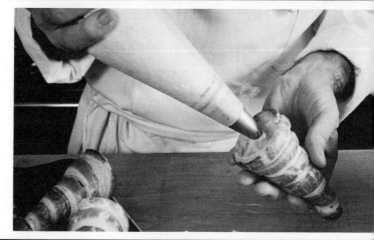

42. Incorporation à la Spatule
(Folding in Ingredients)

MANY RECIPES, primarily baking recipes, call for folding. The goal is to incorporate something delicate, usually whipped egg whites or cream, into a thicker mixture while retaining the fluffiness and airy quality in the mixture.

1. Use a wooden or rubber spatula, or even a metal one, and slide it flat on top of the mixture.

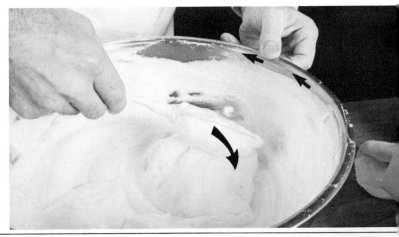

2. Then, cutting side down, go through the mixture and straighten out the spatula underneath it.

3. Twist the spatula again to come out on the top cutting side up. While you perform the whole circle with one hand, spin the bowl toward you with the other hand. The motions should be simultaneous. Do not overfold.

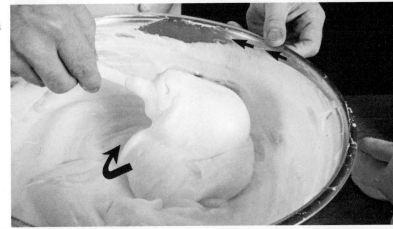

43. Séparation des Oeufs *(Separating Eggs)*

WHEN YOU ARE SEPARATING EGGS, you often end up with an excess of yolk or white. The egg whites, almost pure albumin, freeze well. Defrosted egg whites whip even better than fresh egg whites, and they do not pick up odors. The yolk, however, high in fat, does not freeze well. Unless the temperature goes as low as −20 degrees, bacteria will grow in the egg yolk. In addition, yolks easily become freezer burnt. However, they can be kept for a couple of days in the refrigerator covered with a layer of water to prevent a skin from forming on top. Pour the water off before using.

1. To separate the yolk from the white, crack the egg on the edge of the bowl. Open the egg, keeping one half upright to hold the yolk. Let the white drop into the bowl.

2. Pour the yolk into the empty half shell, letting more white drop into the bowl as you are transferring the yolk from one shell to the other.

3. An alternate method is to pour the egg into your hand and let the white drip through your fingers.

44. Oeufs Pochés *(Poaching Eggs)*

WHEN MAKING POACHED EGGS, the fresher the eggs the better. The older the eggs, the more the whites will tend to spread in the water. A dash of vinegar (white vinegar preferably, to avoid discoloration of the eggs) is added to the water to help firm the egg white. Salt is omitted because it has the reverse effect and tends to thin down the white. Poached eggs lend themselves to an infinite number of combinations, from the very simple poached egg on toast, to the sophisticated eggs Benedict, served with ham, hollandaise sauce and truffles. Eggs can be poached several hours, even a day, ahead (as most restaurants do), eliminating any last-minute panic when you want to serve people at once.

1. To poach 6 eggs, place 2½ to 3 quarts of water and ¼ cup white vinegar in a large saucepan. Bring to a boil; then, reduce to a simmer. Break one egg at a time on the side of the saucepan. Holding it as closely as you can to the water (to avoid splashing), open it with both thumbs and let it slide into the water. Drop your eggs at the place where the water is simmering so that they don't go down into the water too fast and stick to the bottom.

2. If you are afraid of burning your fingers, break the eggs in a saucer or bowl and slide them into the water. Go as fast as you can so that the difference in cooking time is not too great between the first and the last egg. Keep the water at a bare simmer, or let it "shiver," as it is said in France.

3. As soon as all the eggs are in the water, drag the bottom of a large slotted spoon across the surface of the water to move the eggs about a bit and keep them from sticking to the bottom of the pan. Once some of the whites have hardened, the eggs will not stick any more.

4. Large eggs take approximately 3 to 4 minutes of cooking. If you like them more runny or more set, the timing should be changed accordingly. Check the eggs by lifting them, one at a time, with a slotted spoon and pressing them slightly with your fingers. The whites should be set, but the yolks soft to the touch.

5. As soon as an egg is cooked, transfer it to a bowl of iced water. This stops the cooking and washes the vinegar off.

6. When the eggs are cold, lift each one from the water and trim off the hanging pieces with a knife or a pair of scissors. Place in a bowl of fresh cold water.

7. Drain well if you use them cold, or keep refrigerated in cold water. They will keep for at least a couple of days. To use hot, place in a strainer, lower into boiling water for approximately 1 minute, drain and serve immediately.

45. Oeufs en Gelée *(Eggs in Aspic)*

THIS IS A PERFECT FIRST COURSE for a summer dinner. The bottom of the molds can be garnished with ham, chicken, tongue, or decorated with tarragon, tomato, truffles and the like. Poach the eggs, technique 44, and make a strong, crystal-clear aspic, technique 39.

1. Place a bowl of melted aspic in an ice-water bath to accelerate the coagulation process. Stir until it becomes syrupy. Pour about ⅜ inch of aspic in the bottom of small individual molds and let it firm up in the refrigerator. Decorate the top of the aspic to your fancy. The eggs pictured here are decorated with blanched tarragon leaves and little pieces of tomato skin.

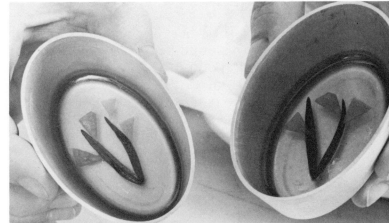

2. Place the well-drained, cold poached eggs on top of the decoration. Cool some more aspic and, when it becomes syrupy, pour enough on top and around to cover the eggs completely. Refrigerate. When cold, and set, unmold and arrange on a platter with chopped aspic around the eggs.

46. Omelettes *(Omelets)*

OMELET MAKING is both very simple and very difficult. A perfect omelet is golden in color on top, delicate and creamy in the center. In addition to fresh eggs and sweet butter, there are three other major ingredients: the right pan, practice and high heat. It is essential to have an 8- to 10-inch omelet pan, "well seasoned" to inhibit sticking, with rounded, sloping shoulders that give the omelet a nice shape and help it slide easily onto the plate when cooked. Be sure to use the highest possible heat, be careful not to overbeat the eggs and do not use too much butter, or the omelet will be wrinkled. The whole operation should not take you more than 1 minute.

PLAIN OMELET

1. Using a fork, beat 3 whole eggs with salt and freshly ground pepper until well mixed. Add 1 tablespoon water (optional) to lighten the omelet. Place 1 tablespoon sweet butter in the pan on high heat. When the foaming has subsided, and the butter has a nice hazelnut color, pour in the eggs. They should sizzle. Let the eggs coagulate for about 6 to 8 seconds.

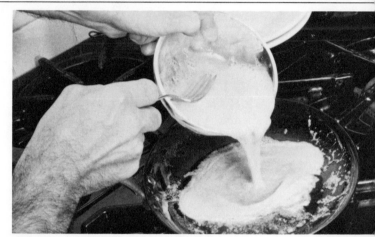

2. With the flat side of a fork in one hand, stir the eggs in a circular motion. Simultaneously, with the other hand, shake the pan back and forth in a continuous movement so that the eggs coagulate uniformly. Lift up the pan slightly while the eggs are cooking so that the "scrambled" eggs end up piled up toward the front of the pan. If the pan is kept flat, and the whole surface is covered with a uniform layer of eggs, then the omelet will roll like a jelly roll or a carpet, and it will not be moist inside.

3. Fold the lower "lips" back onto the omelet, shaping it in a nice half-moon shape as you go along.

4. Run your fork along the side of the pan under the front of the omelet.

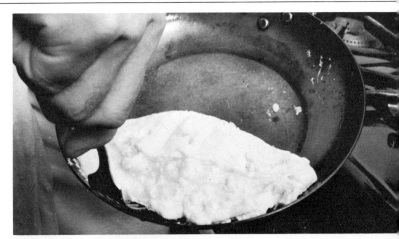

5. Tap the handle of the pan to encourage the omelet to lift up in the front

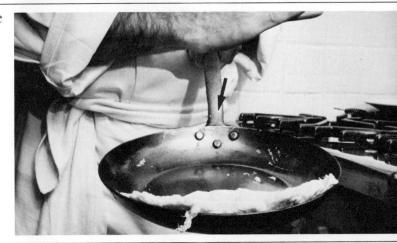

6. and, using the fork, fold the upper lip onto the center, taking care to see that it comes to a point at each end.

7. At this time, the omelet can be stuffed. Arrange the solid pieces, whether you use chicken livers, creamed chicken, spinach or whatever, in a line along the center of the omelet.

8. Changing hands, hold the serving plate vertically against the side of the pan and invert the omelet onto the plate. Pour the sauce, if any, around the omelet.

ALTERNATE WAY TO STUFF AN OMELET

9. Make a plain omelet and turn it onto a plate. With the point of a knife, make an incision lengthwise in the center of the omelet. Using a spoon, stuff the opening. Pour sauce, if any, all around the omelet.

10. From left to right: stuffed, flat and plain omelets.

47. Oeufs Mimosa *(Stuffed Eggs)*

STUFFED HARD-BOILED EGGS ARE an excellent garnish for cold salmon or other fish. They can also be served as a luncheon first course, or as an hors d'oeuvre for a buffet.

1. Be careful when cooking hard-boiled eggs. They should be lowered into boiling water and allowed to barely simmer for 10 to 12 minutes, depending on size. Then the eggs should be placed in cold water to stop the cooking and avoid the greenish discoloration around the yolk. Trim the eggs at both ends, cut into halves and "seat" the pieces on their cut ends. (Very fresh eggs are hard to peel because of their acidity but this diminishes after the eggs are 2 days old.)

2. Remove the yolks (without breaking the whites) and push through a metal sieve with the help of a sturdy spoon.

3. Add 1 tablespoon of soft sweet butter or mayonnaise for every 3 egg yolks. Season with salt and pepper and mix well. The mixture should be soft and homogenous. Fit a pastry bag with a fluted tube, technique 41, and fill up the white halves with the mixture.

4. Decorate the tops with capers. Refrigerate until serving time.

Shellfish and Fish

48. Huîtres *(Oysters)*

AFICIONADOS PREFER OYSTERS RAW on the half shell with a dash of lemon, or a *mignonnette* sauce made by mixing together ½ cup good red wine vinegar, ¼ cup chopped shallots, ½ teaspoon coarsely ground black pepper and a dash of salt. (Crushed peppercorn is called *mignonnette;* hence, the name of the sauce.) These fine mollusks should be used, as all shellfish, only if they are alive and fresh. Despite the fact that restaurants sometimes wash oysters to get rid of any lurking bits of shell that might present problems to their patrons, once oysters are opened, they should never be washed. Their taste becomes flat and insipid. Oysters are usually larger and fatter in the United States than they are in France. The "green" flat oysters of France, the *Belons* and *Marennes,* do not have counterparts in this country. Oysters are usually poached in their own broth. Be sure not to overcook these delicate shellfish or they will toughen. As soon as the edges of the oyster whiten and curl up, they are cooked enough.

1. To open an oyster, only the point of the knife (and you need an oyster knife) is used. Hold the oyster with a thick potholder to protect your hand. With the oyster in the palm of your hand, push the point of the knife about ½ inch deep into the "hinge" (the pointed side of the oyster), between the "lid" and the body of the oyster.

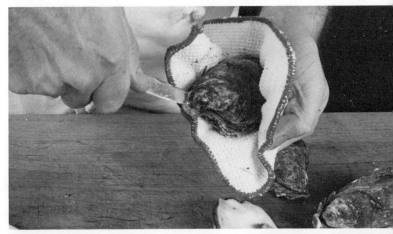

2. Once the lid has been penetrated (this can take a considerable amount of pressure), push down. The lid should pop open. Lift up the top shell, cutting the muscle attached to it.

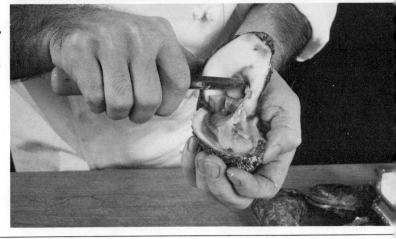

3. If the oyster is too hard to open at the hinge (the Malpeque from the cold waters of Canada are easier to open than the bluepoints which are pictured here), insert the knife about 1 inch on the curved side of the oyster between the lid and the body. Twist the blade to pry the oyster open. Cut the muscle from the lid.

4. Slide your knife under the oyster to sever the muscle. The oyster is now loose in the shell. Place flat on a bed of chopped ice or directly on the plate.

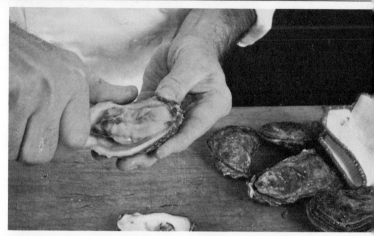

5. Oysters and clams. Serve with buttered black bread, lemon wedges or *mignonnette* sauce.

49. Clams

WHERE THE OYSTER KNIFE is pointed and the tip is usually curved, the clam knife is straight, rounded at the tip, and sharp on one side. Personally, I prefer to use a regular paring knife to open clams. Cherrystones and little necks (the smallest of the hard clam clan) are commonly served on the half shell, although they are often cooked in the shell (clams casino and Rockefeller), or outside the shell (clam fritters, spaghetti and clam sauce). Like oysters, clams should not be overcooked. There are only two alternatives when it comes to cooking clams: to poach them only a few minutes to avoid toughening, or to cook them a couple of hours to have them tender. Cooked in between the two, they will be very rubbery. This principle applies to meat as well. Beef should be cooked rapidly (a steak) or braised (a stew); in between, the meat is, paradoxically, overcooked and undercooked at the same time.

1. Holding the clam firmly in the palm of your hand, place the sharp side of the knife blade at the seam, slightly on the "bulged" side where it is easier to open, and, using the tips of your fingers in back of the blade, tighten your grip, "pulling" the blade up through the seam. The muscle has to be severed for the clam to open.

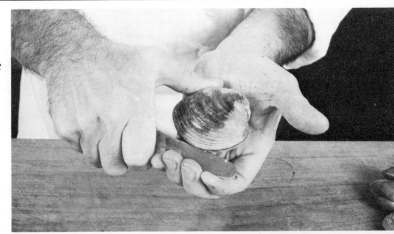

2. Force the clam open. Run the knife along the top shell to free the meat.

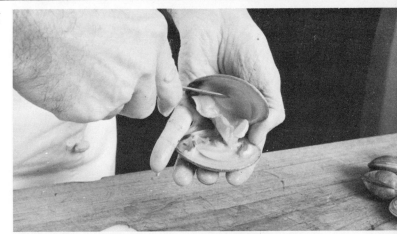

3. Break the top shell off by twisting it. Discard. You may work over a bowl to salvage the drippings.

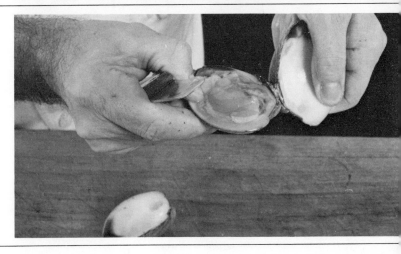

4. To free the clam completely from the shell, run the knife under the meat and sever the muscle. Place on a flat plate. Do not wash. Serve with lemon, *mignonnette,* or a cocktail sauce and buttered bread.

50. Oursins *(Sea Urchins)*

UNFORTUNATELY, THIS SEA DELICACY is rarely available in fish stores or restaurants, even though it is commonly found off the coasts of the United States. They are popular in France, and are usually eaten raw with bread and butter. They exhale a prevalent odor of iodine, and the roe (the only part eaten) are reminiscent of nuts, butter and salt all together.

1. Bottom and top of a sea urchin.

2. The needles are straight and hard in fresh sea urchins.

3. Hold the sea urchin with a potholder. Insert the point of a pair of scissors into the "mouth" (the soft depression on one side). Cut one-third down the shell, then, turn the scissors and cut around the shell.

4. Lift up the "lid."

5. The mouth of the sea urchin is attached to the lid. Discard.

6. With a teaspoon, lift up the roe and eat with bread and butter. (They can also be used to make mousse or as a garnish.) Fishermen in France open the sea urchin and immerse it in seawater, shaking it to clean the inside. Everything washes out except the roe which is attached to the "wall" of the shell. They dip sticks of buttered bread into the roe and eat them.

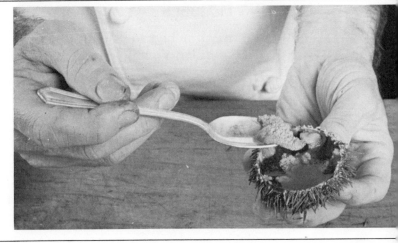

7. Plate of sea urchins.

51. Moules *(Mussels)*

MUSSELS, SO PREVALENT IN FRANCE, have never, unfortunately, had the popularity they deserve in this country, although we have them in great abundance all along the New England and mid-Atlantic shores. The best mussels are the ones found in cold waters. They are sold by weight—about 12 average-sized mussels to a pound—and any aficionado can easily consume at least 1½ pounds.

There are a number of ways to serve mussels. The least sophisticated and easiest way to prepare them is *marinière* (sailor-style). This is how you frequently find them in the bistros in France—plain and in the shell. For something a little more sophisticated and richer, you can try them *poulette* (with a cream sauce). For this dish, the shell is separated and only the half shell with the meat in it is kept. In some recipes the meat is removed entirely from the shell after cooking and used to make a *pilaff de moules* or combined with a *rémoulade* or a light well-seasoned mayonnaise and served as a salad for a first course. Billi-bi, one of the best possible soups, can be made from the broth the mussels cook in, with the addition of wine, cream and herbs.

CLEANING MUSSELS

1. Mussels are attached to one another by a "cord" or "beard" which looks like old wet hay or grass. Nowadays, mussels are often sold half cleaned (that is, with the beard removed), even though they die rapidly without their life-sustaining cord. Even the live ones lose a lot of moisture and end up being small, dry and very yellowish, instead of plump, moist and pale beige in color. If you plan to keep them a few days, buy the uncleaned type.

2. With a small paring knife, scrape off the dirt and most of the encrustations that are on the shell. Cut off, or pull off, the beard. Place in cold water and rub the mussels against each other to clean the shells further.

3. Press each one on a bias to determine if it is full of mud or sand. If so, the shells will slide open and, obviously, these are to be discarded.

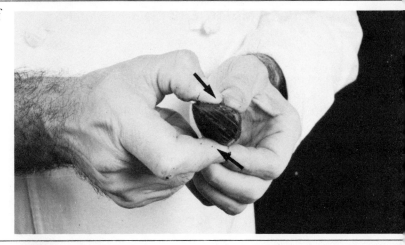

4. Certain mussels are open. This does not mean that they are bad. The spoiled ones smell strongly, contrary to the fresh mussels which smell pleasantly of iodine and seaweed. If you touch the inside muscle and edge with the point of a knife

5. the fresh mussel will close immediately. As long as the shell is moving the mussel is still alive. Place the mussels again in a lot of cold water with salt (a handful of salt per gallon of water), and let them sit for 1 hour so that they throw off any sand that escaped the first washing (there will always be a minimal amount of sand left in them).

6. Wash again one or two more times. The mussels are now ready to cook.

MOULES MARINIÈRE (*Mussels Sailor-Style*)

5 pounds clean mussels
1 cup chopped onion
1 clove garlic, peeled, washed and chopped
½ cup chopped parsley
½ teaspoon freshly ground pepper
Dash of thyme
1 bay leaf
Dash of salt
2 tablespoons butter
1 cup dry white wine

This recipe will serve 6.

1. Combine all ingredients in a large pot, cover, place on high heat and bring to a boil.

2. Keep cooking for approximately 10 minutes. Twice while they are cooking, lift the kettle with both hands, your thumbs holding the cover, and shake the kettle in an up-and-down motion to toss the mussels. They should all open. Do not overcook or they will toughen. Serve in large deep plates or in bowls with some of the broth on top.

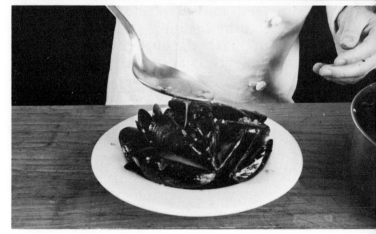

MOULES POULETTE (*Mussels with Cream Sauce*)

Cook as for *moules marinière*. Separate the shells, arranging the halves with the meat on plates. Melt 2 tablespoons butter in a saucepan and mix in 3 tablespoons flour. Add the broth, leaving any sandy residue in the bottom, and bring to a boil, mixing with a whisk. Let simmer 2 minutes. Add 1 cup heavy cream and bring to a boil again. Add salt and pepper if needed. Cook a few minutes and spoon sauce over the mussels.

PILAF DE MOULES (*Pilaf of Mussels*)

1. Cook as for *moules marinière*. When the mussels are cooked, remove the meat from the shell and trim (optional, see trimming mussels). Prepare the sauce *poulette* and set aside. In a saucepan, sauté ⅓ cup chopped onion in 1 tablespoon butter for 1 minute. Add 1½ cups Carolina type rice, stir, add 3 cups chicken stock, salt and pepper and bring to a boil. Cover and cook in a 400-degree preheated oven for 20 minutes.

2. Butter a small bowl and place approximately 3 tablespoons of rice in the bottom and up the sides, making a "nest."

3. Add about 8 to 10 mussels, 2 tablespoons of the *poulette* sauce and

4. cover with more rice, enough to fill up the bowl.

5. Press the mixture with a spoon to pack it together well.

6. Place a serving plate on top of the bowl and

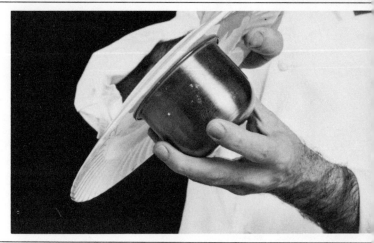

7. invert so the bowl now rests on the plate.

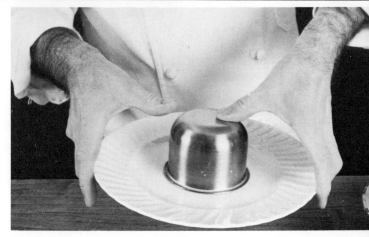

8. Remove the bowl, pour some of the sauce around the pilaf and decorate with a piece of fresh parsley.

9. From right to left: *pilaf de moules, moules poulette* and *moules marinière.*

TRIMMING MUSSELS

1. When serving mussels out of the shell, you might want to remove the brown edge all around the mussel.

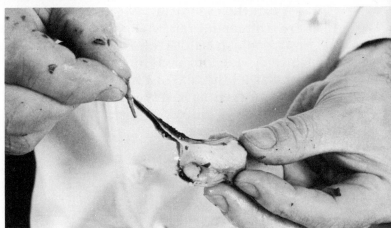

2. This border is tough, especially in large mussels. Pull it and it will come off easily. Discard. It is perfectly all right to serve mussels untrimmed; it's just not quite as elegant.

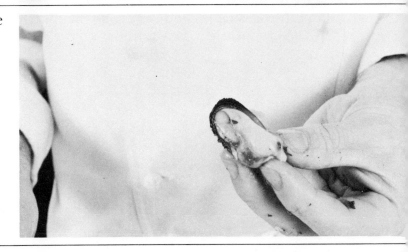

52. Crabes *(Crabs)*

THE COMMON, BLUE HARD-SHELL CRAB is usually boiled in a well-seasoned broth and eaten on newspapers directly at the table. (In summer, when the crab discards his shell, the soft-shell crab is one of the best delicacies to be found in the United States.) Hard-shell crabs are inexpensive, tasty and readily available. They are also excellent in stew, sautéed with hot oil Chinese style, *provençal* with garlic and tomatoes, or *américaine* with a peppery wine and tomato sauce.

1. To prepare for stew, hold the live crab with a potholder and break the large claws off.

2. Turn the crab over. The crab pictured here is a female crab, which is considered the best. You can tell it's a female by the "skirt" which is wide and ends in a point. The male crab has a long, narrow tail instead of a skirt and doesn't have roe inside, but only the tomalley, or liver.

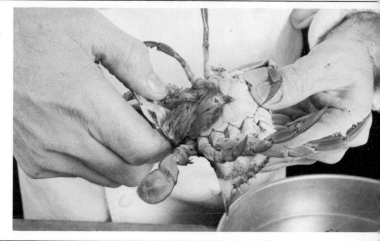

3. Lift the skirt up and twist to break it off. If the crab is dirty, brush under cold water.

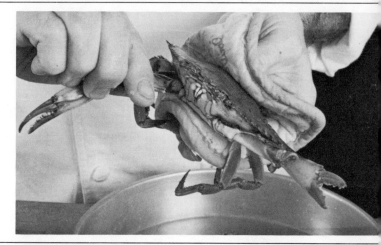

4. Starting next to the fin end and, using your thumb, pry open the shell.

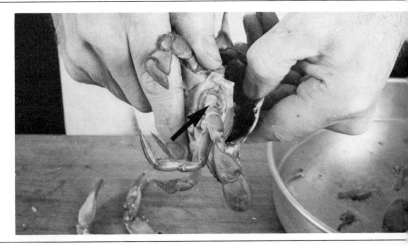

5. If you find it difficult to pull apart, use a teaspoon to pry the shell open.

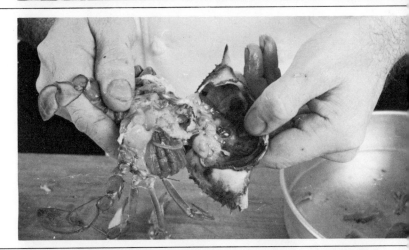

6. Separate the body from the shell.

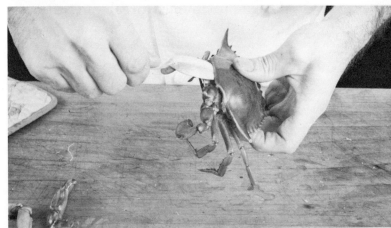

7. Reserve the roe and tomalley attached to the front of the shell. The roe are bright orange and the liver is pale green.

8. Reserve the roe attached to the center of the body. Remove the spongy appendages that adhere to each side of the body.

9. Using your thumbs, break the body into halves.

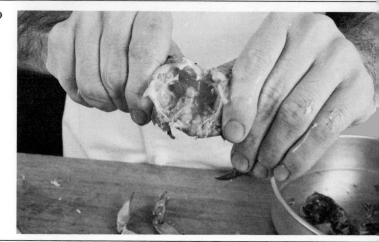

10. The pieces should smell pleasantly, and the flesh should be white and plump. It is near the back fin that the largest morsel of meat is found.

11. Using a meat pounder, break the large claws.

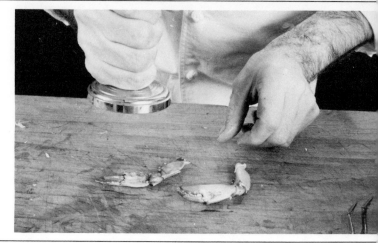

12. Crab ready to stew or sauté. On the left, the two halves of the body, the cracked claws, and the roe and tomalley (used to season and thicken the sauce), and, on the right, the skirt and the shell to be discarded.

53. Homard *(Lobster)*

FRESHNESS IS EXTREMELY IMPORTANT with lobster and other shellfish, and the only way to assure a lobster's freshness is to buy it alive. There are three basic ways of cooking lobster: boiling or steaming, stewing and broiling. The lobster is cut differently depending on which way you cook it.

BROILED LOBSTER

1. Place the live lobster on its back. Plunge a large knife right into the middle of the body and cut down the tail without going through the outside shell.

2. Using both hands, crack the lobster open.

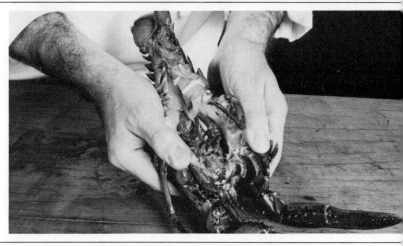

3. Remove sac (stomach) between the eyes and discard. This is usually full of gravel.

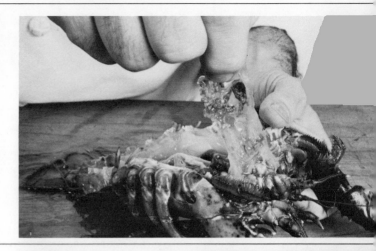

4. Save the liquid, the roe (if any), and the tomalley (liver).

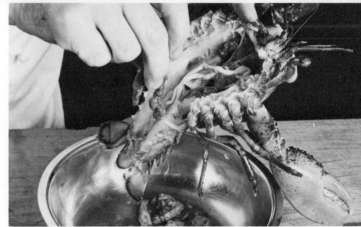

5. Crack claws and big leg joints with a meat pounder or a hammer.

6. An alternate method is to place the lobster on its back and split the body without going through the outside shell. Split the tail into halves. Using both hands, crack the lobster open.

7. Roll each half of the tail back onto itself. Remove the sac, reserve liquid, roe and tomalley, and crack the claws.

STEWED LOBSTER

1. Holding the live lobster firmly with one hand, break off or cut the large claw and small legs on one side of the lobster.

2. Repeat on the other side. Move your knife down and out to separate the claws easily. Crack the claws with a hammer.

3. Insert the point of a large knife under the shell of the body and cut on each side to

4. separate the tail from the body. You can also just break it off.

5. Split the body in half, following the line on the middle of the back. Discard the sac and reserve the liquid, roe and tomalley. Cut the tail into three chunks.

BOILED OR STEAMED LOBSTER

1. After the lobster has been cooked in a strong vegetable stock and cooled in the stock, make a small incision with the point of a large knife between the eyes.

2. Let the liquid run out of the lobster through the opening.

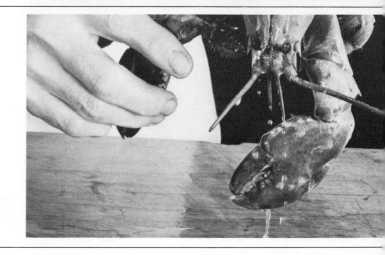

3. Plunge the knife straight down into the body and cut down, following the line on the middle of the back.

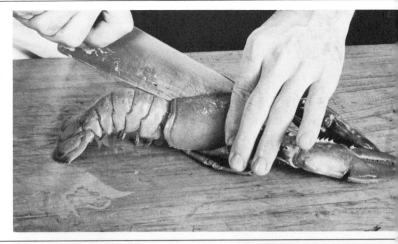

4. Split the tail in half, pushing with both hands on the blade of the knife. Remove the sac and the intestine (a small black thread along the tail).

5. From right to left: boiled lobster, lobster cut for stew and 2 lobsters cut for broiling. Boiled lobsters are usually served cold with mayonnaise, or lukewarm with butter or hollandaise. Lobsters cut for stew are used to make dishes like lobster Newburg and *américaine.* Broiled lobsters are usually seasoned with salt and pepper. The tomalley, roe and liquid are mixed with butter and paprika and spread on the meat. The lobster is then cooked in a very hot oven (450 degrees), or placed under the broiler for 10 to 12 minutes. Do not overcook.

54. Escargots *(Snails)*

EATEN BY THE ROMAN SYBARITES who knew how to fatten them, escargots are a delicacy, unfortunately rarely available fresh in the United States. Although most snails come from snail farms, wild ones are still available at local markets in the countryside throughout France. The two varieties eaten are the succulent "big white" from Burgundy, called vineyard snails because of their fondness for grape leaves and vines, and the smaller garden snails, called the "small gray." The best and most tender snails are picked up at the end of winter. They are called *les dormants,* the sleepers, because they spend the winter in hibernation. Fresh snails are starved for at least 48 hours, in case they have eaten herbs which may be toxic to people. They are then soaked in a mixture of water, salt, vinegar and flour and allowed to disgorge for one hour. They are then washed in cold water, blanched in boiling water, and washed again in cold water. They are pulled from the shell and the lower part of the intestine, the cloaca, is removed. Finally, the snails are simmered in white wine, chicken stock and herbs for 3 to 4 hours. At this point, they are, more or less, at the state you find them in cans. The most popular way of serving snails is with garlic butter *à la bourguignonne.*

ESCARGOTS BOURGUIGNONNE

3 *dozen snails*
2 *sticks (½ pound) sweet butter, softened*
3 *cloves garlic, peeled, crushed and chopped very fine (2 teaspoons)*
4 *tablespoons chopped parsley*
1 *teaspoon Pernod or Richard (or another anise-flavored liqueur)*
½ *cup dry white wine*
1½ *slices fresh bread, crumbed in the blender*
1 *teaspoon salt*
½ *teaspoon freshly ground white pepper*

Mix together all of the ingredients except the snails.

You can vary the recipe by adding chopped shallots, almonds, chives and so on. You could omit the anise liqueur, the wine and the bread.

1. There are two kinds of shells, the real snail shells pictured in the foreground, and the porcelain imitations shown in the back, which are washed and reused in restaurants. The real shells are often washed and reused, but it is not an easy job to wash them properly, and they often smell rancid. Mushroom caps, as well as artichoke bottoms, are used as receptacles for snails.

2. Place ½ teaspoon of the butter mixture in the bottom of each shell and

3. push the snail in, rounded side first.

4. Cover with more of the butter mixture, at least 1½ to 2 teaspoons more.

5. When using the porcelain shells, proceed in the same manner.

6. Snails in porcelain and real shells, oven ready.

7. Place in a 400-degree preheated oven and bake for 12 to 14 minutes. Be extra careful not to burn the garlic butter. Bring the snails, bubbling hot, to the table.

8. The snails are served on a plate from the special *escargotière* (snail dish) in which they were cooked. To eat snails, a special fork and tongs are used.

9. Hold the snail shell with the tongs and pull the snail out with the thin, narrow fork.

10. Pour the extra butter left in the shell into the snail dish, and use your bread to soak up the butter.

55. Quenelles de Brochet *(Pike Quenelles)*

A QUENELLE IS A SUPERFINE DUMPLING usually made from fish, but sometimes made from veal or poultry as well as shellfish and potatoes. We will limit ourselves to fish quenelles here.

There are basically two different fish quenelles—the *quenelles mousseline* and the *quenelles lyonnaise*. The *quenelles mousseline* are made with heavy cream, egg white and the flesh of the fish (trout or sole is often used). They are quite light, akin to a fish mousse. The *quenelles lyonnaise,* perhaps the most celebrated, are made from essentially the same ingredients with the addition of a *panade,* a smooth thick paste used to give the quenelle its special velvety texture. The *quenelles lyonnaise* are made with pike and often with beef kidney fat, but in the version that follows butter is used. Sometimes chopped truffles are added to the mixture. The recipe calls for a 1½-pound fresh pike (the most common is the yellow pike from lakes) and yields 20 to 25 quenelles about 3 ounces each. The raw quenelle dough can be frozen. (Defrost slowly in the refrigerator when ready to use.) Quenelles are served in small earthenware casseroles (called Dutch terrines) all puffed up in their sauce, customarily with a *Nantua* (crayfish) sauce, or with a white wine sauce or a fish sauce.

THE PANADE

2 *cups milk*
½ *stick butter*
½ *teaspoon salt*
¼ *teaspoon freshly ground white pepper*
11 *ounces flour (2½ cups)*

To make the *panade,* place the milk, butter, salt and pepper in a saucepan. Bring to a boil and add the flour all at once (see technique 147, steps 1 and 2). Mix. Cook a few minutes to dry. Place the *panade* flat on a dish, cover with plastic wrap and let cool.

THE FISH MIXTURE

1. Separate the head from a 1½-pound fresh pike, cutting underneath the gills on each side.

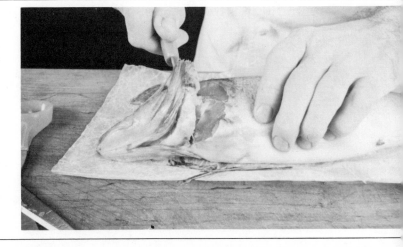

2. Cut along the back fins and follow the central bone with your knife. Repeat on the other side to lift up the second fillet.

3. Remove the skin by holding your knife at an angle and moving it left and right as well as forward as you pull on the skin with the other hand.

4. Cut the fillets into pieces and

5. blend in a food processor or blender.

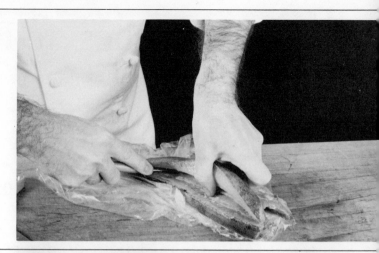

6. Push the fish through a fine sieve to remove any leftover sinews or bones.

7. Scrape the flesh as it comes through the sieve. If you find steps 6 and 7 too tedious, they may be omitted.

6 *large eggs or 7 small ones*
1 *pound sweet butter, softened*
1 *tablespoon salt*
¼ *teaspoon freshly ground white pepper*
⅛ *teaspoon grated nutmeg*

8. Cut the cool *panade* into pieces and blend with the eggs in the food processor. When the mixture is smooth, add the fish, butter, salt, pepper and nutmeg. Mix all the ingredients with a large spoon. Place the mixture, in several batches, back into the food processor to have it well homogenized. Refrigerate overnight covered.

9. There are a number of different ways to form the quenelles. One is to fill up a pastry bag, fitted with a large plain tube, with the quenelle mixture. Then butter a saucepan and pipe the quenelles directly into the saucepan.

10. Wet your fingers and push the "tails" of the quenelles down. Pour hot, salted water on top and bring to a simmer. Do not boil. The quenelles will rise to the surface of the water. Poach for a good 12 minutes without boiling. (If allowed to boil, the quenelles will expand and then deflate. At serving time they will not puff again.) Remove the quenelles with a slotted spoon and place into iced water.

11. In the method pictured here, the quenelles are "molded" with two spoons. Bring a pot of salted water to a boil. Reduce to a simmer. Fill one spoon with the mixture and shape it by rolling it up along the sides of the dish. Repeat several times to round the top of the quenelles.

12. Using the other spoon, scoop the dough from the first spoon, following the curved shape of the receptacle.

13. Repeat, changing spoons as many times as you need to in order to have a neat, well-shaped quenelle. Dip the empty spoon in the water as you go so that the dough slides easily from the spoon.

14. When the quenelle is shaped, hold your spoon very close to the water and let the quenelle fall. Poach following the directions in step 10.

15. A third method, and to my taste the best, is to roll the quenelle dough in flour and shape. Flour your board generously. Place the dough on the table and roll into a long stick. Roll the dough back and forth, moving your hands apart at the same time, to elongate the stick.

16. Dip the blade of a small knife in flour to avoid sticking and cut the stick at an angle into lozengelike pieces.

17. With your hand curved, use your palm to roll the quenelle back and forth to give it a smooth elongated football shape.

18. For tubular-shaped quenelles, roll the dough into a long stick and cut into pieces.

19. Flour your fingers and flatten the ends.

20. Hold a saucepan lid upside down by the handle. Place the lid at the edge of the table and roll the quenelles off the table and onto the lid.

21. Let the quenelles roll down into the salted, simmering water. As the water simmers, the quenelles will rise to the surface, and while cooking, will roll. Do not cover; do not boil; do not let the quenelles expand (see step 10).

22. Place in iced water when cooked. When cold, lift from the iced water and store in a covered container in the refrigerator. It is in this form that they are usually bought in the *charcuterie* in France. Reheat, covered, with your favorite sauce, or bake in the oven. Serve all puffed up, like a soufflé.

56. Gravlax à la Française
(Salt-Cured Salmon with Green Peppercorns)

GRAVLAX, OR GRAVLAKS, is a Scandinavian salmon dish. It is customarily made by boning out a fresh salmon and pickling it with lots of sugar and a dash of salt. It is heavily seasoned with dill. After a day or so, the fillets are sliced and served raw with a sweet mustard and dill sauce. Our version, *à la française,* is pickled with salt instead of sugar and is seasoned with a number of fresh herbs and a lot of green peppercorns. It is served sprinkled with capers, virgin oil and a dash of vinegar. One 7- to 8-pound salmon will serve about 30 persons.

1. Choose the freshest possible salmon with bright and glossy eyes and red, plump gills. Cut off the head, sliding your knife under the bone near the gills.

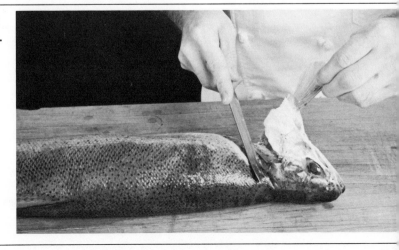

2. Using a sharp knife, start cutting along, and just above, the backbone.

3. Follow the central bone. Try to leave as little meat as possible on the bone.

4. Do not cut through, but follow the shape of the rib cage, sliding your knife, almost flat, along the ribs. Finish by "lifting up" the whole fillet.

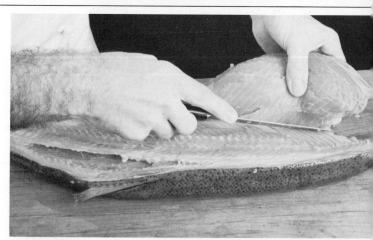

5. Cut under the backbone and follow the same method as described in steps 3 and 4. The central bone is now on top of the knife.

6. Go slowly and be careful not to cut into the meat with your knife. Keep the blade almost flat. Separate the flesh and the rib cage, without going through the ribs.

7. Central bone completely separated. Note the rib cage.

8. Using small pliers, pull out the bones which go straight down in a line, almost in the center of each fillet. Start at the head. (This is the same technique used to clean smoked salmon.)

9. You can feel the bones by rubbing the tip of one finger from the head down to the tail of the fillet. The bones go about three-quarters down the fillet and there are about 30.

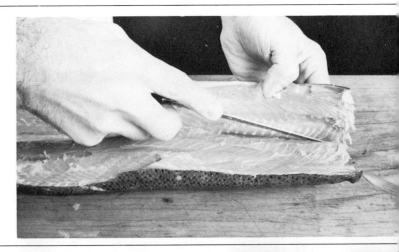

10. Using a large, stiff knife, begin to remove the skin.

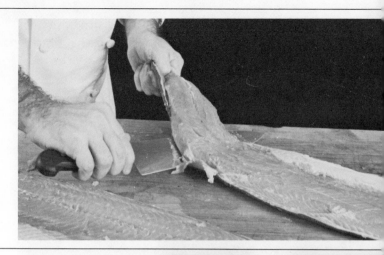

11. Keep the blade on a 30-degree angle so you do not cut through the skin. Pull on the skin with one hand, and cut forward in jigsaw fashion, scraping the skin clear of all meat.

12. Remove the skin and discard.

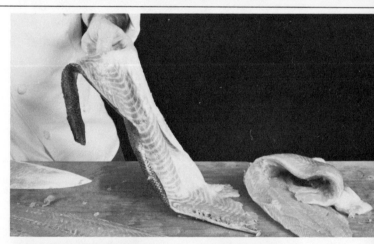

13. Remove, as thin as you possibly can, the white skin on the inside and thinner side of each fillet.

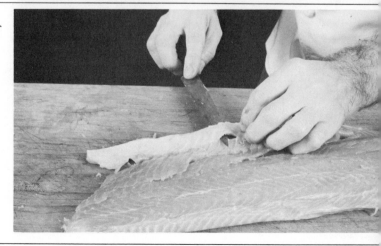

14. Turn the fillets over. All along the central line you will notice a dark brownish strip of flesh. Cut if off, going all the way down the center line.

15. Two fillets: in the foreground, the inside; in the background, the outside. The meat should be completely pink and cleaned of brown meat, bones and gristle. Seven to 8 pounds of salmon will yield two fillets between 2¼ and 2½ pounds each.

16. For each fillet, mix together ⅓ cup coarse (kosher) salt and 2 teaspoons granulated sugar. Place the fillets on a large piece of aluminum foil. Rub the salt and sugar mixture on both sides of the fillet. Reduce the salt and sugar mixture if the fillets are smaller.

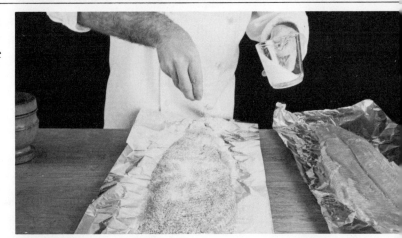

17. Cover with another sheet of foil and fold the edges carefully.

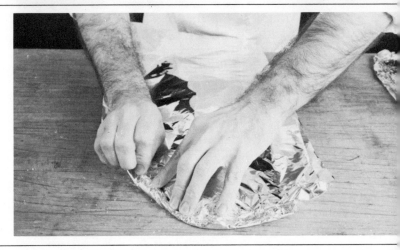

18. The fillets should be well wrapped and tight in the foil. Place on a tray in the refrigerator for a day and a half. Turn the fillet upside down and let pickle for another day and a half. (If the fillets are smaller or thinner, cut the curing time to 2 days instead of 3.)

19. After 3 days, unwrap the fillets. Mash 4 tablespoons green peppercorns (you need the soft green canned peppercorns from Madagascar) into a purée. Chop ½ cup of fresh herbs (chervil, tarragon and thyme mixed together). Spread on both sides of the fillets (¼ cup for one fillet). (If green peppercorns are not available, you can use a tablespoon of coarsely ground black peppercorn instead.)

20. Wrap again in foil and place between 2 cookie sheets. Place about 8 to 10 pounds of weight on top of the cookie sheets to flatten the fillets. Keep refrigerated and pressed for 12 to 24 hours. Slice, technique 115, and serve. (The peppercorns and herbs may discolor the salmon in spots. This does not impair its flavor.)

57. Saumon Poché en Gelée

(Poached Salmon Glazed with Aspic)

THERE IS NOTHING MORE GLORIOUS than a large, decorated, glazed salmon for a buffet. It is not difficult to make but it requires some time and effort. You will need a fish poacher, preferably one that is made of tin or stainless steel because aluminum tends to discolor the broth. For a 6½- to 7-pound salmon, the poacher should be 28 to 30 inches long. Make the vegetable stock and poach the salmon in it one day ahead. (If there's any salmon left over, the meat can be molded in aspic and served very attractively with vegetable garnishes as described in the next technique.)

2 *cups coarsely chopped green of leek*
2 *cups diced carrots*
2 *cups coarsely chopped leafy celery*
2 *tablespoons salt*
1 *teaspoon black peppercorns*
4 *bay leaves*
2 *thyme leaves*

1. Place all the ingredients in a large kettle, cover with water and boil on a high heat for 30 minutes. Pour the stock and vegetables into the fish poacher.

2. Place the removable perforated rack on top of the vegetables. Lay the fish on top and fill with cold water, enough to cover the fish. The stock should be barely lukewarm. Bring to a simmer on medium to high heat. As soon as the stock starts simmering, reduce the heat to very low and let the fish poach (just under a simmer) for 30 minutes. (This is equal to 10 minutes per inch of thickness at the thickest point.) Remove from heat and let the fish cool off gently in the broth overnight.

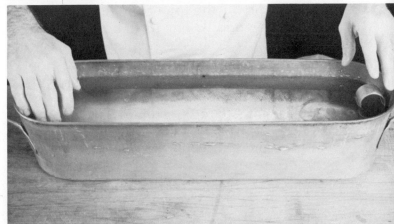

3. Lift from the broth. (The salmon should be intact. If it is split, it boiled too fast.) Let it drain and set for a good hour. Then slide the salmon onto the working table. Cut through the thick skin in a decorative pattern near the head.

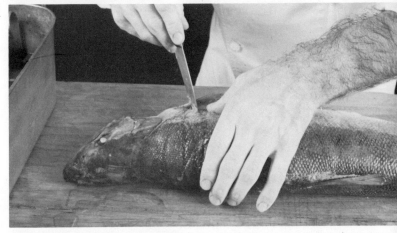

4. Pull the skin off. It should come easily.

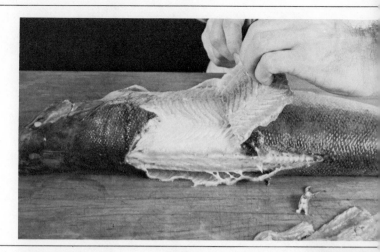

5. Using a small pair of pliers or tweezers, pull off the bones that stick out along the back of the fish.

6. Scrape off the top of the flesh, especially along the middle line to remove darkish brown fatty flesh. The salmon should be nice and pink all over. When the salmon is all cleaned, slide it onto a large serving platter. If you do not own a platter large enough to accommodate the salmon, cut an oval piece of plywood, pad with a towel, cover with a piece of white cloth and staple underneath.

7. Using vegetable flowers, technique 11, decorate the salmon. First, place long strips of blanched green of leeks near the head and tail to outline the edge of the skin. Next, place strips down both sides of the salmon to frame the area to be decorated.

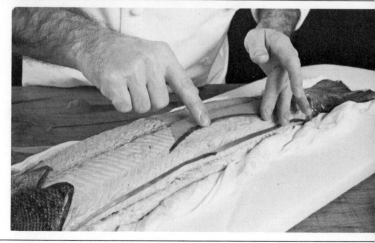

8. Make a flowerpot with thin slices of cooked carrots and green of leek.

9. Make flowers using your imagination. Simulate the eye of the fish with the white of a hard-boiled egg and the black of an olive.

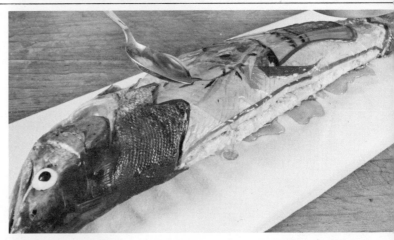

10. Make an aspic with the poaching broth by thoroughly mixing together 5 egg whites, 3 cups greens (a mixture of leeks, scallions, parsley and celery) and 5 to 6 envelopes of plain gelatin. Add 10 cups of strong, flavorful poaching liquid. Bring the mixture to a boil, stirring to avoid scorching. Let it come to a strong boil; then shut the heat off. Let the mixture settle for 10 minutes, then pour through a sieve lined with wet paper towels. Chill the mixture on ice until syrupy, and glaze the salmon. Repeat until the whole surface is coated with aspic.

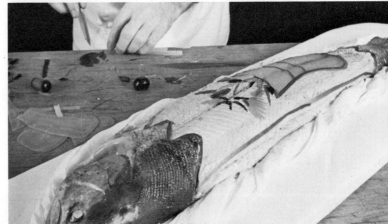

11. Prepare the garnishes. Fill artichoke bottoms, technique 66, with vegetable salad (for recipe, see technique 24, *macédoine*).

12. Slit, without going through, a large wedge of tomato. Pull open and

13. set a quarter of a hard-boiled egg in the opening.

14. Cut two tomatoes in half. Squeeze the seeds and some juice out. Compress the flesh inside to make a receptacle and fill it with the vegetable salad.

15. Decorate the top of the garnishes with strips or cut-outs of tomatoes, leeks, eggs and the like. Decorate around the salmon with lettuce leaves and the garnishes. Carve in the dining room, technique 116.

The salmon will serve 15 to 18.

58. Aspic de Saumon *(Salmon Molded in Aspic)*

THIS DISH IS AN ATTRACTIVE WAY to serve leftover poached salmon. The salmon pieces are suspended in aspic and garnished with eggs, tomatoes and a vegetable salad.

1. Poach a salmon and prepare the aspic following the directions in the preceding technique or use leftover poached salmon if you have it on hand. Pour 1 cup of melted aspic into a mold and roll it in a bowl filled with ice so the aspic coats the side of the mold as it hardens. (Alternatively, you could fill the mold with aspic—you will need a larger quantity—and set it into ice. The outside will solidify first. When the aspic is set all around, but slightly soft in the middle, scoop out the center to leave only an outside layer about ¼ inch thick.)

2. Note how the aspic coats the sides.

3. Add more aspic and keep twisting the pan to thicken the coating on the entire inside of the mold.

4. Garnish the bottom with some pieces of poached salmon and hard-boiled eggs.

5. Add a little more aspic and let it set.

6. Garnish the inside of the mold with salmon arranged on top of the aspic. Add hard-boiled egg, tomato and so on, to decorate to your liking.

7. Fill the center with a vegetable salad (for recipe, see technique 24, *macédoine*).

8. Cover the top with a layer of syrupy aspic. Let it set overnight, if possible.

9. To unmold, pull the solidified mass with the tips of your fingers all around the mold. It should detach itself easily from the side.

10. When the edges are loosened, turn the mold upside down on a platter and cover with a towel wrung in hot water.

11. After barely a minute, the mold should lift off easily.

12. Cut wedges with a thin sharp knife and

13. serve on individual cold plates. You may garnish the aspic with lettuce leaves and tomatoes and serve it with homemade mayonnaise, technique 22.

59. Sole: Entière, Filets, Paupiettes
(Preparing Sole)

YOU WILL FIND SOLE, especially Dover sole, featured in fine fish stores and restaurants, and rightly so, for this is probably the most versatile of fish. Dover sole is not found in North American waters and is imported, fresh or frozen, from Europe, the best being caught in the English Channel. It is the best of the small "flat" fish family (which includes grey sole, lemon sole, flounder, fluke and dab, to cite the most known), and it can be prepared in more than a hundred different ways. It is excellent broiled, poached whole or filleted, in mousses, *paupiettes,* sautéed in butter, deep-fried and baked, to give you a few examples. If Dover sole is not available in your market, apply the recipe to its kith and kin, especially the grey or lemon sole which are the firmest, though they are not firm enough to be char-broiled as the Dover sole could be. A 1-pound fresh sole will give you approximately 6 ounces of flesh after cleaning and filleting.

WHOLE

1. To prepare the Dover sole for poaching, broiling or sautéeing whole, place black skin up and cut the very tip of the tail. Loosen the black skin on the tail by scraping it enough so that you can take hold of the skin ·with your fingers.

2. Take a firm grip on the skin and

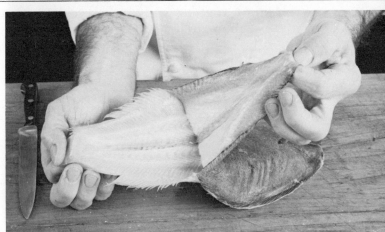

3. pull it off in one piece. Discard.

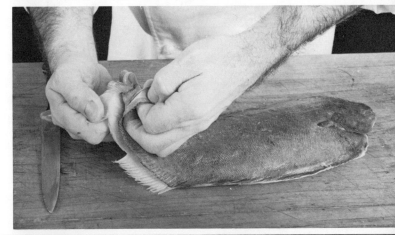

4. Detach the head close to the gills cutting on a diagonal.

5. Using sturdy fish shears, trim the protruding fins on both sides.

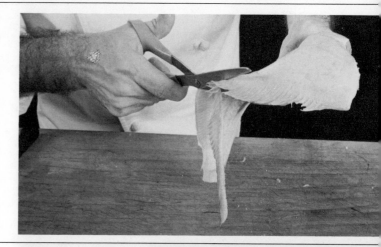

6. Using the handle of the knife, push out the roe. If you can, pull the roe out in one piece. Reserve to fry or sauté.

7. Using a regular knife, a fish scaler or an empty scallop shell, scale the white (also called the blind) side. When the fish is cooked whole, the white skin is left on because it is tender, and it makes a delicious and crusty surface when broiled or sautéed.

FILLETS AND PAUPIETTES

1. Remove the black skin and head as described in the preceding steps 1–4. Cut through the fillet to the bone to mark the contour of the flesh.

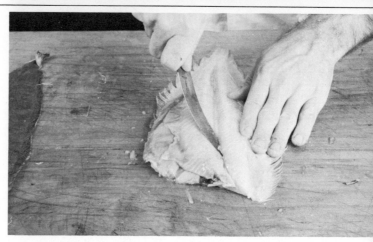

2. Slide a fillet of sole knife, which has a special thin, sharp and very flexible blade, under the central bone in the middle (apply pressure to flex the blade so that it slides along the central bone) and detach the fillet from underneath. Repeat with the other side, sliding the blade on the flat ribs. You now have 2 single fillets taken from the top of the sole.

3. Turn the sole over and fillet the other side. The correctly filleted sole yields 4 single fillets, 2 on each side. The cleaned, central bone and fins are excellent for stock or fish *fumet*.

4. For *paupiettes*, the fillets are rolled, starting with the thickest end. Be sure that the white, fleshy side which touched the central bone, is on the outside of the *paupiette*. Rolled this way, the *paupiette* will contract during cooking and keep its shape. Rolled the wrong way, it will open during cooking.

5. When served flat, the fillets are *ciselés* to retain their natural shape; i.e., little slits are made on top to prevent them from contracting while they cook.

6. Cut only the top layer of the fillets on the sinewy side.

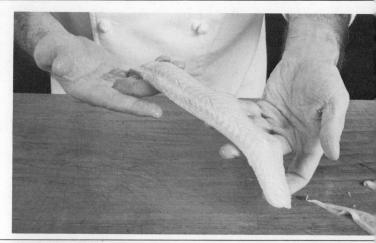

7. Fillets, stuffed or unstuffed, can be folded in half with the slits inside and served poached, with or without a sauce.

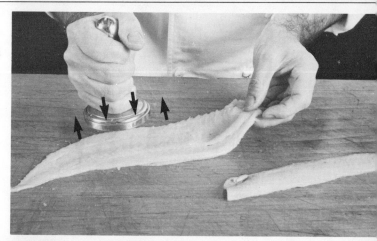

8. Fillets should be pounded when used to line a mold. Pound gently to avoid tearing the meat apart. The motion should be down and toward you (see technique 96, steps 4 and 5).

9. Arrange in a *savarin* mold to make a lining for a mousse or a quenelle mixture, technique 55.

60. Sole Bercy *(Baked Sole with Mushrooms and Parsley)*

1 1¼-pound Dover sole
3 tablespoons sweet butter
2 tablespoons chopped shallots
¾ teaspoon salt
¼ teaspoon freshly ground white pepper
4 large mushrooms, sliced (1 cup loosely packed)
3 tablespoons chopped fresh parsley
⅓ cup dry white wine
1 tablespoon flour
⅓ cup heavy cream
5 or 6 drops of lemon juice

Following technique 59, whole sole, steps 1–7, clean the sole, leaving the white skin on.

1. Rub a gratin dish with 1 tablespoon butter. Sprinkle shallots on top, along with salt and pepper.

2. Arrange the sole on top, and add another tablespoon butter.

3. Top with the mushrooms, 2 tablespoons parsley and the wine.

4. Place a buttered piece of wax paper on top and place in a 450-degree preheated oven for 10 minutes.

5. At this point, the sole should be done. Lift the sole up with a large spatula and place on a plate.

6. Using the blade of a knife, "push off" the bones on either side of the fillets. They should come off easily.

7. Lift up the top fillets of the sole from the central bone and

8. place in a gratin dish or serving platter.

9. Remove the central bone in one piece and

10. place the second half of the sole on top of the first half. The sole is now completely boned and reconstituted. Cover the sole with the wax paper and keep warm in the oven.

11. Melt 1 tablespoon butter in a saucepan, add the flour and cook for 1 minute on low heat. Add the drippings of the sole and bring to a boil, stirring with a whisk. Add the cream, bring to a boil and simmer for 2 minutes. Correct seasonings with salt and pepper, if needed. Add 5 or 6 drops of lemon juice to the sauce.

12. Remove the sole from the oven and coat with the sauce.

13. Sprinkle with remaining parsley and serve immediately.

This recipe serves 2 as a first course.

61. Sole Meunière *(Sole Sautéed in Butter)*

WHEREAS THE SOLE BERCY is cooked with the little side bones intact (they are removed after cooking, technique 60, step 6), *sole meunière* is cooked without them. The reason is that where the trimmings enhance the stock the *sole bercy* is cooked in, they just absorb the butter used to sauté the *sole meunière*. They do not add any extra flavor to the meat of the sole. Therefore, even though the sole will look smaller, it is preferable to remove the side bones before cooking.

1. Clean the sole (technique 59, steps 1–7), leaving the white skin on. With a pair of scissors, remove the bones on the side of the fillets.

2. Sprinkle the sole with salt and a small dash of pepper. Dredge in flour.

3. Melt ⅓ stick of butter in a skillet. Place sole in the hot butter, skin side down, and cook on medium to low heat for 6 to 7 minutes on each side.

4. Bring the skillet directly to the table. Using a spoon and fork, lift up the top fillets and place on each side of the sole.

5. Remove the central bone and discard.

6. Place the bottom fillets on a hot plate and cover with the top fillets. The sole is reconstructed and completely boned.

7. Add 1 tablespoon of hot brown gravy all around (optional) and the drippings of the skillet.

8. Cover with slices of lemon dipped in chopped parsley (see lemon slices for fish, technique 19) and serve immediately.

This recipe serves 2 as a first course.

62. Préparation de la Truite
(Cleaning and Boning Trout)

THE RIGHT WAY TO STUFF A TROUT WHOLE is to bone it and stuff it through the back. In this case, the trout shouldn't be opened and gutted in front as is usually done, but through the gill. If you are not a fisherman, it's not easy to come upon trout that haven't been gutted in the usual manner. However, a reliable fish store should be able to order them for you (usually alive) with some advance notice.

1. To gut the trout, insert your index finger into the opening of the gill, hook the gill and pull.

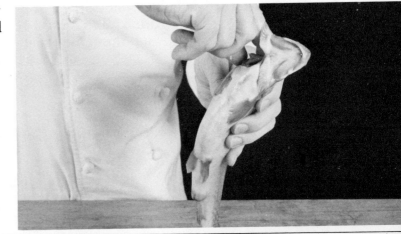

2. The gill will come out with the gut attached to it. Run water into the cavity to clean the inside of the fish as well as you possibly can without opening it.

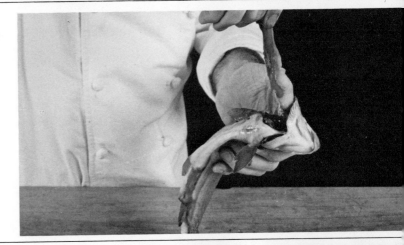

3. Trim the fins off.

4. Place the trout on the table and, holding it flat with one hand, start cutting along and just above the backbone.

5. Do not cut through, but follow the shape of the rib cage, sliding your knife, almost flat, along the ribs to detach the meat from the bone.

6. Repeat on the other side of the bone to detach the other fillet from the rib cage.

7. Sever the bone at the tail and pull to detach from the body. Sever at the head. Stuff and cook, following the recipe in technique 65, or use one of your own.

63. Paupiettes de Truites *(Rolled Trout)*

1. For *paupiettes* of trout, you can buy trout that has been gutted through the belly—the usual way. Separate the fillets from the bone, technique 56, steps 2–6, and sever from the tail end.

2. Remove the central bone near the head.

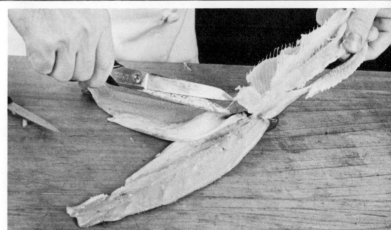

3. Roll each fillet so that the skin shows on the outside.

4. Rolled up trout, ready to cook. Trout are often prepared this way when they are to be poached and served cold in aspic.

64. Truite Amandine *(Trout with Almonds)*

1. In this technique, you can use trout that has been gutted in the usual way and boned through the opening of the belly. Slide the blade of a thin, sharp paring knife behind the rib cage, and detach the ribs from the flesh.

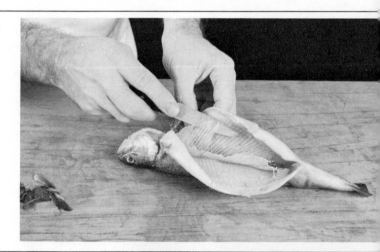

2. Repeat on the other side.

3. Continue to separate the meat from the central bone without going through the skin of the back.

4. Pull the bone loose, detaching it from the fish. Sever at the tail end and

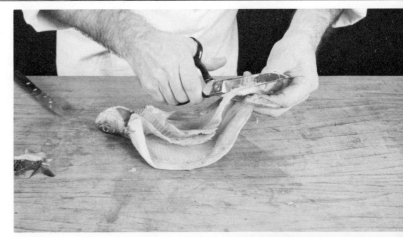

5. near the head.

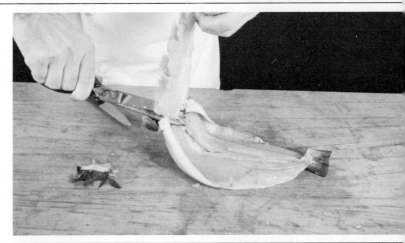

6. Fold the fish in half and

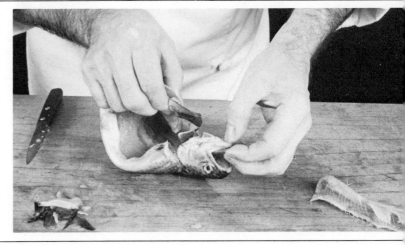

7. push the tail through the mouth.

8. Sprinkle the trout with salt, pepper and dredge lightly in flour. Melt 3 tablespoons butter in a heavy skillet, and when hot, place the fish in skillet, skin side down, and cook on medium to low heat for 5 to 6 minutes on each side. The skin should be crisp and nicely browned.

9. Place the trout on a warm plate and add 1 tablespoon sliced almonds to the drippings. Cook the almonds for about 1 minute in the hot butter. Spoon almond and drippings mixture over the trout.

10. Sprinkle with a few drops of lemon juice and decorate with slices of lemon dipped in chopped parsley (see lemon slices for fish, technique 19). Serve immediately.

Serve 1 trout per person.

65. Truites Farcies à la Crème

(Stuffed Trout with Cream Sauce)

THE STUFFING

¾ *pound (12 ounces) fillet of fresh fish (it*
   can be sole, trout, pike or even whiting)
2 *egg whites*
1 *cup heavy cream*
¾ *teaspoon salt*
¼ *teaspoon freshly ground white pepper*
1 *tablespoon fresh tarragon (or ½ teaspoon dry)*
2 *tablespoons chopped fresh parsley*

Cut the fillets in small pieces. Place in the container of a food processor (or use a blender, making the mousse in several batches). Add the egg whites and blend until smooth. With the motor still on, add the cream slowly, letting the mixture blend well. Add the salt, pepper and herbs; blend well. Set aside and refrigerate.

THE TROUT

4 *1-pound trout*
10 *mushrooms*
½ *cup chopped shallots*
1 *cup julienne of carrots, blanched in boiling*
   water for 2 to 3 minutes, drained
2 *teaspoons salt*
½ *teaspoon freshly ground white pepper*
2 *cups dry white wine*
½ *stick sweet butter, plus 2 tablespoons for the*
   roux

1½ *tablespoons flour*
1 *cup heavy cream*
1 *tablespoon* glace de viande *(meat glaze),*
   optional

Bone and clean the 4 trout through the back following the directions in technique 62. Set aside. Preheat the oven to 400 degrees.

1. Cut the caps of the mushrooms into slices.

2. Stack the slices together and cut into juliennes. You should have about a cup. Use the stems for soup, stew, purée and the like.

3. Butter the bottom of a roasting pan generously.

4. Sprinkle with some of the mushrooms, shallots, carrots, salt and pepper.

5. Place the mousse in a pastry bag fitted with a plain tube. Stuff the 4 trout.

6. Arrange the trout on the bed of vegetables. To prevent the stuffing from moving, place a piece of wax paper against each trout.

7. Place the trout on top and fold the paper to cover the fish. If the trout is opened on both sides, wrap the paper all around to keep the stuffing inside.

8. Cover with the remaining vegetable garnishes, salt and pepper.

9. Add the wine. Butter half of a piece of wax paper. Fold the unbuttered half over the buttered half,

10. then unfold. The paper is now completely coated with butter. Place the ½ stick butter in pieces on top of the trout.

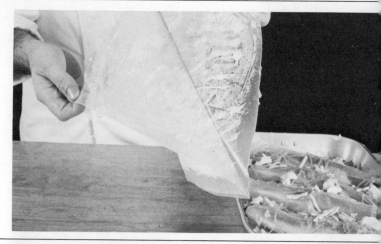

11. Cover with the buttered paper and bring to a boil on top of the stove. Place in the preheated oven for 15 minutes.

12. Lift the trout up from the poaching liquid and place on a serving platter. Pull the skin off from one side.

13. Turn and pull the skin from the other side.

14. Using a slotted spoon, place the julienne of vegetables on top of fish.

15. Cover with the wax paper and keep warm in the oven.

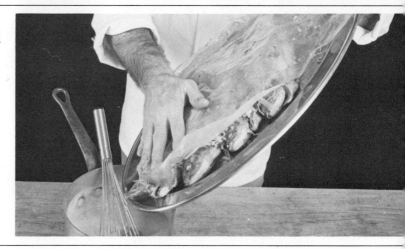

16. Melt the 2 tablespoons butter in a heavy skillet. Add the flour, mix and cook 1 minute on low heat. Pour the poaching liquid into the roux, mix well and bring to a boil. Let simmer for 2 minutes and add the cream. Bring to a boil and reduce the heat. Add the *glace de viande* and simmer for 2 minutes.

17. Remove the trout from the oven. You will notice that some liquid has accumulated around the fish. Add the liquid to the sauce and mix well.

18. Taste the sauce for seasoning. It may need salt and pepper. Coat the trout with the sauce.

19. Serve immediately.

This recipe serves 8.

Vegetables

66. Artichauts et Fonds d'Artichauts *(Artichokes and Artichoke Hearts)*

ALTHOUGH ARTICHOKES have been widely cultivated in France since the middle of the sixteenth century (Rabelais mentions them), they are not a common vegetable on the American table. Cooked artichokes can be served cold as a first course, lukewarm with hollandaise or melted butter as a vegetable, or hot stuffed with meat or other vegetables. The small, young artichokes, especially the Provence or the Tuscany violet, are eaten raw with salt and butter or with a vinaigrette.

WHOLE

1. A good-sized artichoke, Breton Stocky or Lyon Green, weighs about 8 ounces. Cut the stem off with a knife, or break it at the base (this helps pull out of the heart the stringy fibers that develop in overmatured artichokes).

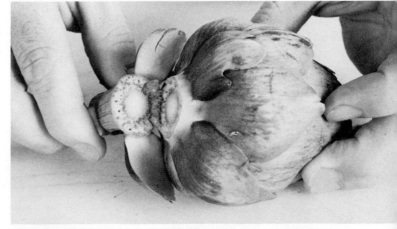

2. Cut off at least 1½ inches of the top.

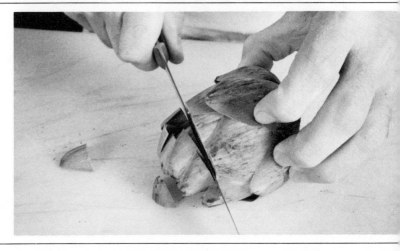

3. Cut off about one-third of the top of each leaf. The ends are very tough, bitter and often thorny. The reason is also aesthetic.

4. To prevent discoloration (artichokes turn dark very fast), tie a slice of lemon to the bottom of the artichoke where the stem is cut. Restaurants that cook artichokes several days ahead use this technique to keep the bottom white until serving time. The technique is optional.

5. Place the artichoke in a large amount of boiling, salted water. Place a wet towel directly on top of the artichoke to keep it wet and immersed during cooking. Boil as fast as possible for 40 to 50 minutes, depending on the size. Do not cover. Artichokes tend to become bitter if covered during cooking. To test for doneness, pull out a leaf; if done, it pulls out easily. Do not overcook. Place under cold water (see step 10, technique 67) to cool.

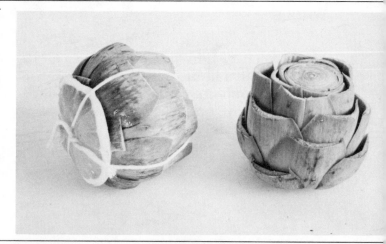

6. Avoid refrigerating artichokes for it changes the taste. Serve not too cold. To serve lukewarm, lower into hot water for 2 to 3 minutes. Drain. Spread the outside leaves at the top enough to slide your fingers inside and around the center leaves.

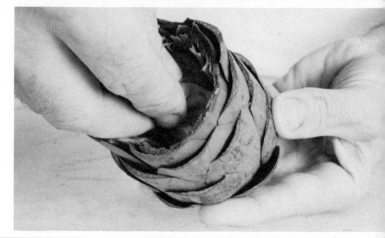

7. Pull out the central leaves; they should come out in one piece like a small funnel or cone. Now, the "choke" is exposed.

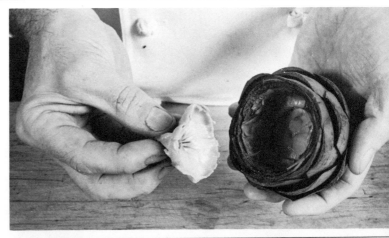

8. Using your fingers, or a teaspoon, remove the hairy choke from the cavity.

9. Replace the central leaves upside down on the opened top of the artichoke and garnish with curly parsley. Serve on a tulip napkin, technique 36, or directly on plate.

HEARTS

1. The artichoke bottom or heart is extensively used as a garnish or in the making of a dish. It can be filled with purée of smoked salmon or tomatoes, as well as with poached eggs or cooked beef marrow. Many restaurants use canned artichoke bottoms but the difference is like night and day. Break the stem and cut the leaves all around the base of the artichoke. Trim as closely as you can manage without taking "meat" from the heart itself. This is a delicate technique.

2. Cut the central core of the leaves just above the heart. Leave the choke attached; it will be removed after cooking.

3. Trim the remaining greenish leaves and pieces all around the heart.

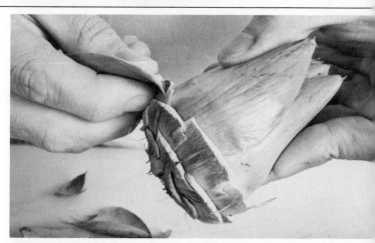

4. If you find it difficult to execute step 2, instead of cutting around the heart, you can break the leaves off at the base. Be careful not to pull out pieces of meat when breaking the leaves off.

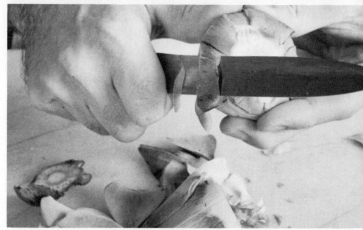

5. Trim all of the green off as evenly as you can manage.

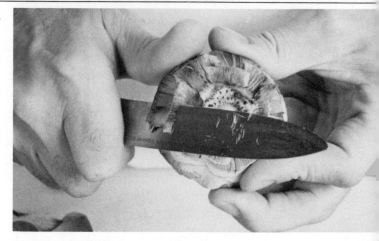

6. Rub with lemon to avoid discoloration. If a recipe calls for pieces of artichoke bottom, separate the heart into 6 equal wedges and remove the choke, using a small paring knife. Cook according to your recipe. To cook 6 artichoke bottoms, place 3 cups water, 2 tablespoons vegetable oil, the juice of 1 lemon and ½ teaspoon salt in a saucepan. Bring to a boil. Add the heart and simmer for 20 to 30 minutes.

7. The heart should be tender when pierced with the point of a knife. Let cool enough to handle and remove the choke with a spoon. It should slide off easily if the artichoke is cooked enough. Cover the hearts with the cooking liquid and refrigerate. They will keep at least one week refrigerated. Use as needed.

67. Asperges *(Asparagus)*

ASPARAGUS HAS BEEN commonly cultivated in Europe from the seventeenth century on. The large white, fleshy Argenteuil is considered one of the best, although rarely available in the United States. The commonly found varieties are the Italian purple (with almost violet-colored tips) and the green Mary Washington type. There are countless ways of cooking and serving asparagus. The best is the simplest, boiled and served plain with vinaigrette, hollandaise or melted butter.

1. The fresh stalks are firm, not wrinkled, and the tips are tightly closed. To make the whole spear edible, the asparagus must be peeled. Use a small paring knife or a vegetable peeler.

2. Determine by scratching with your nail the place where the outer skin is getting fibrous and tough. It is usually 1 or 2 inches under the tip. Holding the asparagus at the root end, peel from the tip down toward the root until you touch your finger. Peel, rotating the asparagus as you go along so that the whole spear is peeled.

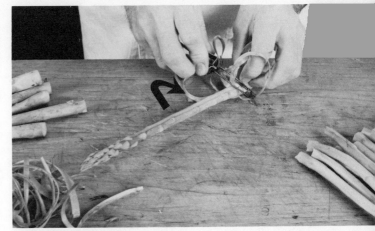

3. Cut or break the stalk at the end of the peel.

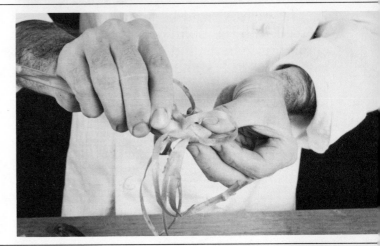

4. Asparagus are often bundled into a portion of about 10 or 12 thin stalks. Grab a handful and align the tips by leveling them on the flat table.

5. Holding the spears firmly in one hand, wrap your middle finger with soft kitchen string.

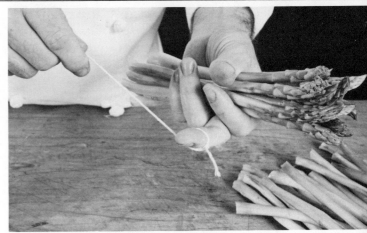

6. Start bundling the lower part of the bunch. Be sure to make it tight. (This is one reason why you should not use string that is too thin and might cut.)

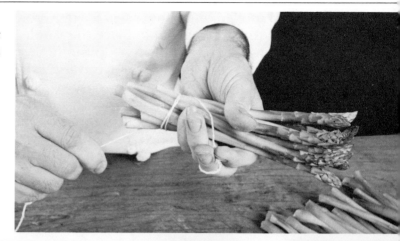

7. Come across, still holding the bundle tight and

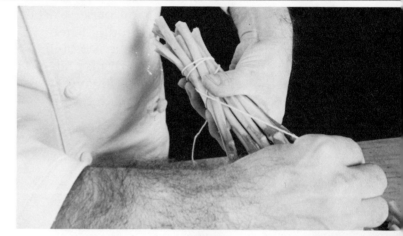

8. tie the front, lower than the tips. Secure with a double knot.

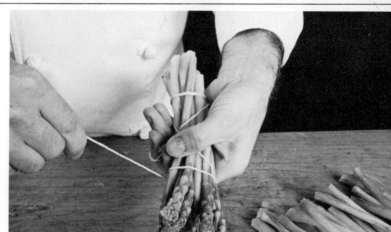

9. Trim the spears at the root end. The asparagus are now the same length. Bring a large pot of salted water to a rolling boil. Lower the asparagus into the water and cover them until it starts boiling again; uncover. If the cover is left on during the whole cooking time, the asparagus will turn yellowish. Boil, depending on size, from 6 to 10 minutes. They should still be crunchy, but cooked enough. Lift the bundle from the boiling water and serve immediately.

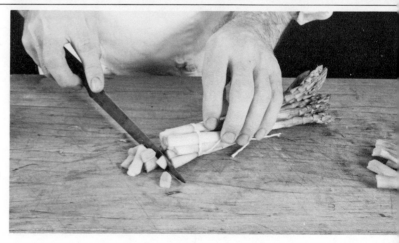

10. If cooked ahead or served cold, as soon as the asparagus is done, place the whole kettle under cold water to stop the cooking. To prevent breaking the asparagus, place a spoon across the pot to divert the force of the water so it falls gently on the tender tips. (If only a small amount of asparagus is to be cooked, place ½ inch water in a skillet. Spread the asparagus in one layer and cook, covered, for 4 minutes. Lift out the asparagus and let cool on a plate.)

11. Drain the asparagus on paper towels. To serve warm, place a bundle, when needed, in a sieve and lower into boiling water for about 1 minute. Drain and serve immediately. To serve cold, arrange the spears on a large, oblong platter and

12. garnish the ends with a bunch of curly parsley.

68. Purée de Carottes *(Puree of Carrots)*

PUREE OF FRESH VEGETABLES makes an elegant accompaniment to saddle of lamb, creamed chicken, veal roast and other dishes.

1. Place 3 pounds of peeled carrots in a kettle. Cover with water and add 2 teaspoons salt. Bring to a boil and simmer for about 20 minutes. The carrots should be tender to the point of a knife. Drain. Line a bowl with cheesecloth.

2. Place the carrots in a food mill and strain on top of the cheesecloth.

3. Tie the four corners of the cheesecloth.

4. Push a stick through it and

5. let it hang in a deep vessel to drain the pulp of excess moisture. Let it hang for 2 hours.

6. Lift and press to extrude more liquid. Discard the liquid or use for soup.

7. Place the pulp in a saucepan. Add ⅓ cup heavy cream, 2 tablespoons sweet butter, 1 teaspoon salt and ¼ teaspoon freshly ground white pepper. Heat slowly on low heat and serve hot.

This recipe yields 6 to 8 servings.

69. Chou-fleur *(Cauliflower)*

IT MAY COME AS A SURPRISE to many Americans to learn that in France cauliflower is a very popular vegetable. It can be eaten raw with a spicy dressing, used in soup, pickled, combined with cream sauce and cheese or browned in butter.

1. In choosing cauliflower, be sure the heads are very white and very firm with small, compact flowers squeezed together. Separate the leaves from the stem with a paring knife.

2. Separate the flowerets from the central core by cutting around each one with your knife.

3. If the cauliflower is old, pull off the tough, outer layer from the stem of each floweret with a small paring knife. Drop the cauliflower into a large pot of salted water and boil 10 to 12 minutes until the stem can be pierced with the point of a knife. Immediately place the whole pot under cold, running water to stop the cooking. Protect the tender flowerets from the heavy stream of cold water by resting a large spoon on the kettle to divert the water's force (see step 10, technique 67). When cool, drain thoroughly and cover with plastic wrap.

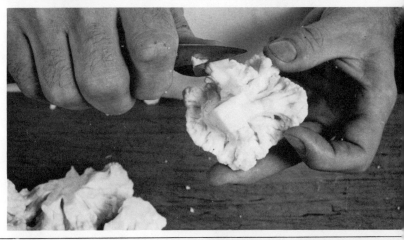

4. To sauté cauliflower, place the cooked flowerets, head side down, in foaming butter. Sprinkle with salt and pepper. Bring to medium heat and cook for a few minutes, until the flowerets are nicely brown. Turn each piece on the other side and brown for a few minutes more.

5. Arrange the cauliflower on a platter in a circle so that the flowerets are facing the outside of the plate.

6. Keep piling up flowerets to reconstruct a whole head of cauliflower.

7. Cauliflower ready to serve. Sprinkle with parsley and serve immediately.

70. Crêpes de Maïs *(Corn Crêpes)*

WHOLE EARS OF CORN are excellent poached (not boiled) in salted water, or cooked in aluminum foil on top of the barbecue. A puree of the pulp is very elegant served with veal or lamb. (Melt sweet butter in a saucepan, add the pulp, salt and pepper and simmer a few minutes, just enough for the starch to tighten and the puree to thicken into a creamy mixture. You may add some cream or some white sauce to extend it.) With the pulp, one can also make excellent crêpes.

6 medium-sized ears of corn
4½ tablespoons flour
4 large eggs
1 teaspoon salt
¼ teaspoon freshly ground white pepper
½ cup heavy cream
½ stick (4 tablespoons) melted sweet butter

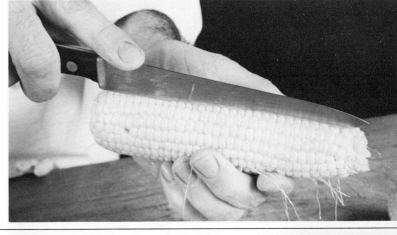

1. Holding the cleaned ear of corn in one hand, using a sharp knife, cut through the middle of each row of kernels. The object is to open each kernel so the pulp can be "pushed" out.

2. Stand the ear straight up. Using the back (dull side) of the knife, scrape the pulp out of the opened kernels, turning the ear as you go along. You should have approximately 1½ cups of pulp. Mix all ingredients thoroughly, starting with the pulp and the flour. Make the crêpes, technique 168, steps 2–8. The crêpes will be very delicate and fragile to handle. Serve as soon as possible as a vegetable or as a garnish for your favorite meat.

This recipe yields approximately 20 crêpes.

71. Céleri-rave *(Celeriac or Celery Root)*

CELERIAC OR CELERY ROOT, usually available in Italian markets, is not the root of the common stalk celery. Though it tastes like celery, it is a different plant. It is excellent cooked, but is commonly served raw in julienne with an oil and mustard sauce.

1. Peel the celeriac with a knife or a vegetable peeler.

2. Cut the celeriac in half through the root. Remove the spongy flesh in the center near the stem end.

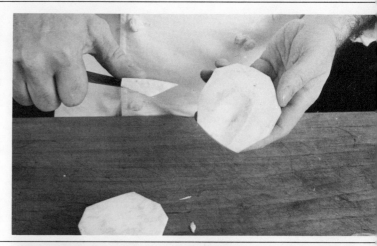

3. Using a knife or a *mandoline,* slice into ⅛-inch slices.

4. Stack a few slices together and cut into a fine julienne. Make a mayonnaise, technique 22, but triple the amount of mustard and double the vinegar. Mix with the celeriac and add more salt and pepper. Make the salad at least one hour in advance. Serve cool, but not ice cold.

72. Salade de Concombres *(Cucumber Salad)*

FIRST CULTIVATED more than 3,000 years ago, cucumbers are widely used in the United States as well as in many European countries and India. Cucumbers can be served raw as a salad, cooked or stuffed as a vegetable, or pickled to use as a condiment. However, it is raw in a summer salad (or as a salad ingredient) that cucumbers are most frequently served.

3 cucumbers
1 tablespoon coarse salt
4 tablespoons sour cream
1½ tablespoons lemon juice
½ teaspoon freshly ground white pepper
2 tablespoons peanut oil
2 tablespoons chopped fresh dill

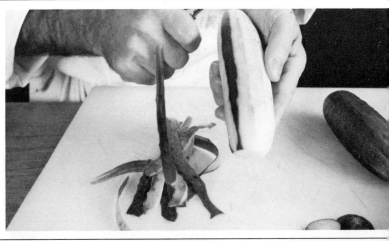

1. Store-bought cucumbers are often coated with a chemical to retard spoilage, and it is better to peel them using a vegetable peeler. You don't have to peel the cucumber if you grow your own.

2. Cut into halves lengthwise. You may slice the cucumber with the seeds, season it and serve that way. However, it is more elegant to remove the seeds. Use a teaspoon.

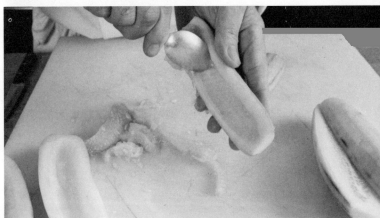

3. Slice into ⅛-inch or ¼-inch slices. You should have about 5 cups.

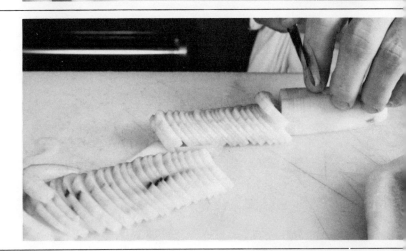

4. Place in a colander and sprinkle with coarse salt. Mix well. Let the cucumber macerate for at least 1 to 2 hours at room temperature. The salt, you will discover, draws the juices from the cucumbers, making them limp, and, paradoxically, very crisp at the same time.

5. Drain, rinse under cold water and press lightly to extract excess moisture. Combine the sour cream, lemon juice and freshly ground white pepper in a bowl. Add the peanut oil, beating with a wire whisk. Combine with the cucumber and the fresh dill. Do not use more salt. Prepared this way, the cucumbers will stay crisp for several days.

 This recipe yields 6 to 8 servings.

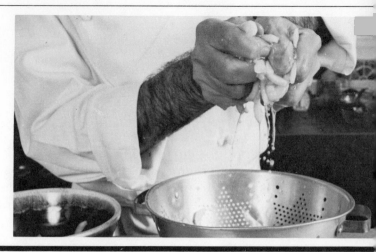

73. Laitues Braisées *(Braised Lettuce)*

BOSTON LETTUCE makes a splendid and unusual cooked vegetable which goes well with veal, as well as chicken and beef. Although lettuce is customarily braised with carrots, onions and herbs, it is excellent boiled in water and finished with butter. One large head of lettuce will serve 2 as a garnish.

1. Remove any bruised leaves from the lettuce and wash in cold water, spreading the leaves gently under the stream of the water to remove any sand. Drop the lettuce into a large kettle of boiling, salted water and cover until it comes to a boil again. Uncover; if left covered, the lettuce will lose its vivid green color and turn yellowish. Place a wet paper towel on top of the lettuce; this will keep the lettuce underwater and help cook it evenly all around.

2. Let boil for 15 to 20 minutes, until the core of the lettuce feels tender to the point of a knife; it should be tender, not mushy. Immediately place the lettuce under cold running water. When cold, remove the lettuce.

3. Be sure not to disturb the natural shape of the lettuce. Squeeze gently to extrude the excess water.

4. Cut the smaller heads into 3 equal-sized pieces.

5. For a larger head, cut in quarters.

6. Place a piece, outside down, on the table and flatten the leafy end gently with a knife.

7. Turn the leafy green part onto the center of the lettuce and,

8. holding it with the point of the knife, fold the core end over it.

9. Trim the core. You should have a nice little package, slightly triangular. Sprinkle lightly with salt and pepper.

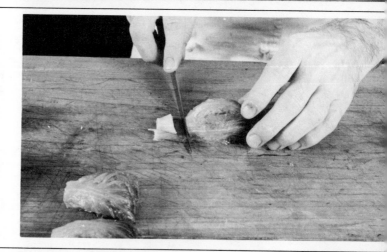

10. Melt some butter in a large skillet. When hot, place the lettuce pieces, folded side up, one next to the other, in the skillet. Do not crowd the skillet. Cook on medium heat 6 to 8 minutes until slightly brown. Turn gently and cook 4 to 5 minutes on the other side.

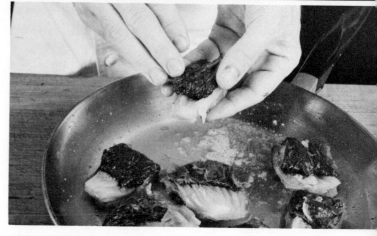

11. Arrange on a serving platter, folded side down. You may coat the lettuce with a good brown gravy, 1 tablespoon per lettuce, and sprinkle some butter cooked to a hazelnut color *(beurre noisette)* on top just before serving.

74. Soufflé de Gourilos *(Escarole Soufflé)*

A SOUFFLÉ, from the verb *souffler* (to breathe, inflate or puff up), is nothing more than a thick white sauce into which egg yolks, flavoring and, finally, beaten egg whites are incorporated. The small air bubbles in the whites expand during baking, pushing it up to magnificent heights. To make this soufflé, you will need a 1½-quart soufflé mold.

4½ *tablespoons sweet butter, plus 1 teaspoon to coat the mold*
¼ *cup grated Parmesan cheese*
3 *scallions, cleaned, washed and sliced thin*
1 *head escarole, trimmed of most of the green leafy part*
1½ *teaspoons salt*
⅓ *cup water*
4½ *tablespoons flour*
1¼ *cups milk*
¼ *teaspoon freshly ground black pepper*
4 *drops Tabasco sauce*

3 *egg yolks*
½ *teaspoon Worcestershire sauce*
1 *cup grated Cheddar cheese, plus strips, optional*
7 *egg whites*

1. Butter the mold with 1 teaspoon soft butter. Be sure it is well coated all around.

2. Add the Parmesan cheese and

3. turn the mold around so that the cheese sticks to the butter. Let the extra cheese fall into a bowl.

4. Refrigerate the coated soufflé mold. A very cold mold helps the soufflé rise straight. Keep your fingers out of the mold. If you smear the coating you may disturb the rising of the mixture.

5. Slice the trimmed escarole coarsely. (Trimmed escarole, called *gourilos* in French, can also be braised in butter or served in a cream sauce.)

6. Melt 1 tablespoon butter in a saucepan and sauté the sliced scallions for 30 to 40 seconds. Add the escarole, ½ teaspoon salt and the water. Cover and cook for 5 to 6 minutes on high heat. Uncover and continue cooking for a few minutes until all liquid has been evaporated.

7. Melt the remaining butter in a saucepan and add the flour. Cook for 1 minute on low heat. Add the milk, 1 teaspoon salt, pepper, Tabasco sauce and bring to a boil, stirring with a whisk. As soon as it reaches the boiling point, the sauce will thicken. Boil on low heat for 1 minute, still stirring to avoid scorching. Add the yolks and mix well.

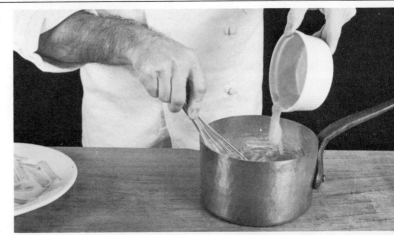

8. Add the salad mixture and

9. stir with a spatula. Add the Worcestershire sauce and the grated Cheddar cheese.

10. To whip the whites by hand, use a large balloon whip. It should be flexible, long, with a lot of wires, so that the whites are lifted up with each stroke. Use a copper or stainless steel bowl. The equipment should be immaculate. A greasy bowl or yolk particle in the whites will prevent them from whipping.

11. Beat with a strong motion, making a complete circle with each stroke, and lifting up the whole bulk of whites. (Cream is beaten more gently. If you beat cream as hard as you do egg whites, it would turn into butter.)

12. As soon as the whites hold a peak, but are still "wet," place about one-third in the white sauce–escarole mixture and mix with the whisk. Work as fast as you can, because as soon as you stop beating the whites, they start to break down and become grainy.

13. Using a spatula, fold the remaining whites and escarole mixture together.

14. Fill the soufflé mold to the edges. At this point, the soufflé can be refrigerated, and will keep for at least a couple of hours. At baking time, sprinkle the reserved Parmesan cheese on top and place on a cookie sheet in a 375-degree preheated oven. Reduce the heat to 350 degrees and bake for 30 minutes.

15. Five minutes before the soufflé is done, you may arrange strips of cheese on top, forming a decorative pattern, and place back in the oven to melt the cheese. Serve immediately.

16. A soufflé (especially if it is collapsed) can be served unmolded. Run a knife around the edges, pulling the soufflé into the mold at the same time, to free it from the mold.

17. Invert and remove the mold.

18. Serve in wedges with or without a light cream sauce.

This recipe serves 6 to 8.

75. Champignons Farcis *(Stuffed Mushrooms)*

MUSHROOM CAPS can be stuffed with meat, fish, shellfish, vegetables or most anything. Snails with garlic butter are often served in mushroom caps. The caps are cooked before they are stuffed.

23 large mushrooms
Salt and freshly ground black pepper
1 tablespoon peanut oil
3 to 4 shallots
3 tablespoons butter
⅓ cup fresh bread crumbs
1 tablespoon grated Parmesan cheese
½ teaspoon paprika
1 tablespoon melted butter

1. Break the stems off 20 large mushrooms. Place the caps, hollow side up, on a cookie sheet. Sprinkle with salt and peanut oil. Place in a 425-degree preheated oven for 10 to 12 minutes. Remove from the oven and turn the caps, hollow side down, to empty them of any liquid.

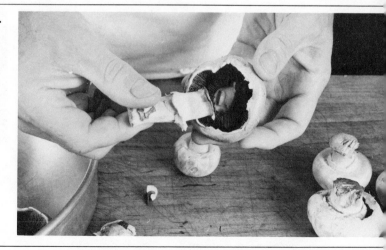

2. Chop the stems and the extra mushrooms very fine. You should have a good 3 cups. Chop the shallots (about 1½ tablespoons chopped). Place 3 tablespoons butter in a saucepan, add the shallots and cook for about 1 minute. Add the chopped mushrooms, salt and pepper and cook until most of the liquid has evaporated and the mixture is dry enough to hold a shape. Let it cool for 10 minutes.

3. Using a spoon, fill the caps so that each cap is rounded on top. Mix together the bread crumbs, Parmesan cheese, paprika and 1 tablespoon of melted butter.

4. Press some bread crumb mixture on top of the stuffed caps,

5. or dip the caps, stuffed side down, into the mixture so that the whole top is heavily coated with the mixture. Place the mushrooms, stuffed side up, under a hot broiler for 3 to 4 minutes, or until nicely browned.

   This recipe serves 4 to 6 as a garnish.

76. Pommes Parisienne *(Fried Potato Balls)*

THE POTATO IS PROBABLY the greatest food contribution that the New World made to the Old. It was introduced in France in the second half of the sixteenth century, but was first used as a decorative plant. It was popularized by an agronomist named Parmentier during the eighteenth century. Hence, in classic cooking, any dish *Parmentier* includes potatoes. The potato is a versatile vegetable; it can be boiled, sautéed, baked, fried, steamed, broiled, stewed and so on.

1. Peel large white potatoes. Keep in cold water to avoid discoloration. Push a round melon ball cutter down into the potato with your thumb as far as it will go.

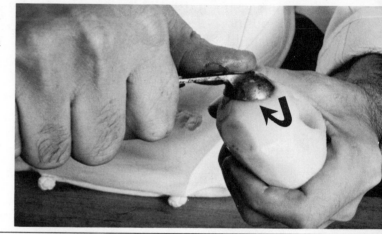

2. Still pressing the tool into the potato, pivot the cutter in a downward motion to scoop out a ball. Repeat, using as much of the potato as you possibly can. Place in cold water again to avoid discoloration. Use trimmings for soup or mashed potatoes. Blanch the balls in boiling water for 2 minutes, drain and fry in a butter and oil mixture.

77. Pommes Anna *(Sliced Potato Cake)*

1. This is a very presentable dish for a party. Begin by trimming the potatoes all around to make long cylinders.

2. Use the trimmings in soup or croquettes or mashed potatoes.

3. Slice by hand or machine into ⅛-inch slices. Sauté the slices in butter and oil for a few minutes.

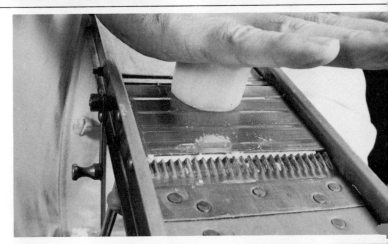

4. Arrange the slices in the bottom of a frying pan or cake pan. A nonstick surface is the best. Place the potato slices any old way on top of the bottom layer. Season with salt and pepper and bake in a 425-degree preheated oven for 30 to 45 minutes. Let rest a few minutes, run a knife around the potatoes and unmold. Remove any slices that stick to the bottom, and replace where they belong on the "cake."

78. Pommes Poisson *(Potato Rounds)*

1. If you don't have small potatoes, cut medium-sized potatoes in half or large potatoes into chunks.

2. Trim all the edges (use trimmings for soup and the like).

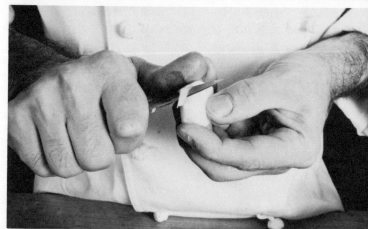

3. These potatoes are basically the same as the *pommes à l'Anglaise* (see page 200), but they are rounded and hold their shape better when boiled. They can also be sautéed or fried.

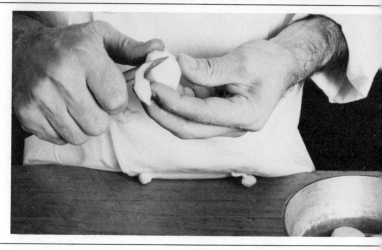

79. Pommes Cocotte et Anglaise

(Potato Ovals)

COCOTTE

1. Cut large potatoes in half. Cut each half into two pieces.

2. Cut the quarters into equal elongated pieces.

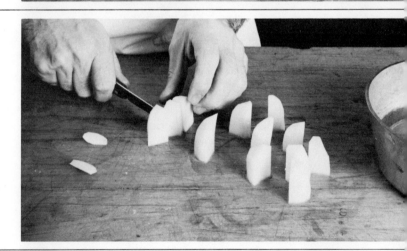

3. Trim or "turn" each piece into a little football-shaped potato. These are *pommes cocotte*. They are blanched for 1 minute in boiling water, drained and sautéed in butter and oil and served as garnish for roast, steak and the like.

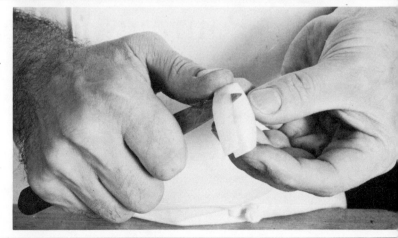

ANGLAISE

1. Trim potatoes at both ends and cut into large elongated chunks.

2. Trim each piece into a football-shaped potato. These potatoes can be steamed or boiled (*pommes à l'anglaise*), blanched and fried (*pommes château*), or cooked with butter and a little bit of water (*pommes fondantes*).

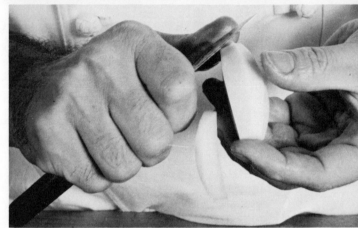

3. Left to right: *pommes poisson, pommes cocotte, pommes à l'anglaise, pommes parisienne*. Shaping the potatoes ensures proper cooking but is essentially done for aesthetic reasons. These kinds of potatoes should be cooked as closely as possible to the moment they will be eaten. If cooked ahead, they will taste reheated.

80. Pommes Pailles, Allumettes et Pont-Neuf *(Potato Sticks)*

DEEP-FRIED POTATOES take on different names depending on the shapes they are cut into before cooking. Though three kinds of potatoes shown here are all cut into sticks, the sizes are different and hence, the names.

1. Peel each potato and trim to look like a parallelepiped.

2. Cut it into ⅜-inch slices.

3. Stack the slices together and cut into ⅜-inch sticks for matchstick potatoes (*allumettes*) or into ¾- to 1-inch sticks for the *pont-neuf*.

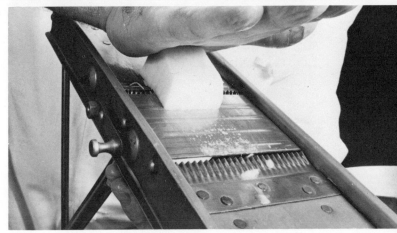

4. The straw potatoes (*pommes pailles*) can be cut by hand or with a *mandoline*.

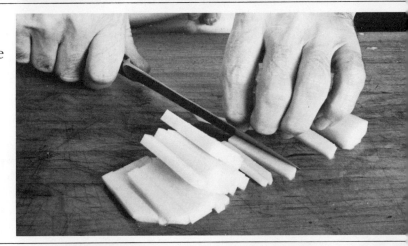

5. Left to right: straw, *pont-neuf* and match-stick potatoes.

81. Pommes Gaufrettes *(Waffled Potatoes)*

1. The *gaufrettes* potatoes are cut with the *mandoline* which is a special vegetable cutter. Using the side with the wrinkled or "teeth" blade, hold the potato with the palm of your hand and cut straight down.

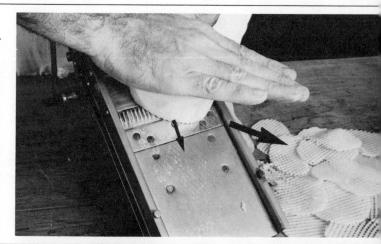

2. Turn the potato 90 degrees. Your fingers are now facing the other direction. Cut straight down. Turn the potato 90 degrees for the next slice. You are crisscrossing the slices.

3. *Gaufrettes* potatoes ready to be deep fried. If the holes are not evident, the slices are too thick. If the potato slice does not hold together, but is all stringy, the slices are too thin. Adjust the thickness accordingly. Wash the potato slices, dry and deep fry in 375-degree oil.

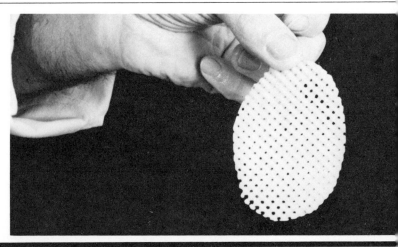

82. Pommes Dauphine *(Cream Puff Potatoes)*

DAUPHINE OR CREAM PUFF POTATOES are made from equal amounts of *pâte à choux* (cream puff dough) and plain mashed potatoes. They are truly excellent served soon after being fried but soften if they're held too long. The *pâte à choux*, technique 147, can be made several days ahead, leaving you with just the potatoes to do.

1. Place the peeled potatoes in cold salted water. Boil and cook until done. Drain and push through a food mill. Mix the plain mashed potatoes with an equal amount of the *pâte à choux*. Fit a pastry bag with a fluted tube and fill, technique 41.

2. For potato crowns, lay out strips of wax paper or parchment paper and pipe circles onto the paper.

3. Dip the sheet of paper in the hot oil (340 degrees) and the potatoes will slide off into the oil. Cook, turning the potatoes every 2 minutes, for about 8 to 10 minutes. Dry on paper towels and sprinkle with salt.

4. For potato sticks, rest the tip of the pastry bag on the edge of the fryer. Squeeze the dough out, cutting it into strips by sliding the blade of a knife across the opening of the tube. Dip your knife in the hot oil to prevent sticking. Cook for 5 to 6 minutes in 340-degree oil. Drain on paper towels and salt.

5. For potato puffs, use a teaspoon to scoop some dough. Get as close as you possibly can to the hot oil (to avoid splashing), and push the dough off the spoon with your fingers.

6. Scrape the dough from the tip of your finger with the spoon, pushing it into the hot oil. Cook for 8 to 10 minutes in 340-degree oil, drain on paper towels and salt.

7. Three different shapes of *pommes dauphine*. Serve as soon as cooked to prevent softening.

83. Pommes Soufflées *(Puffed Potato Slices)*

MAKING THE PUFF, OR INFLATED, POTATO, called *pommes soufflées,* is a delicate operation. If the potatoes have too much moisture, as new potatoes often have, they will not puff. If they are soft and marbled, as old potatoes frequently are, they will not puff either. Ordinarily 15 to 20 percent of any one batch stays flat. In restaurants, the flat ones are served to the help as regular fried potatoes.

According to *Larousse Gastronomique,* the recipe was discovered accidentally in 1837 at the inauguration ceremonies for a railroad service to a small town near Paris. A local restaurant prepared a meal, including fried potatoes, for the official delegation. The train was late and the chef removed the potatoes from the fryer half cooked. At serving time, he was stupefied to see they puffed as he dipped them back in the hot oil. The chemist Chevreul worked out the chemical reasons and a recipe was compiled.

1. In restaurants, the first cooking of the potatoes takes place during the morning or afternoon preparation. They are dipped again in hot oil just before serving. Peel the potatoes and trim each one into the shape of a cylinder. (They can also be trimmed into a tube or a rectangle.) Use the trimmings in soup, puree, hash browns and the like.

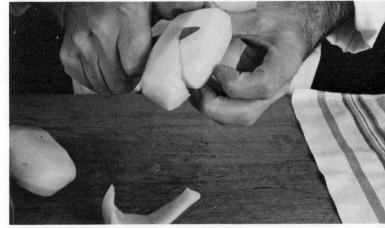

2. Trim the ends of the potatoes. The slices should be the same size and shape to insure proper cooking, and for aesthetic reasons.

3. Using a slicer or a knife, cut the potatoes into ¼- to ⅜-inch-thick slices. Wash the potato slices in cold water and dry well with paper towels.

4. Pour vegetable oil, about 2½ to 3 inches deep, into two saucepans. Heat one to 325 degrees and the other to 375 degrees. Drop 15 to 20 slices into the 325-degree fryer and shake back and forth on the heat for 6 to 7 minutes (an asbestos pad will make the shaking easier by helping the pan to slide). Be careful not to splash oil on your hands while shaking the pan. You have to get a rhythm going. After 4 to 5 minutes, the slices should come to the surface and blisters should start to appear on them. Keep shaking another minute.

5. Stop shaking the pan. Using a skimmer, remove a few slices at a time. Let drain and soften for 5 to 6 seconds, then dip into the 375-degree fryer. The potatoes should swell instantly. Do not let them brown unless you are serving them at this point. As they puff up, transfer to a pan lined with a paper towel to drain. Finish the whole batch in this manner.

6. You will notice they deflate as you place them on the towel. Pick out the ones that puffed up and arrange them on the pan. Eat or discard the other slices. Covered with a paper towel, the good ones will keep at room temperature for several hours.

7. At serving time, drop the slices in the 375-degree fryer, moving them around with a skimmer so that they brown evenly. They should be very crisp to stay puffed. (During the first cooking, the surface of the slices becomes watertight. When the slices are dropped into hot oil, the water "imprisoned" inside tries to escape, pushing from the center, making the potato puff up.) Sprinkle with salt and serve immediately on folded napkins, technique 36.

84. Nouilles Vertes *(Green Noodles)*

PASTA IS NOT COMPLICATED TO MAKE. Although it is made here by hand, the small pasta machines make the process quite easy and give very good results too. Use 3 cups of flour instead of 2¾ if you are using a machine. Green noodles, usually made with spinach, and sometimes Swiss chard leaves, are beautiful with a cream sauce and tomatoes. The spinach does not give much taste to the pasta. Pasta can be made with all-purpose flour, although a mixture of unbleached, hi-gluten flour and semolina flour gives a better texture and bite to the pasta.

1 *pound fresh spinach*
2¾ *cups flour (semolina, semolina and hi-gluten, or all-purpose)*
3 *large eggs, lightly beaten*
½ *teaspoon salt*
2 *tablespoons good olive oil*

Cook the spinach in salted, boiling water for 6 to 8 minutes. Strain and cool off under cold water. When cold, press with your hands to extrude as much water as possible. Chop, blend or mash into fine pieces. You will have between ½ and ⅔ cup of spinach purée.

1. Place the flour in the middle of the work table and create a well in the center. Add remaining ingredients to the well. Start mixing with your fingers.

2. Using a dough scraper, gather all the ingredients into a solid, compact mass.

3. Knead the dough with your hands for 2 to 3 minutes until nice and smooth. Place in a plastic bag and let "rest" in the refrigerator for at least 30 minutes.

4. Flour the table generously. Divide the dough into 4 pieces.

5. Roll each piece into a thin wheel, pushing on the rolling pin to spread the edges of the dough.

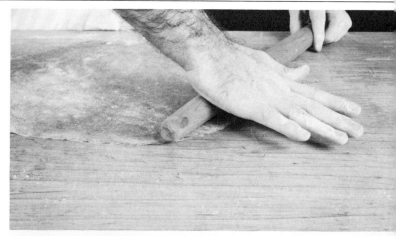

6. Keep rolling with one hand, "pulling" the dough with the other hand to stretch it.

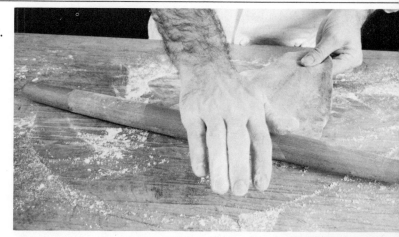

7. When thin enough (no more than ⅛ inch), hang the dough on the rolling pin or

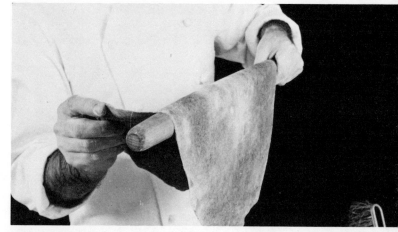

8. on a broomstick, or on the back of a chair lined with wax paper, and let it dry and stretch for a good 30 to 45 minutes.

9. Sprinkle the table with flour and stack the four pieces of dough on top of one another, being sure to flour generously between each layer.

10. Roll the layers into a cylinder and

11. cut into ¼- to ½-inch slices.

12. Separate the noodles. Cook in a lot of boiling salted water for no more than 3½ to 4 minutes. Serve with butter, cheese or your favorite sauce. If you don't use right away, let them dry on a towel to absorb the moisture. Keep in mind that the longer they dry the longer they will need to cook.

Poultry and Meat

108.	Ris de Veau	*Sweetbreads*
109.	Cervelles	*Brains*
110.	Saucisson et Saucisse	*Salami and Sausage*
111.	Jambon en Gelée	*Ham in Aspic*
112.	Pâté Maison	*Pork Liver Forcemeat*
113.	Terrine de Ris de Veau	*Sweetbread Terrine*
114.	Pâté de Faisan en Croûte	*Pheasant Pâté in Crust*

85. Préparation du Pigeon et Autres Volailles *(Cleaning Squab and Other Poultry)*

ALTHOUGH THIS TECHNIQUE of cleaning can be applied to all poultry, it is illustrated with squab because squab usually comes uncleaned. Unless you hunt pheasant or duck, buy your fowl at a farm or raise your own, most birds you encounter in butcher shops and supermarkets are all emptied and cleaned.

1. Cut the feet off the squab just under the joint. Holding it on its back, cut the tips sticking out at the first joint of each wing. This is primarily for aesthetics.

2. Holding the skin tightly squeezed around the neck, make a long incision to expose the bone.

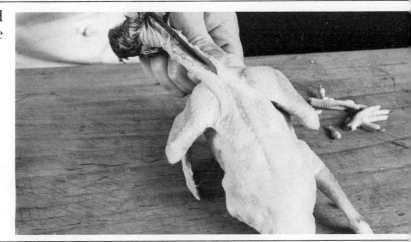

3. Separate the neck from the skin and crop (the loose saclike first stomach) by pulling with both hands.

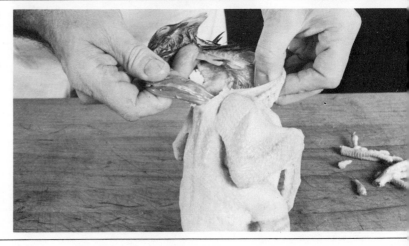

4. Cut the neck at the base, near the body, and the skin next to the head. Separate the neck from the head.

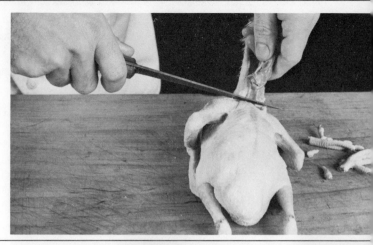

5. Pull out the crop and the viscera from the skin of the neck.

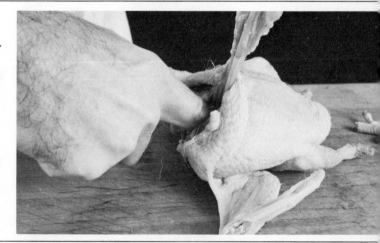

6. Lifting up the crop and viscera in the direction opposite the backbone, slide one finger underneath the crop. Slide the finger along and on each side of the backbone to get the guts and lungs loose.

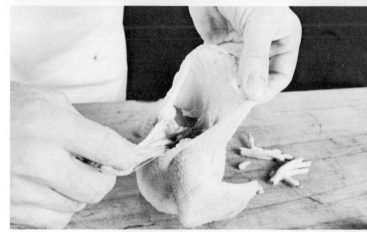

7. Sever the crop near the opening and fold the neck skin onto the back of the bird.

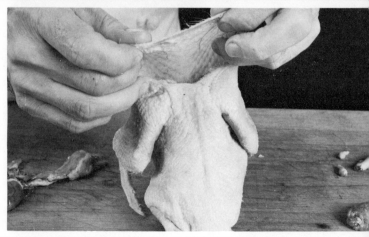

8. Cut a piece from the opening above the tail and

9. slit the skin open to the tip of the breastbone.

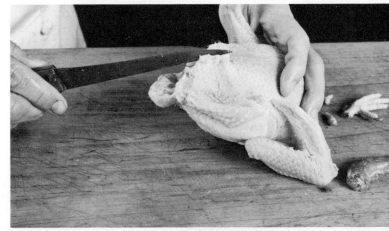

10. Pull the insides out. All the entrails should come out easily in one long piece.

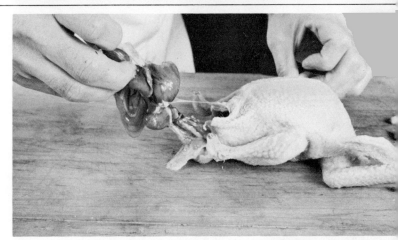

11. Reserve the little lumps of fat on each side of the opening. Separate the heart and liver. Remove the gall—the green part of the liver. (Squab liver does not contain gall though most other poultry does.) The gall is in a pouch attached to the liver. Do not break it open. Remove in one piece and discard. Slit the gizzard (the second stomach) on the thick and fleshy side until you feel the inside which is harder.

12. Open it and remove the pouch inside.

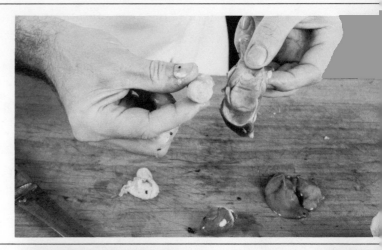

13. Make a hole on each side of the opening and slide the tip of the drumstick inside to hold the leg.

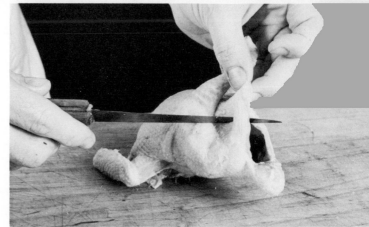

14. Squab trussed, technique 87, and oven ready. From left to right: fat, cleaned gizzard, heart and neck. (The liver is in front.)

86. Pigeon Crapaudine *(Toadlike Squab)*

S QUAB CRAPAUDINE is usually served with deep-fried potatoes and garnished with watercress. Clean the squab following the directions in the preceding technique.

1. Holding the bird on its back, cut above the legs, alongside the breastbone. Do not cut through the backbone.

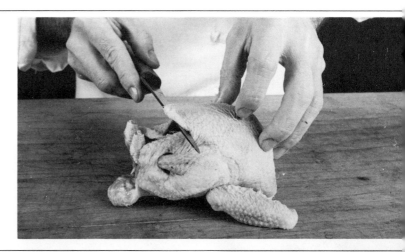

2. Separate the bird at the cut and

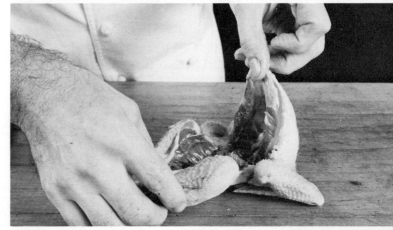

3. crack the back open.

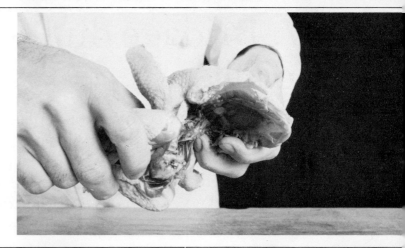

4. Turn the squab cut side down and flatten it with the heel of your hand.

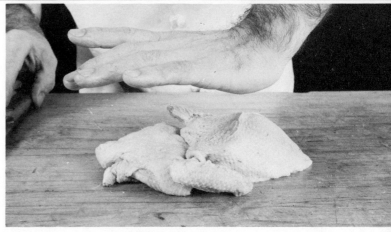

5. The tip of the drumstick can be secured through the skin of the back or it can be held upright by positioning a skewer through the wing and thighs. Place the squabs on a roasting pan. Sprinkle with salt and pepper and place in a 450-degree preheated oven. For 1¼- to 1½-pound squab, bake 25 minutes, about 12 minutes on each side.

6. Brush the squabs with 1 teaspoon of good mustard (Dijon-type) and sprinkle each with 1 tablespoon fresh bread crumbs. Baste with the drippings to moisten the bread and place under broiler for 4 to 5 minutes until nicely brown. Make the "eyes" with pieces of hard-boiled egg whites and pieces of black olive.

87. Bridage du Poulet et Autres Volailles *(Trussing Chicken and Other Poultry)*

WHAT, ESSENTIALLY, is the purpose of trussing a bird? It is so that once properly tied, and I emphasize properly, the bird will keep its shape, will be easier to manipulate and will roast evenly throughout. Here are several methods of trussing. Methods 1 and 2 use trussing needles; the first is for ordinary chicken and the like; the second is for larger fowl, such as capons and turkey. Method 3 is a way of trussing without a needle.

METHOD 1

1. Cut the tips of the wings.

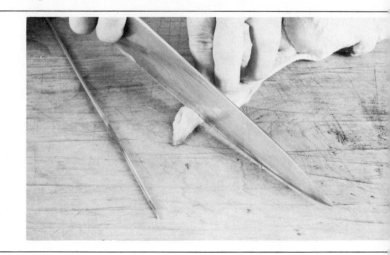

2. Cut the other small tips at the first joint. The removal of these little extremities is more for aesthetics than anything else.

3. Tuck the first section of the wings under.

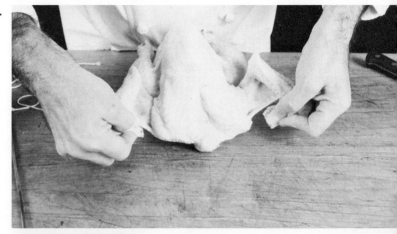

4. Push the legs toward the breast. If you keep the legs tucked tight on the side of the bird, they will push the breast up and make it plump.

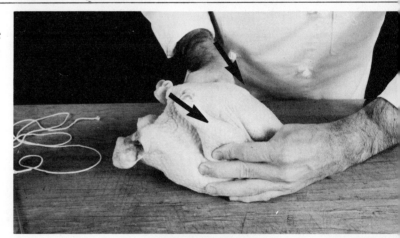

5. Thread the needle with a long piece of soft string (not too thin) and make a knot at the eye. Lift up the drumstick and insert the needle in the "soft" spot in the lower part of the backbone. Be sure to insert the needle in the right place so that the string is anchored into the bone rather than in the skin.

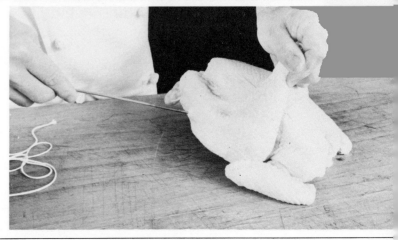

6. Come out at the point where the thigh and drumstick join.

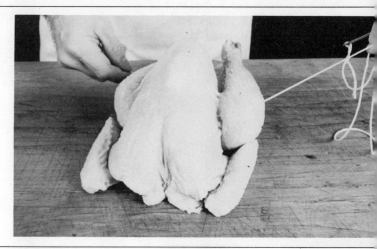

7. Turn the chicken on its breast. Push the needle through the wing section, the loose neck skin, the skin of the back and the other wing.

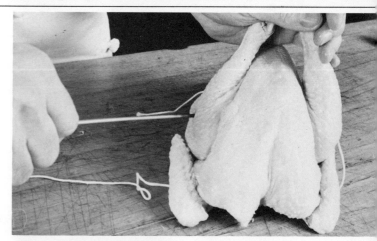

8. Place the chicken on its back and push the needle in the middle joint of the leg, through the lower back, a reverse operation of steps 6 and 5.

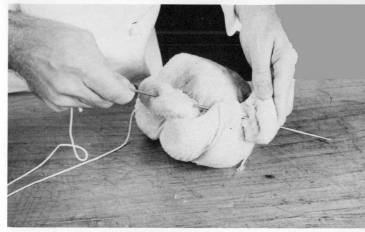

9. Lift up the skin of the tail end and push the needle through. It is important that the needle go through the lower part of the skin because it makes a small tight loop that holds the drumstick in place.

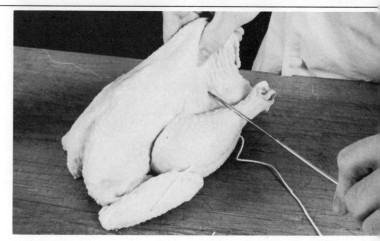

10. Pull both ends of string tight, securing with a double knot.

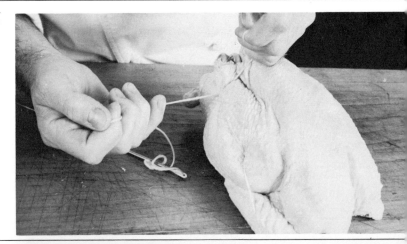

11. Chicken, trussed and oven ready.

METHOD 2

1. Lift the drumstick and push the needle through the body at the joint of the thigh and drumstick. Come out at the corresponding joint on the other side.

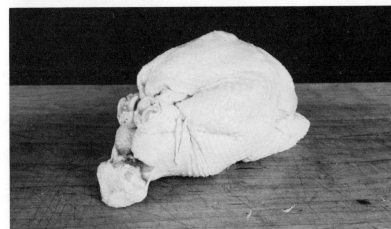

2. Turn the capon on its breast and push the needle through one wing section, the loose skin of the neck and the back skin, then the other wing.

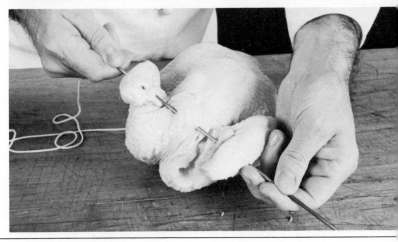

3. Pull the string tight and secure with a double knot. Cut the string. The front part of the bird is trussed.

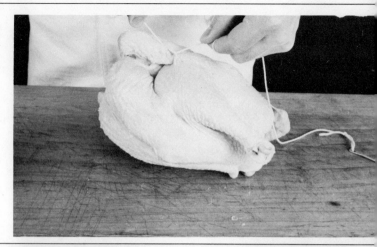

4. Next, push the needle straight across through the lower back next to the tail.

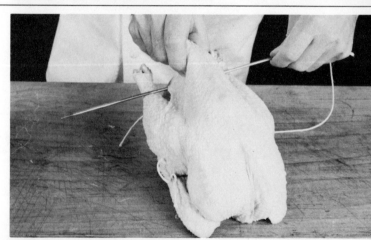

5. Lift up the loose skin under the tip of the breast and go through with the needle. Secure with a tight double knot.

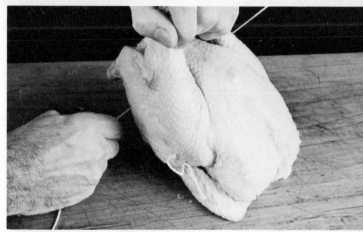

6. Capon trussed with two strings, oven ready. The two strings give a tighter-trussed bird.

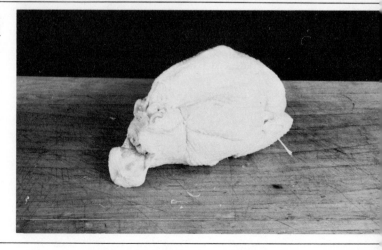

METHOD 3

1. Cut the wings at the second joint. You may also remove the tips of the wings only, and tuck the first section under, as shown in the two preceding methods.

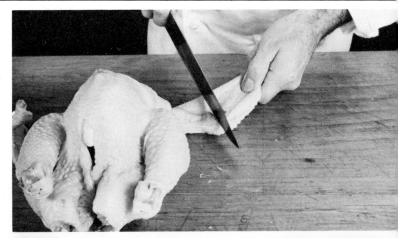

2. Slide the string under the back, next to the tail.

3. Lift the string on both sides and cross it over the top.

4. Slide the string under the tip of the drumstick and pull it tight.

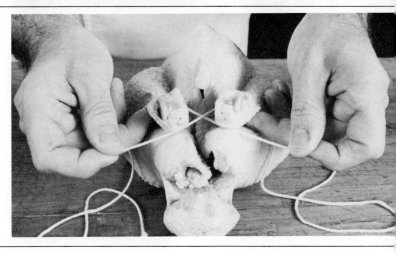

5. Bring the string along both sides of the chicken. Place your thumbs on both sides of the neck, and "push" the chicken forward, pulling up the string at the same time. This step is important; it pushes the breast up.

6. Place the chicken on the breast. Bring one end of the string above the wing and behind the bone of the neck, securing the loose skin of the neck as you go along.

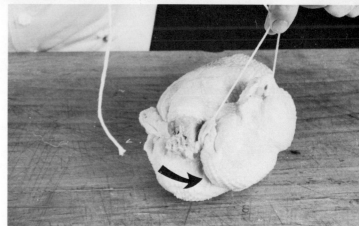

7. Secure tightly with a knot.

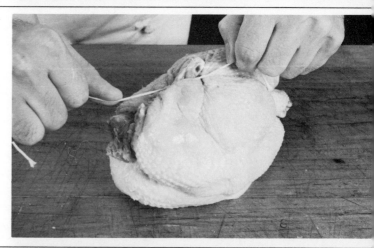

8. Chicken trussed without a needle, oven ready.

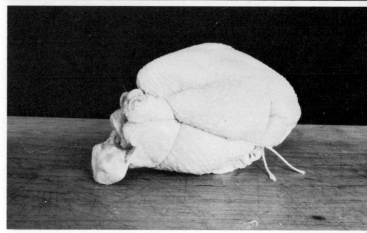

88. Poulet pour Griller *(Preparing Chicken for Broiling)*

CHICKENS THAT ARE TO BE BROILED, barbecued or charcoal-broiled should be cut in the way that offers maximum surface to the heat.

1. Holding the chicken on its side, cut through the backbone on one side of the neck with a sturdy sharp knife.

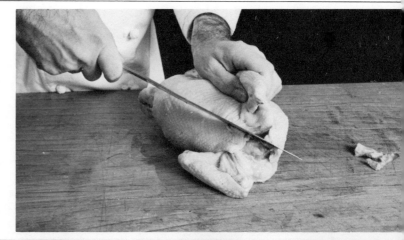

2. Pull the chicken open and

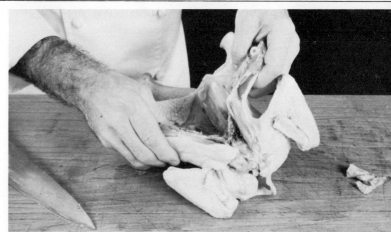

3. separate the backbone by cutting on the other side of the neck bone down to the tail. Reserve the pieces of bone for stock.

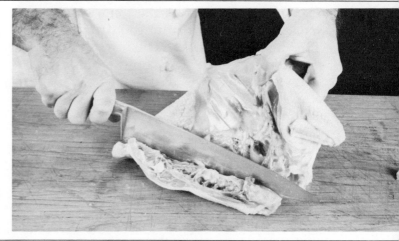

4. Place the chicken flat, skin side down, and using a meat pounder, flatten it.

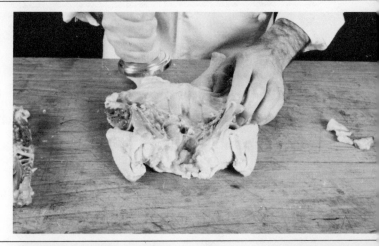

5. Remove the shoulder bones that stick up by cutting at the joint.

6. Remove the rib cage on each side.

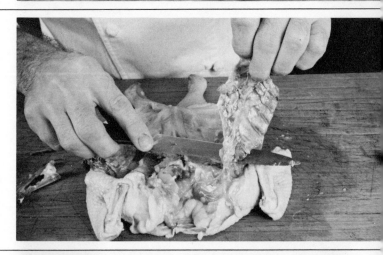

7. Make an incision at the joint which separates the thigh from the drumstick. This helps the chicken cook evenly (the thickest part of the leg would otherwise take longer to cook).

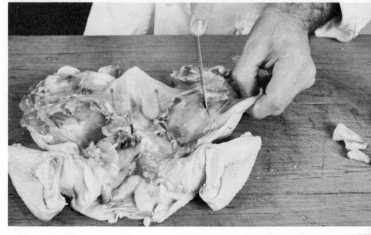

8. Cut a hole through the skin between the point of the breast and the thigh.

9. Push the tip of the drumstick

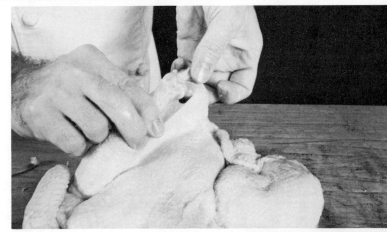

10. through the hole to secure the leg.

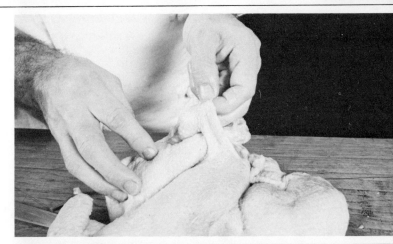

11. Chicken ready to broil. Sprinkle with salt and pepper and brush with vegetable oil before cooking. Cook skin side up. For chicken *grillé à la diable,* bake the chicken in a 450-degree preheated oven—a 3- to 3½-pound roaster won't take more than 35 minutes—coat with mustard and bread crumbs and finish under the broiler. (See step 6, technique 86.)

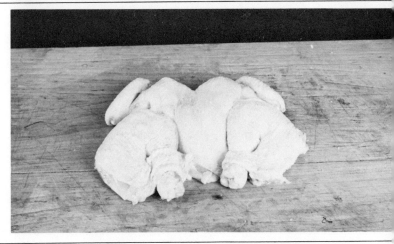

89. Poulet pour Sauter *(Preparing Chicken for Stews)*

THERE ARE LITERALLY hundreds of recipes that call for cut-up chicken. Chicken can be cut "off the bone" (the backbone), which is the more elegant method, or with the bone in. The second yields more pieces and is, therefore, more economical.

OFF THE BONE

1. A chicken can be cut off the bone into quarters (2 legs and 2 single breasts), into 5 pieces (2 legs, 2 wings, 1 breast), or into 7 pieces, if the chicken is large enough (about 3½ pounds), by separating the legs into thighs and drumsticks. Begin by cutting the wing at the second joint, leaving only the first section attached to the chicken.

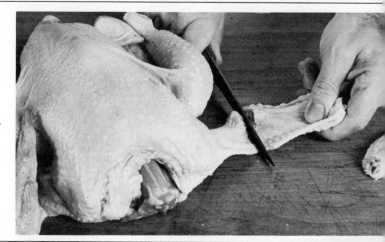

2. Place the chicken on its side and, with a small sharp knife, cut the skin all around the leg.

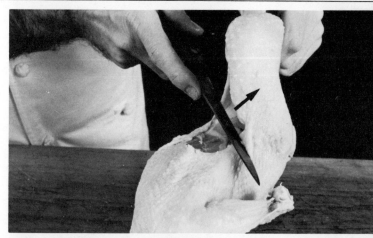

3. Open the leg to expose the joint where the thigh is attached to the body. Cut through the joint.

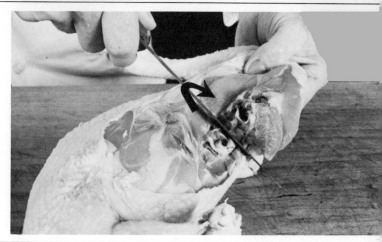

4. Holding the chicken firmly with one hand, pull the leg until it separates from the body.

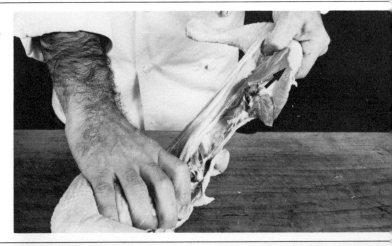

5. Cut off the tip of the drumstick and

6. push down on the meat to expose the bone. Separate the thigh and drumstick at the joint. Cut the other leg in the same manner.

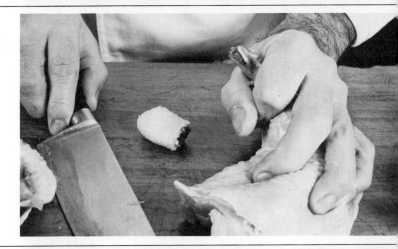

7. With the chicken on its side, pull back the wing. With your knife, find the joint where the wing is attached to the body and cut through with the point of your knife.

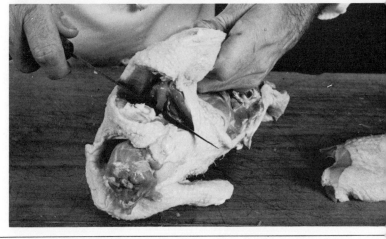

8. Cut down along the breast so part of the white meat is attached to the wing.

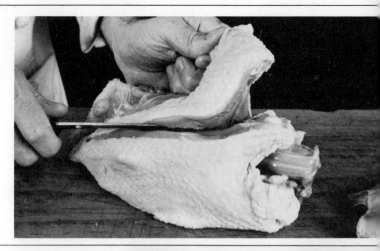

9. Then, holding the chicken firmly with one hand, pull the wing section out. Repeat on the other side.

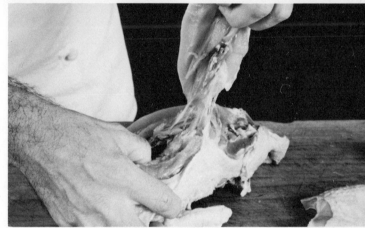

10. Trim the end bone of the wings.

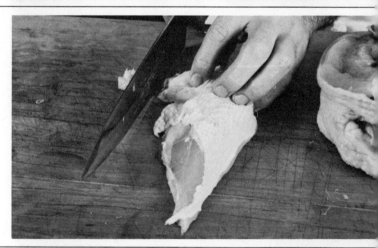

11. Separate the breast (in fact, the sternum; *bréchet* in French) from the carcass. Use the carcass, neck and tip of bones for stock or sauces.

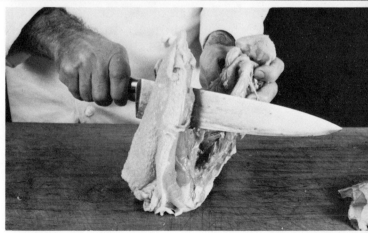

12. Chicken ready to sauté.

BONE IN

1. Remove the first joint of both wings. Then, with a heavy knife, cut through the center of the breast and through the back on one side of the backbone to separate the chicken into halves.

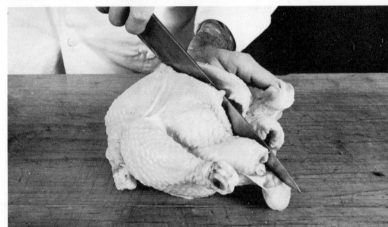

2. Remove the backbone and tail from the half it is attached to.

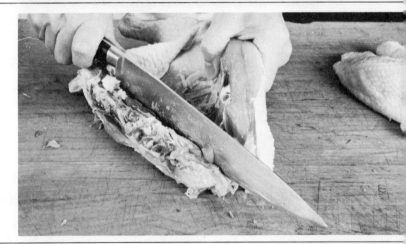

3. Separate the leg from the wing, going right through the bones with the large knife.

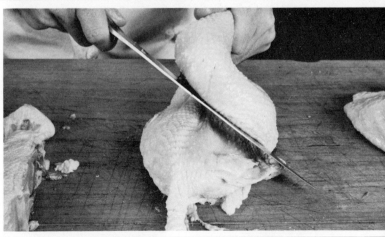

4. Cut each breast and leg into halves.

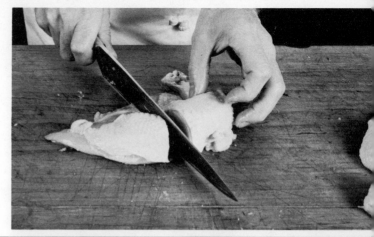

5. Chicken ready for stewing or frying.

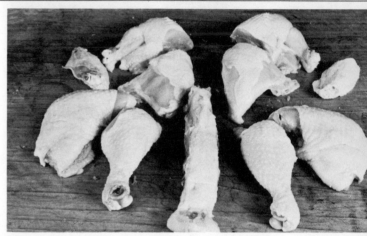

90. Poulet en Saucisse *(Chicken Sausage)*

A GALANTINE is a boned bird, usually a duck or chicken, filled with a force-meat mixture and alternate layers of liver, *lardon,* truffles and the like. The boned, stuffed bird is poached in broth, cooled off and served with its own aspic. A *ballottine* is essentially the same except the stuffed bird is roasted instead of poached and served hot with a sauce. A simplified version, the *poulet en saucisse,* is not quite a galantine or a *ballottine,* but it partakes of both. The most tedious part of the preparation is boning the chicken. The meat is completely separated from the carcass and left in one piece.

BONING THE CHICKEN

1. Using a 3- to 3¼-pound roasting chicken, remove the wings at the second joint and reserve. Lift up the skin of the neck to expose the flesh and, using the point of a small knife, follow the contour of the wishbone to get it loose.

2. Pull the wishbone out.

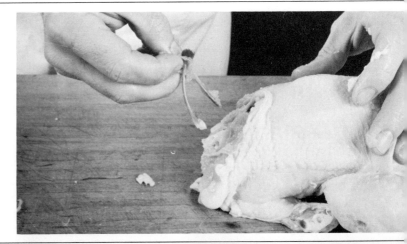

3. Place the chicken on its breast, and cut down the backbone to expose the meat.

4. Following the carcass with your knife, begin cutting the meat from the bone. Cut the joint at the shoulder (see arrow). Cut on top and around the breastbone and down on the other side. This is not really complicated; you simply separate the meat from the bone as you go. Do not worry about the leg, shoulder and wing bones.

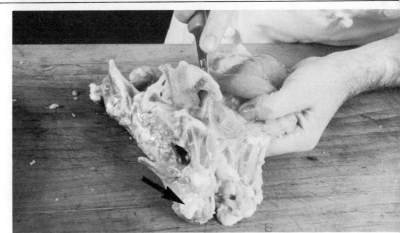

5. Remove the carcass in one piece.

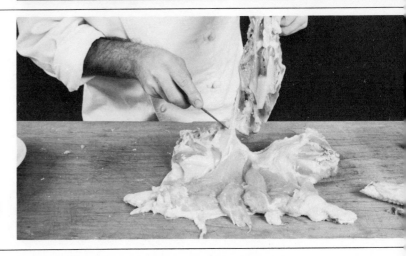

6. Cut around the bone of the thigh to free it of meat. Holding the tip in one hand, scrape with your knife, "pushing" the meat from the bone. Separate the thighbone at the joint between the thigh and drumstick. The drumstick bone is left in.

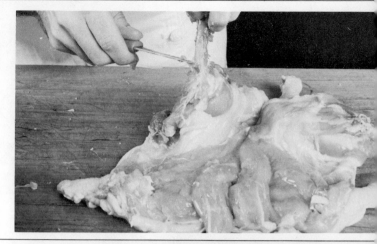

7. With a large knife, cut the tip of the drumstick and

8. "push" the flesh back to expose the bone.

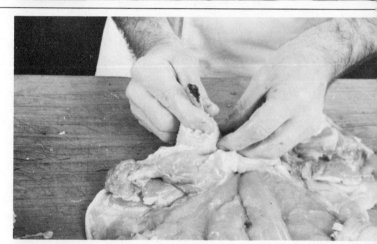

9. Cut the tip of the wing bones.

10. You will notice that there are 2 fillets loose on the breast. Pull them off and position them lower than the breast, where there is no meat on the skin. Most of the surface should be lined with meat.

THE POACHING BROTH

Wings, bones, neck and gizzard
1 carrot, peeled and coarsely sliced
1 onion, peeled and coarsely sliced
1 celery rib, coarsely sliced
2 bay leaves
¼ teaspoon thyme
½ teaspoon salt

Place the wing pieces, bones, neck and gizzard in a kettle, cover with cold water and add the remaining ingredients. Bring to a boil and simmer for 1½ hours.

STUFFING AND COOKING

2 tablespoons sweet butter
½ cup chopped onion
5 ounces mushrooms, chopped fine (1 cup)
1½ teaspoons salt
½ teaspoon freshly ground white pepper
2 large chicken livers
Same amount or weight of chicken fat as of
  chicken livers (lumps from inside the bird)
8 ounces ground pork
1 tablespoon sherry

Melt the butter in a saucepan, add the onion and sauté for 1 minute. Add the mushrooms, ½ teaspoon salt and ¼ teaspoon pepper. Cook until all the liquid is evaporated from the mushrooms and the mixture starts to stick in the pan (about 5 minutes). Set aside and let cool. Cut the livers and chicken fat in small pieces. Place in a food processor or blender and blend until smooth. Add the ground pork, remaining salt and pepper and the sherry. All ingredients should be well blended and the mixture should be smooth.

11. Spread the purée of mushrooms equally on the meat.

12. Then place the liver mixture on top, spreading it with wet fingers. (Wet your fingers by dipping them into cold water.)

13. Bring both sides of the skin toward the center.

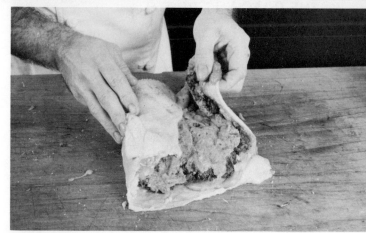

14. Pull the skin of the neck to enclose the stuffing.

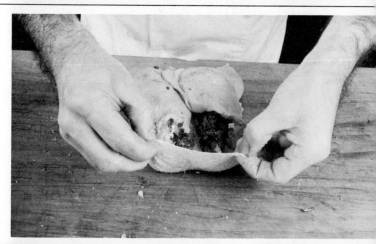

15. Place the chicken on a piece of cheesecloth and

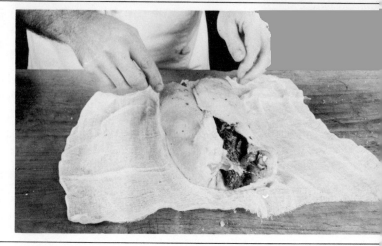

16. wrap carefully. Tie with a string and secure both ends, technique 98.

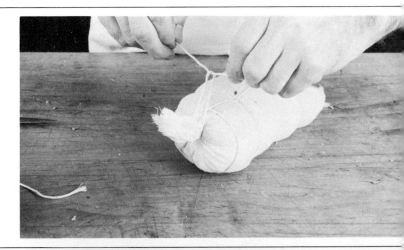

17. Using 2 tablespoons butter and 1 tablespoon vegetable oil, brown the chicken (it will brown through the cheesecloth) in a large skillet on medium to low heat. It will take about 20 minutes.

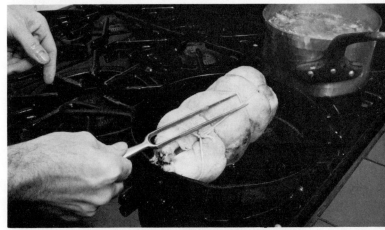

18. Strain the poaching broth. You should have 5 to 6 cups. If you don't, add water as necessary. Place the browned bird in a deep casserole and pour the stock on top. It should come almost to the top of the bird.

19. Bring to a boil, lower the heat and simmer very slowly (it should barely simmer) for 1½ hours. Let the chicken cool in the stock, overnight if possible. Remove from stock

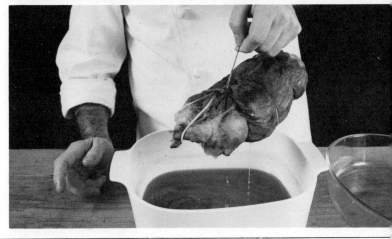

20. and unwrap.

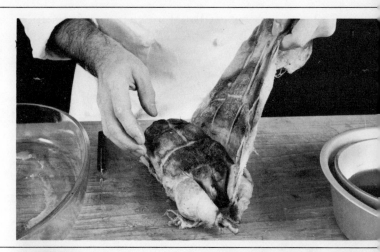

21. Trim the meat around the drumstick bone and pull the drum up. (This is just for appearances; note the last photograph.)

22. Twist and pull off the bone from the wings.

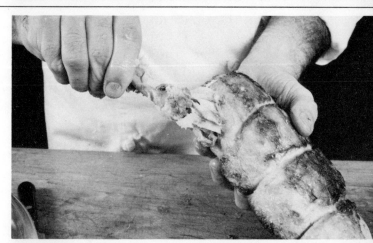

23. Strain the cold stock through a fine sieve to remove the fat. Bring to a boil and reduce on medium heat until you have about 1¼ cups left. It should be reduced enough to make a concentrated natural aspic. Place the reduced stock on ice and mix while cooling. Cut the "sausage" into ½-inch slices.

24. Arrange on a large tray and coat with the aspic when it is oily and almost set. Place paper frills on the legbones, technique 32. For the final presentation, see color plate 5.

The *poulet en saucisse* serves 6 to 8.

91. Préparation et Cuisson des Viandes *(Trimming and Cooking Meat)*

To ascertain the exact degree of doneness when roasting or broiling meat, you need a thorough, practical knowledge of cooking. The professional chef knows by touching, or rather pushing into the meat with his fingers. How the meat springs back clearly reveals the degree to which the meat is cooked. An underdone roast feels soft and mushy; when rare, it feels soft with some bounce; when medium, it feels hard and springy; and when well-done, it feels hard with almost no bounce. However, variations due to differences between cuts, quality and method of cooking make this system difficult for the untrained.

Another method—cooking meat so many minutes to the pound—is also unreliable because it doesn't take into account the temperature of the oven, or the cut, shape, quality or preparation of the meat. For instance, a 6-pound rib roast will take close to 2½ hours in a 325-degree oven to be rare and about 1½ hours in a 420-degree oven. At the same temperature, a 3-pound piece of top round will take twice the time required for a 3-pound flank steak because of the difference in shape. One meat may be porous, another may be tight; one may be fatty, the next one may be lean; one is boned out, another is cooked bone in, and so on and on. All these factors modify the cooking of the meat and alter the timing.

A reliable modus operandi is the thermometer, one as thin as possible to avoid making big holes in the meat. Plunge the thermometer into the thickest part of the meat and wait approximately 45 seconds before reading the dial. (Do not use the kind that is left in the meat during the whole cooking time.)

The cooking figures given by manufacturers or the U.S.D.A. are invariably too high. Beef and lamb should be removed from the oven when the internal temperature reaches 110 to 115 degrees for rare, 115 to 120 degrees for medium rare, 130 to 135 degrees for medium, and 155 to 160 degrees if you want it well-done. Veal should be cooked to an internal temperature of

155 to 160 degrees. Poultry and pork should be removed at 160 to 165 degrees. Trichinea, the parasite worms found in pork, are killed at a temperature between 138 and 140 degrees.

It is *imperative* that the meat "rest" before being carved (from 5 to 10 minutes for a small rack of lamb, to 25 minutes for a large rib roast) so the juices can settle, ensuring a nice pink color throughout the meat. A roast beef sliced as soon as it comes out of the oven will be mushy, lukewarm, practically raw in the middle, and grey and dry 1 inch all around the outside. The same piece of meat will be uniformly pink throughout if allowed to settle in a lukewarm place for 15 to 20 minutes.

You will really come to understand meat once you begin trimming it yourself, relying less on your butcher and more on your own skills. It requires some practice, but it will save you money and you will be able to have your meat trimmed the way you like it without extra expense. When it comes to trimming meat the cook and the butcher have different goals. The cook trims differently and trims more.

Once you get to know the principal cuts in one animal, they become quite easy to recognize in other animals, even if the cuts are handled differently. For example, after you have worked on a saddle of lamb, you will know that the lamb loin chops come from the saddle. You will also recognize veal saddle, veal loin chops, pork loin chops, and, in the beef, the shell steak, the tenderloin and the porterhouse steak, all of which come from the same part of the animal. Whether you are served a saddle of venison or a "rabble" (back) of hare, you will recognize where it comes from in the animal.

92. Préparation de la Selle d'Agneau *(Trimming Saddle of Lamb)*

THE SPRING LAMB—the 8- to 12-month-old animal—is preferred for *selle d'agneau*. It has more taste and flavor than baby lamb and hasn't yet acquired the strong flavor of mutton. Baby lamb (which weighs under 20 pounds with skin and head) is usually served around Easter and is always cooked medium, unlike mutton which is cooked well, and spring lamb which should always be served pink.

1. A saddle, the piece between the ribs and the legs, comprises the T-bone with the two loins and two tenderloins. The kidneys are underneath the saddle. This saddle is 9½ pounds, untrimmed.

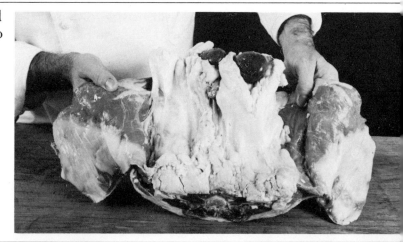

2. Remove the kidneys, including their lump of fat, by cutting and pulling.

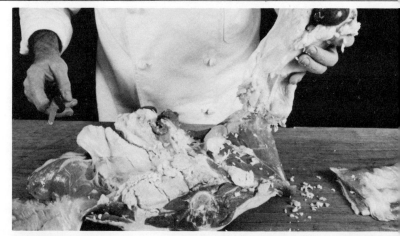

3. Remove each kidney from its envelope of fat.

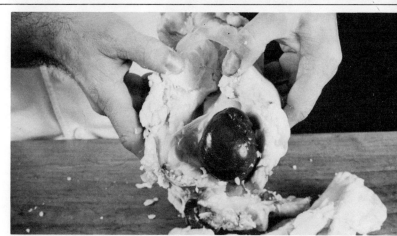

4. Cut the flank or skirt on both sides of the saddle.

5. With the saddle still upside down, trim the strip of sinews and fat along the central bone.

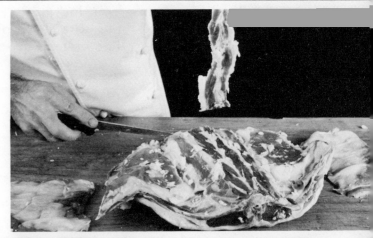

6. Keep trimming the fat on both sides of the tenderloin.

7. Turn the saddle right side up and trim the fat off the back.

8. Keep trimming on both sides of the loins, leaving only a very thin layer of fat on top of the meat.

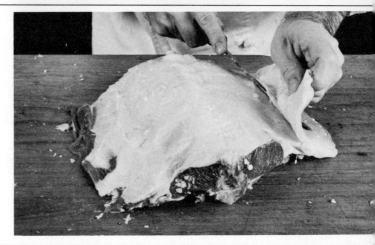

9. Turn the saddle upside down and fold the skirt back onto the tenderloin. (This protects the choice tenderloin from drying during cooking.)

10. Place the saddle right side up and using the point of a knife, prick the large sinew all the way down the spine so that the meat does not contract during cooking.

11. Tie the saddle to secure the skirts underneath.

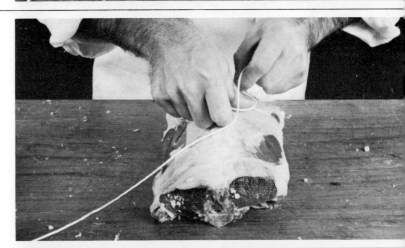

12. Saddle, oven ready. The trimmed saddle weighs 3½ pounds, and the trimmings and kidneys combined weigh 2 pounds. The trimmings make a delicious stew. The kidneys can be broiled or sautéed (technique 107). The fat is discarded.

93. Préparation du Carré d'Agneau *(Trimming Rack of Lamb)*

1. The double rack of lamb, the piece between the saddle and the shoulder, is not as lean on the shoulder side

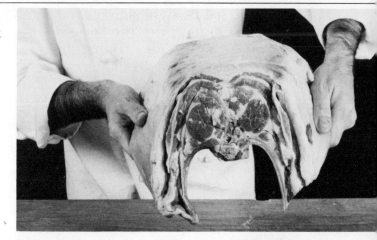

2. as it is on the saddle side. This double rack is 7½ pounds, untrimmed.

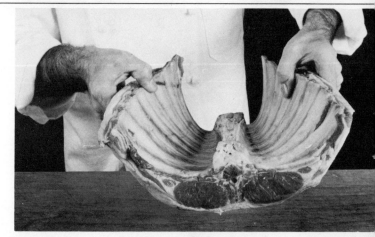

3. The double rack can be split into halves in a few different ways. One is to insert a skewer into the spinal cord and,

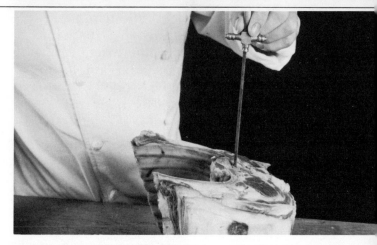

4. using it as a guide, split the double rack in half with a cleaver. However, this method leaves the meat of each rack attached to the backbone, and makes it hard to carve at the table.

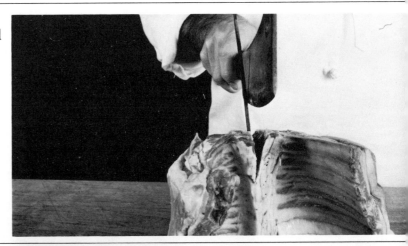

5. Although slightly more involved, this method for splitting the rack is better by far. Using a sturdy sharp knife, cut down on each side of the backbone. Keeping your knife tight along the bone, go as deep as you can. The tip of the knife should go down to the T-bone.

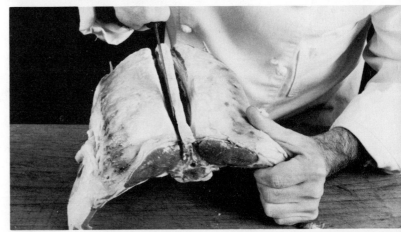

6. Holding the double rack with one hand and working with a cleaver from the inside of the rack, begin to sever one of the racks where it joins the backbone. Do not sever entirely; just make an incision. Stop and go to the other side of the backbone and sever the second rack entirely. Use only the tip of the cleaver and be sure not to cut into the meat which should stay attached to the rack.

7. Go back to the incision on the first side and separate with the cleaver. The incision makes the job easier.

8. Two single racks with the detached central backbone.

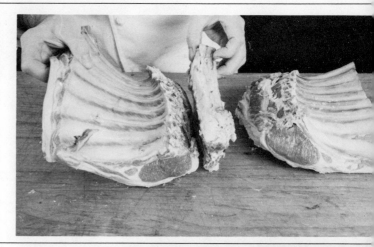

9. Trim the ends of the ribs (trimmings are used in stew).

10. Trim the fat along the rib cage.

11. Trim the fat from the top of the rack and

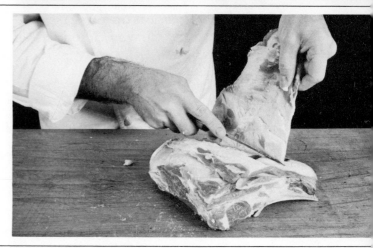

12. remove the shoulder blade.

13. Then trim the big sinew near the loin.

14. Rack, oven ready, 1½ to 1¾ pounds each.

15. You can trim about an inch and a half of fat and meat from between each rib to dress up the rack.

16. Paper frills, technique 32, can be placed over each trimmed bone at serving time.

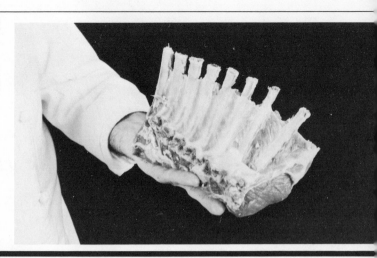

94. Côtes d'Agneau *(Lamb Chops)*

1. Trim and separate a double rack as explained in the preceding technique. Separate each rack into individual chops by cutting between each rib.

2. For thin chops, make one chop from each rib. For thicker chops, cut one chop with 2 ribs, then remove one of the ribs.

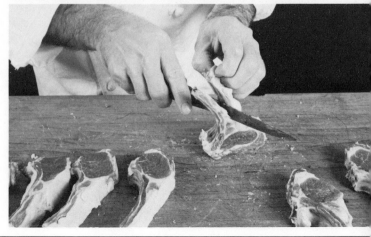

3. Cut the layer of fat along the rib.

4. Holding the chop in one hand, cut the fat above the "eye" all the way around the rib.

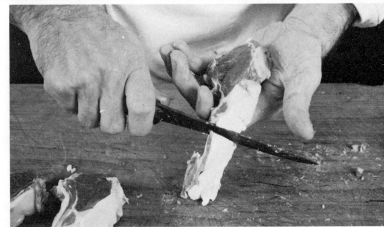

5. "Scrape" it off with your knife to expose a clean bone.

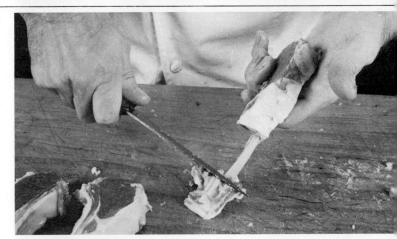

6. Flatten the chop slightly.

7. Trim a chunk of the fat above the eye.

8. Chops from one rack. Note that the 2 chops on the left in the back row are nicer. They are cut from the end of the rack that is near the saddle. These are called the "first" or "prime" chops. The other chops in the same row are cut toward the shoulder and are called "second" or "lower" chops. It is customary, as shown in front, to serve one first and one second chop to each guest.

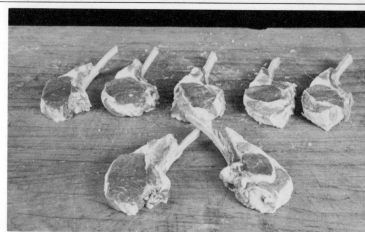

95. Préparation du Gigot
(Trimming Leg of Lamb)

1. A whole untrimmed leg of lamb with the hipbone weighs approximately 7½ to 8 pounds. Use a spring lamb, i.e., a lamb from 8 to 12 months old.

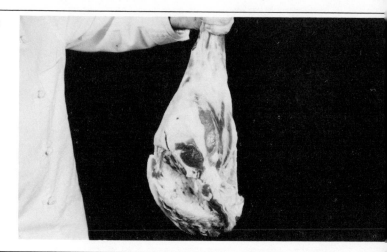

2. Place the leg on its back and insert a thin, sharp, sturdy knife along the hipbone. Follow the bone as closely as you can.

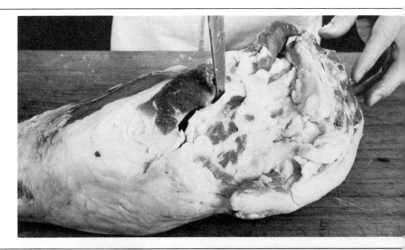

3. Cut inside the socket of the hip joint (you will see the tip of the femur). Remove the tail and the hipbone in one piece. Discard or keep for stock.

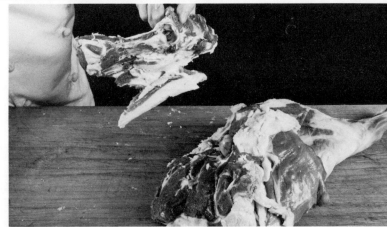

4. Trim the fat along one side of the leg.

5. Then trim the fat along the other side.

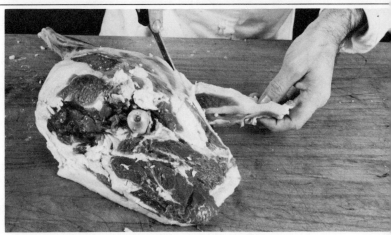

6. Holding the leg by the shank, cut the meat all around the bone.

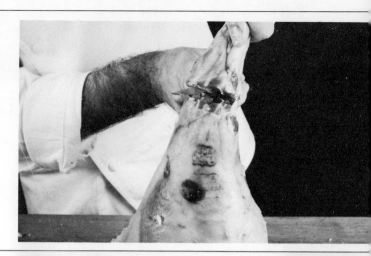

7. With the leg flat, remove the meat from the tip of the bone. You should have 2 or 3 inches of exposed bone.

8. Using a saw, cut off the knotty tip of the bone. The bare bone is decorative and serves as a handle, which makes carving easier.

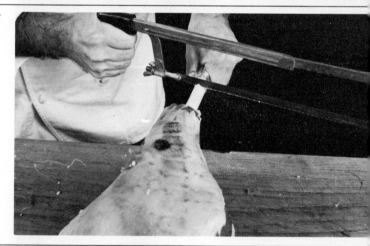

9. Trim the top of the leg of fat, leaving a layer about ¼ inch thick.

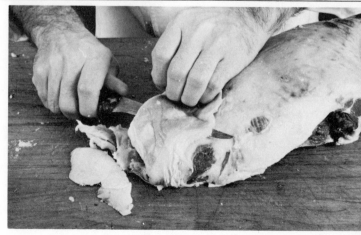

10. The leg can be roasted whole or a piece can be removed and used for stew. (This shortened leg is called *gigot raccourci* in French.)

11. Leg of lamb, oven ready.

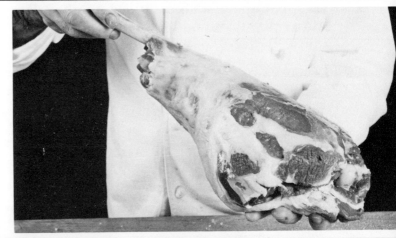

96. Escalope de Veau Viennoise
(Breaded Veal Scaloppine)

FOR VEAL SCALOPPINE, you should use first-quality veal *(plume de veau)*, usually the cuts from the top sirloin or the loin. The meat should be without fat or gristle. Each scaloppine should weigh about 5 to 6 ounces and should be pounded paper thin into a slice about 10 inches in diameter.

1. Use a long sharp knife. Holding your hand flat on the meat to direct the knife, and cutting on a slant,

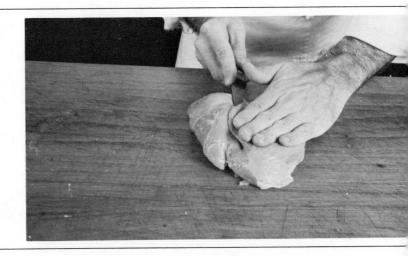

2. slice about ¼ inch down the meat. Do not separate the slice from the meat.

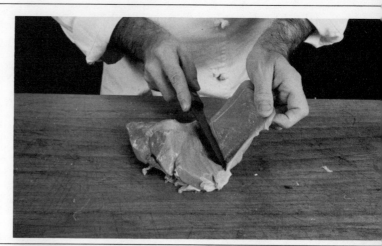

3. Open the first slice and cut another slice through, separating it from the bulk of the meat. Both scallops should hold together. (You can also cut a ½-inch-thick slice, place it flat on the table and butterfly it to obtain the same result.)

4. Using a meat pounder, thin out the veal by pounding down and out from the center toward the edges. The meat should not be crushed, but thinned down. Wetting the pounder with cold water helps it slide on top of the scallops without making holes in the meat.

5. Pounding is the most delicate operation in the recipe. If you do not have a good meat pounder, or if you do not feel confident about the procedure, ask your butcher to prepare the scallops for you. After it is pounded, dip in flour lightly, shaking off any excess.

6. Beat together 1 egg, 1 tablespoon vegetable oil, 1 tablespoon water, salt and pepper and dip both sides of the scallop in the mixture. Squeeze out excess with your fingers.

7. Prepare fresh bread crumbs in the blender and spread on the table. Dip the veal on both sides, pressing on it slightly to make the crumbs adhere well. Shake off any excess.

8. Pat the breaded veal with the flat side of a large knife.

9. Mark a crisscross lattice on top with a knife. Refrigerate until cooking time. The breaded veal is cooked in a large frying pan in a mixture of butter and vegetable oil. Start with the marked side down. After 4 to 5 minutes on medium heat, turn and cook for the same amount of time. In the *viennoise* style, it is served with melted butter and decorated with chopped hard-boiled eggs, capers, lemon slices and anchovies.

97. Paupiettes de Veau *(Rolled Veal)*

A PAUPIETTE is a thin piece of meat or fish that is pounded, rolled and usually stuffed and then braised. *Paupiettes de veau* are sometimes called *oiseaux sans tête* (headless birds) because of the resemblance to stuffed quail or woodcock. This recipe serves four.

THE STUFFING

1 *tablespoon sweet butter*
½ *cup chopped mushrooms*
½ *cup chopped onion*
¼ *cup chopped celery*
1 *clove garlic, peeled, crushed and chopped fine*
1 *pound ground pork shoulder*
2 *tablespoons chopped parsley*
½ *teaspoon salt*
¼ *teaspoon freshly ground black pepper*

Melt the butter in a saucepan, add the mushrooms and cook for 1 minute on medium heat. Add the onion and celery and sauté for 2 minutes. Remove from the heat and stir in the remaining ingredients. Stuff and cook the scaloppines as described below.

THE VEAL

1. Holding your hand flat on the meat to direct the knife,

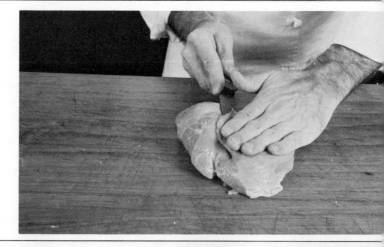

2. cut 8 scaloppines, about 2½ ounces each. Pound each piece into a paper-thin slice about 6 to 8 inches in diameter. (See steps 4 and 5 in the preceding technique.)

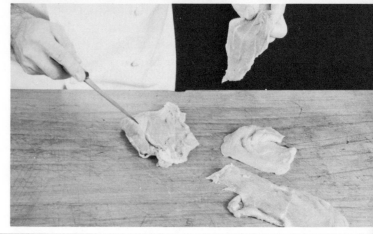

3. Place 2 tablespoons stuffing in the middle of each scaloppine.

4. Wrap the stuffing carefully and

5. tie with string. Cook according to recipe below.

6. *Paupiettes* ready to cook and scaloppine ready to sauté or to bread.

TO COMPLETE THE DISH

4 *tablespoons sweet butter*
1 *cup thinly sliced onion*
3 *cloves garlic, peeled, crushed*
  and chopped
½ *cup dry white wine*
1 *teaspoon salt*
½ *teaspoon freshly ground black pepper*
1 *teaspoon arrowroot*
2 *tablespoons cold water*
1 *tablespoon chopped parsley*

You will need a large casserole with a cover. Melt 2 tablespoons of butter in the casserole, brown the *paupiettes* on all sides and set aside. In a skillet, melt the remaining 2 table-spoons butter, add the onion and sauté for 3 to 4 minutes. Add the garlic and sauté 1 minute longer.

Pour the onion mixture over the *paupiettes*, then deglaze the skillet with the wine and add this liquid to the casserole with the salt and pepper. Bring to a boil, then reduce heat and simmer, covered, over low heat for 25 minutes. With a slotted spoon, transfer the *paupiettes* to a platter and remove the strings. Keep warm.

Mix the arrowroot and the cold water into a smooth paste and stir into the braising liquid. Bring to a boil and taste; add salt and pepper, if needed. Pour the sauce over the *paupiettes,* sprinkle with parsley and serve immediately, two to a person.

98. Ficelage du Rôti *(Tying a Roast)*

THERE IS NO REASON to tie a roast if it is a solid piece of meat, such as a bottom round. However, to fasten lard leaves around a piece of meat, or to assemble loose pieces of meat, tying is necessary if the meat is to hold together while cooking and after.

1. Gather or roll the meat into the desired shape.

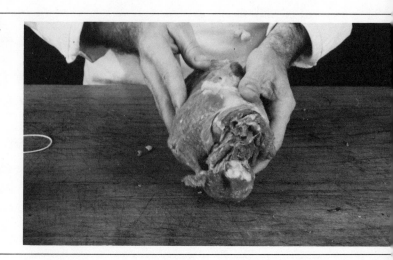

2. Slide thick, soft kitchen string (thin thread will cut through meat) under the roast and tie at the end close to you. Do not cut the string off.

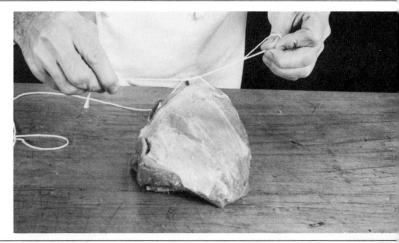

3. Make a loop around your opened fingers and

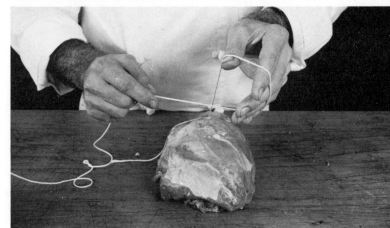

4. slide the opened loop under the roast about 2 inches in front of the first ligature.

5. Pull the string up to tighten the loop. Repeat, making a loop every 2 inches.

6. Slide the string under the roast and make a single loop at each ligature to fasten the roast underneath.

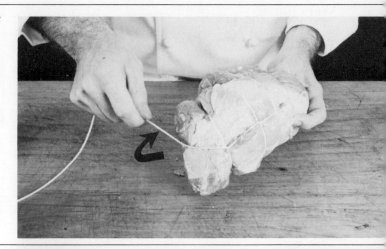

7. Bring the string around and make the last knot at the first ligature. Cook according to your favorite recipe. Remove the string before serving.

99. Poitrine de Veau Farcie
(Stuffed Veal Breast)

Veal breast is an inexpensive and versatile cut of meat. It can be roasted; it can be divided into short ribs *(tendrons)* and braised; and it can be stuffed as shown here. Most recipes for stuffed veal call for a boneless piece of meat. However, the meat is easier to bone after cooking. The ribs slide off effortlessly which helps you recognize when the meat is cooked. They also keep the roast from shrinking and add to its flavor.

A veal breast can weigh from 4½ to 8 pounds and run from about 18 to 25 inches long. The stuffed veal can be braised in the oven or cooked, covered, in a large, deep roasting pan over a flame. If you do not have a pan large enough to accommodate the breast, you may cut it in half. Each piece is then stuffed and tied before braising. Use your favorite stuffing, or the vegetable stuffing suggested below. This recipe will serve 8 to 10.

1 *10-ounce package fresh spinach*
1 *3-ounce piece fresh salted pork (called sweet pickle or corn belly), cut into ¼-inch slices (small* lardons)
2 *carrots, peeled and coarsely chopped (1 cup)*
2 *or 3 onions, chopped (1½ cups)*
1 *celery rib, peeled and coarsely chopped (1 cup)*
1 *or 2 small eggplants, peeled and cut into ½-inch slices (4 cups)*
1 *green pepper, seeded and cut into ½-inch slices (1 cup)*
½ *cup water*
2 *teaspoons salt*
1 *teaspoon freshly ground black pepper*
¼ *teaspoon thyme leaves*
4 *hard-boiled eggs, coarsely chopped*
3 *to 4 cloves garlic, peeled, crushed and chopped fine (1 tablespoon)*
⅓ *cup chopped parsley*
2 *cups fresh bread crumbs*

Cook the spinach in salted, boiling water for 8 to 10 minutes. Drain, run under cold water and press to extrude the water. Chop coarsely.

Place the sliced pork in a large saucepan and cook on medium heat until the pieces are browned and crisp and all the fat is rendered (about 5 minutes). Add the carrots, onion and celery and cook for 3 to 4 minutes. Add the eggplant, green pepper and water. Mix well, cover and let cook until all the water is evaporated and the mixture starts to sizzle again (about 5 to 6 minutes). Add the salt, pepper, thyme and mix well.

Remove from the heat. Add the chopped eggs, spinach, garlic, parsley and bread crumbs. Stir just enough to blend the ingredients together.

1. Use the best veal you can find, pale pink (flesh colored) with white fat. This large breast weighs 7 pounds, bones in.

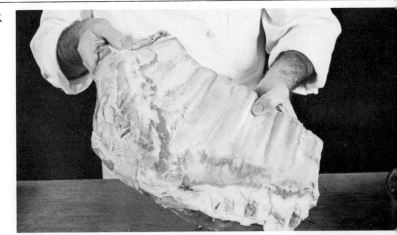

2. Use a small knife to enlarge the opening on the larger side of the breast.

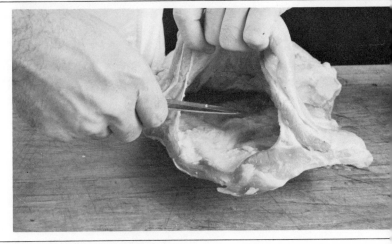

3. Push your hand inside the cavity to loosen the top layer. Push your fingers to the edges all around, but do not go through. You should have a nice deep pocket.

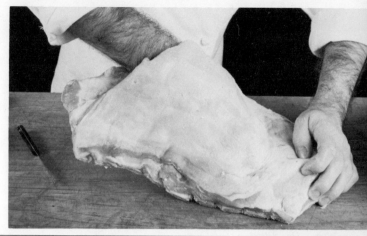

4. Place the stuffing in the cavity.

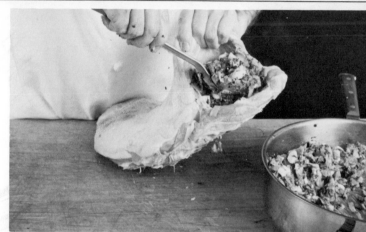

5. Push and pack it with a large spoon.

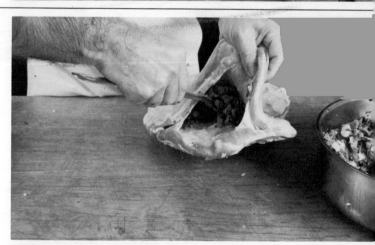

6. Sew the opening with soft kitchen string.

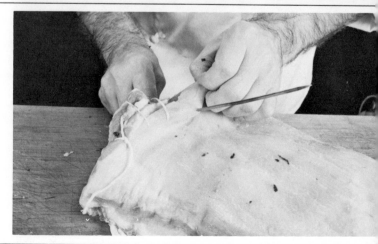

7. Secure with a double knot.

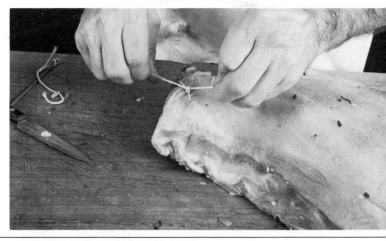

2 *tablespoons butter*
1 *tablespoon olive oil*
1¼ *teaspoons salt*
1 *teaspoon freshly ground black pepper*
3 *medium onions, peeled and halved*
1 *cup water*

In a large roasting pan, melt the butter and add the olive oil. Sprinkle the breast all around with salt and pepper. Brown on all sides on medium to high heat (about 10 minutes). Add the onions. Cover tightly, reduce the heat to very low and cook, covered, on top of the stove for 1 hour. Add a generous cup of water to the pan. Cook, covered, for another hour. You may also place the meat, covered, in a 325-degree preheated oven and bake the same amount of time. At this point, the meat should be tender, and there should be just enough natural juices to serve with the veal. Let the meat "rest" for 15 minutes before carving. Remove the string and slice, following the ribs, into nice portions. You may remove the bone, or serve it with the meat. Pour some of the juice on the slices and serve immediately.

100. Côte de Boeuf *(Rib Roast)*

1. This rib roast has 4 ribs and weighs about 9 pounds untrimmed. A rib roast is fatter on the large side which is closer to the "chuck" or the neck.

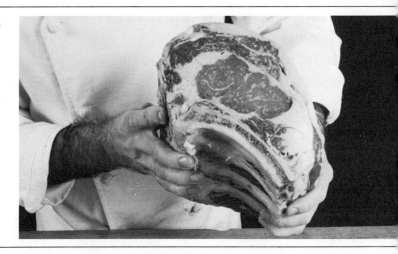

2. It is leaner on the smaller end which goes toward the "sirloin" or the lower back. Hence, it is preferable to buy the ribs closest to the sirloin.

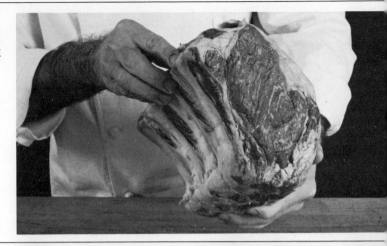

3. Using a sturdy sharp knife, lift up the top layer of fat from the whole roast.

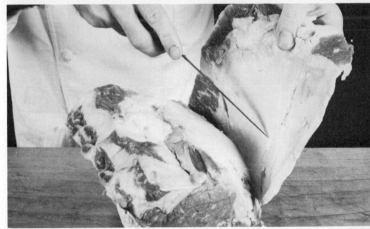

4. Keep cutting down the back of the roast to remove the flat bones. The only bones left should be the ribs.

5. Remove the nerves and large sinews covering the meat.

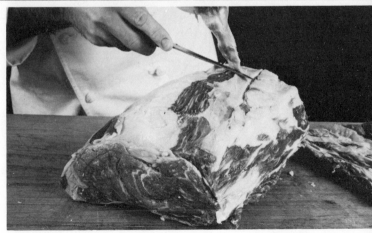

6. Place the top layer of fat on the roast to keep it from drying out during cooking.

7. Tie it with string. When the meat is cooked (110 degrees internal temperature), remove the layer of fat and brown the top of the roast under the broiler for a few minutes. Carve following the directions in technique 121.

101. Préparation du Contre-filet ou Faux Filet *(Trimming Shell Steak)*

1. The shell steak is cut from the beef loin. With a sturdy knife, follow the bones under and behind the loin and separate the "shell roast" from the bone. A 7½-pound bone-in yields 6 pounds boneless.

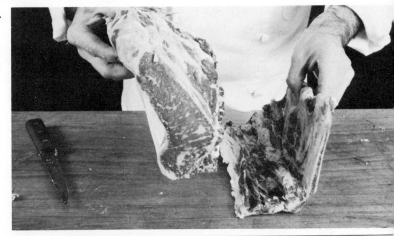

2. Place flat on the table and, using your knife horizontally, trim the large nerves off the meat.

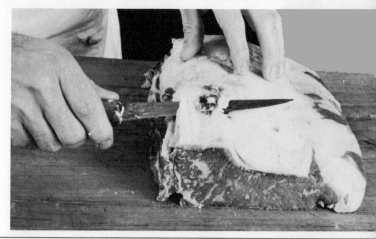

3. Keep trimming until the top of the roast is cleaned of fat and gristle.

4. Cut the fatty end off, leaving some of the fat attached.

5. The roast is 4¼ pounds completely trimmed. You could roast it at this point and serve it rare with its juices, or with a *bordelaise*, truffle or other sauce. Or you can slice it into 8- to 10-ounce steaks.

6. Notice that the "chain"—the sinewy strip along the back of the roast—is left attached to the steak.

102. Steak au Poivre *(Pepper Steak)*

PEPPER STEAK is usually made with an expensive cut such as a shell steak from the beef loin. However, it is quite good made from a hip steak or a shoulder blade steak (also known as a "chicken steak"). An 8- to 10-ounce boneless, well-trimmed steak serves one.

1. If the shell steak is bought ready-cut, trim the fat all around the meat.

2. The choice meat is as tasty as the prime which is often too fatty and rich for my taste.

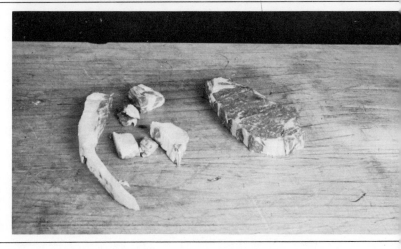

3. Crush whole peppercorns with a rolling pin or the edge of a heavy saucepan by spreading them out and pushing down and forward. You can hear them crack. Repeat until all the little corns are broken. Crushed peppercorn is called *mignonnette* in French cooking. Black peppercorns are preferred, being more flavorful and less pungent than white.

4. Salt the steak on both sides. Spread the *mignonnette* on the working surface and press the steak onto the pieces on both sides. Sauté the steak in hazelnut colored butter, 3 or 4 minutes on each side. The classic way to prepare steak *au poivre* is to deglaze the skillet with cognac, add some brown sauce and finish it with little bits of fresh butter. However, red wine is often added, as well as shallots and sometimes cream. Find your own variations.

103. Préparation du Filet de Boeuf
(Trimming Fillet or Tenderloin)

1. The whole fillet or tenderloin is one of the choicest parts of the beef. Untrimmed, this fillet weighs 9 pounds.

2. Start in the front of the fillet (the larger end), cutting and lifting the fat from the meat.

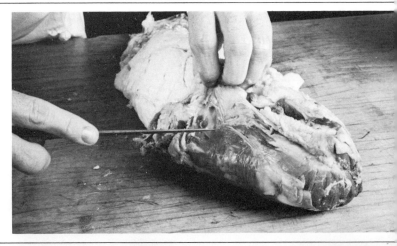

3. When the top layer of fat is loose, pull to separate it from the meat.

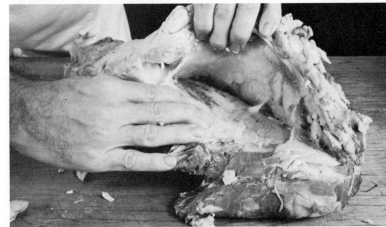

4. Keep pulling the thick layer open.

5. Then trim it off as closely as you can to the meat.

6. The "chain," a long, thin piece of meat that is full of gristle, should be removed although many restaurants and butchers leave it attached.

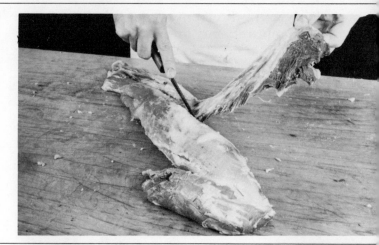

7. Pull the large lump of fat under the "head" of the fillet and

8. sever with your knife.

9. Turn the fillet upside down and pull the long, thin, fatty strip of gristle

10. from the corner under the head to the tail of the fillet. Sever.

11. Placing the fillet back in its upright position, pull off the thin, veil-like layer on top to expose the large sinews.

12. Using a sharp knife held on an angle, remove the sinews which cover the meat.

13. The meat, fat and sinew free, is completely nude. Fold the narrow tail underneath and

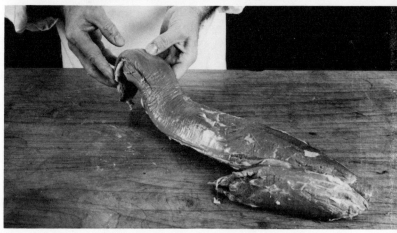

14. secure with a piece of string. Tie up the loose part of the front, also.

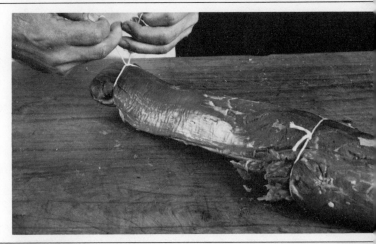

15. Trimmed fillet, oven ready. This fillet weighs 3½ pounds trimmed, a loss of almost two-thirds of its untrimmed weight. Sprinkle with salt and pepper. Melt half a stick of butter in a roasting pan and sear the meat on all sides for about 5 to 6 minutes on high heat. Place in a 425-degree preheated oven for 18 to 20 minutes, basting every 5 minutes. Let "rest" 10 minutes before carving.

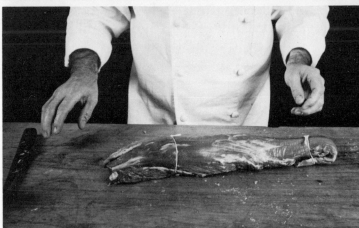

104. Division du Filet de Boeuf
(Cuts of Fillet)

1. When a trimmed beef fillet, technique 103, is not roasted whole, it is cut into a variety of steaks. The tail is cut into tidbits for fondue, or for sautées like stroganoff. Then, the tip of the head and

2. the thinner part of the tail are cut into small (4- to 5-ounce) filets mignons.

3. The center is cut into *tournedos* or *coeur de filet* (heart of fillet), 8 to 9 ounces each.

4. Then the last piece, which weighs about 1¼ pounds, is used as a *chateaubriand* to serve 2 to 3. Place the *chateaubriand* on a kitchen towel.

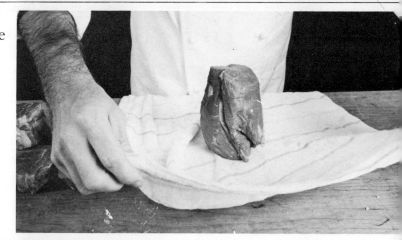

5. Wrap the towel around and, holding it tight,

6. pound it with the flat side of a cleaver to mold it into a thinner and rounder shape.

7. The whole 3½-pound trimmed fillet gave 8 ounces of tidbits, 3 filets mignons, 2 *tournedos* and 1 *chateaubriand*.

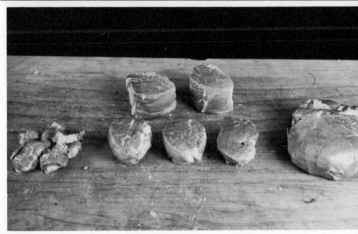

105. Bavette Farcie *(Stuffed Flank Steak)*

Flank is a popular cut of meat and not too expensive. It is usually roasted or charcoal broiled and served thinly sliced, as London broil, technique 123. The meat is fibrous and will be tough if not cut against the grain. However, properly prepared, flank is tasty and juicy. This stuffed flank is served hot, but it is also good cold, cut in thin slices and served without the sauce on a bed of lettuce decorated with tomato wedges, sour French pickles *(cornichons)* and good mustard. A 3- to 3¼-pound untrimmed flank steak (about 2¼ to 2½ pounds trimmed) when stuffed will serve 6 to 8 people.

THE STUFFING

¼ cup vegetable oil
3 tablespoons sweet butter
2½ cups ¼-inch bread cubes, made with white
    bread
1 pound lean ground beef
2 eggs
1 onion, peeled and chopped (¾ cup)
½ celery rib, chopped (½ cup)
2 cloves garlic, peeled, crushed and chopped fine
    (1 teaspoon)

2 tablespoons chopped parsley
1½ teaspoons salt
½ teaspoon freshly ground black pepper
¼ teaspoon crushed thyme or savory

Heat the oil and butter in a skillet and brown the bread cubes. Combine the remaining ingredients in a large bowl and then add bread cubes, mixing in lightly to avoid making a mush. Stuff the flank steak, salt and pepper all around, and cook as directed below.

1. You will probably buy the flank trimmed, or ask the butcher to trim it for you. However, if you buy it untrimmed, your first step is to pull off the thin "skin" on one side and

2. then the fatter skin on the other side. Trim off excess fat at the end.

3. Keeping the flank flat with one hand, cut into the steak lengthwise with a small, sharp paring knife to make a pocket for the stuffing.

4. Lift up the upper "lip" and cut, keeping your blade horizontal. Be careful not to come out at either end.

5. Cut deeper into the steak, but do not cut through to the other side.

6. If you cut through the flank by accident,

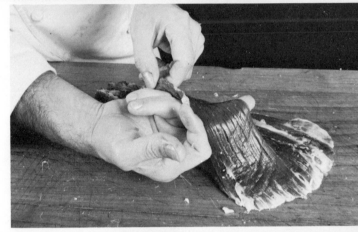

7. slice a thin piece off an end where it won't affect the pocket

8. and use it as a patch to plug the hole; the stuffing will keep it in place.

9. Once your cavity is ready, push the stuffing (your recipe or ours) into the opening, making sure the corners are filled.

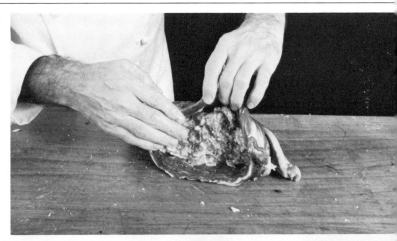

10. Bring the lower lip of the flank against the stuffing.

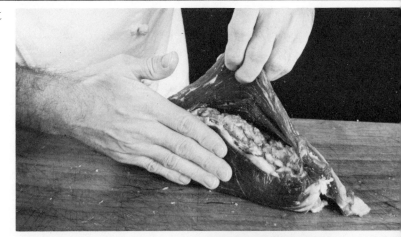

11. Then bring the upper lip down on top to form a nice loaf.

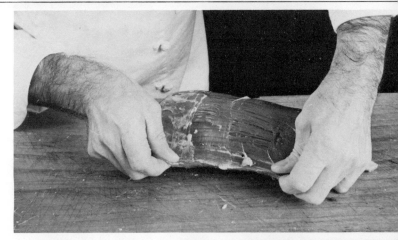

12. Tie the roast, technique 98.

COOKING THE STUFFED FLANK STEAK

1 tablespoon butter
1 tablespoon oil
1 medium carrot, peeled and diced fine (about
    ¾ cup)
1 onion, chopped (about ¾ cup)
2 bay leaves
1 tomato, coarsely chopped (about 1 cup)
1 teaspoon thyme leaves
1 cup water or stock
1 cup dry red wine
2 tablespoons arrowroot
¼ cup cold water
Salt and pepper

You will need a deep, heavy casserole with a cover. Heat the butter and oil in the casserole, and then brown the stuffed meat on all sides. Add carrot, onion, bay leaves, tomato and thyme and cook over moderate heat, uncovered, for 5 minutes. Add water or stock and wine, bring to a boil, cover and braise on a very low heat on top of the stove, or in a 350-degree preheated oven for 1½ hours. Lift meat to a platter, remove strings and keep warm while making the sauce.

Spoon out most of the fat from the surface of the braising liquid in your casserole. Mix the arrowroot with the cold water and then stir into the liquid left in the casserole. Bring to a boil and cook, stirring constantly, until the sauce thickens slightly. Add salt and pepper to taste.

To serve, cut the meat in ½-inch slices (if cut too thick, the meat is tough), one per person, and arrange on a platter with the uncarved part of the roast. Pour 2 or 3 tablespoons of sauce over each serving.

106. Daube de Boeuf en Gelée
(Braised Beef in Aspic)

BEEF FOR BRAISING is usually taken from the bottom round which is part of the leg. The bottom round is divided into two pieces—the eye of the round and the "flat," which is the moister piece of meat and the cut used here. *Daube de boeuf* can be served hot with a sauce, but this recipe is for a cold *daube* in aspic—a beautiful summer buffet dish.

1 5-pound bottom round, studded with fat back
    (technique 23: larding a large cut of meat)
1 12- to 16-ounce piece pork rind
4 cloves garlic, lightly crushed with skin on
2 bay leaves
½ teaspoon thyme leaves
1½ cups coarsely sliced onion
1½ cups coarsely sliced carrots
¾ cup coarsely sliced celery
5 cups good dry red wine (a good dry domestic
    gallon wine is fine)
2 tablespoons butter
2 teaspoons salt

1 teaspoon freshly ground black pepper
3 cups water
2 tablespoons arrowroot diluted with ½ cup
    cold water
2 envelopes plain gelatin moistened with ½ cup
    red wine
2 dozen small glazed onions (technique 6)
2 dozen small cooked turned carrots (see technique
    79)
2 dozen small cooked turned turnips, glazed in
    butter
1 tablespoon cooked peas
1 dozen cooked string beans

1. Place the bottom round in a large vessel. Add the next eight ingredients. Cover with plastic wrap and let the beef marinate for at least 1 day in the refrigerator (2, if possible). Remove the beef and vegetables from the liquid.

2. Melt the butter in a saucepan. Sprinkle the beef with salt and pepper and brown on medium to high heat for about 10 to 12 minutes. Brown thoroughly on all sides.

3. Transfer to a deep casserole.

4. Add the vegetables to the drippings and brown for a good 5 minutes. Add the vegetables and liquid to the meat. Pour the water into the saucepan and boil to melt all the solidified meat drippings. Add to the meat. Bring to a boil, cover and place in a 330-degree preheated oven for 3½ hours.

5. Remove the meat and place in a nice terrine, bowl or earthenware casserole. Strain the juices and scoop as much of the fat from the top as you can. (If you have the time, let the mixture cool and remove the fat after it hardens.) Discard the vegetables. Add the diluted arrowroot and gelatin to the sauce. Bring to a boil.

6. Place about one-third of the vegetable garnishes around the meat. Strain the sauce again and pour over the meat. It should barely cover. Push the vegetables down into the sauce if they rise. Cover the bowl with plastic wrap and refrigerate for a couple of hours until it hardens.

7. When set, arrange the remaining vegetables on top as artfully as you can.

8. Make some aspic, technique 39, with whatever poultry or meat stock you have on hand. Cover the top of the mold with the aspic. Let cool for a few hours before serving.

    This *daube de boeuf* will serve 12 to 15.

107. Rognons *(Kidneys)*

T HE CHOICEST KIDNEYS are veal and lamb kidneys. The kidneys are enclosed in an envelope of fat near the tenderloin (see photographs 1 and 2, technique 92). Unfortunately U.S.D.A. regulations require that veal kidneys be opened and freed of fat and skin before leaving the slaughterhouse. This means they can never be broiled or braised whole, like lamb kidneys. Beef kidneys are usually used for long-simmered stews such as kidney pie.

ROGNONS DE VEAU *(Veal Kidneys)*

1. One single veal kidney cleaned of its fat and skin.

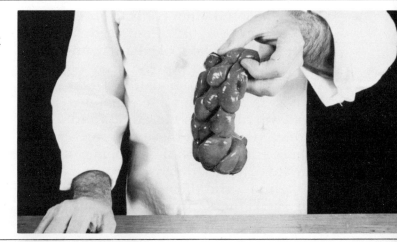

2. Butterfly the kidney into halves lengthwise.

3. Remove most of the strip of fat and gristle which runs through the middle.

4. Cut the kidney into slices if you want to sauté it.

5. On the left: kidney ready to broil or roast whole. On the right: kidney ready to sauté. Kidneys should be cooked a few minutes only at the highest possible heat. They should be pink in the middle. Drain the kidneys in a sieve for a few minutes (pink liquid will run out of the kidneys and should be discarded). After the kidneys are sautéed, a sauce is made with the drippings in the pan. Return the kidneys to the pan only long enough to warm them in the sauce. Do not boil; the kidneys will get as tough as rubber.

ROGNONS D'AGNEAU (*Lamb Kidneys*)

1. Lamb kidneys are usually broiled on a skewer and served with *beurre maître d'hôtel* (technique 21) and watercress. They can also be sautéed and served with a sauce. Remove the thin skin that covers the kidneys if it wasn't removed at the slaughterhouse. Cut the kidney in the middle and butterfly it.

2. Using a skewer, go into the kidney on one side of the center (the small lump of fat) and come up on the other side.

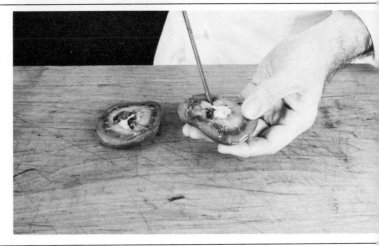

3. Kidneys ready to broil. Sprinkle with salt and pepper and broil (charcoal broiling is the best) on high heat for 2 to 3 minutes on each side. Let "rest" 1 to 2 minutes before serving. They should be pink in the middle.

108. Ris de Veau *(Sweetbreads)*

SWEETBREADS MAY WELL BE THE CHOICEST of the offals. The best sweetbreads are from lamb and calf, but only the calf is available and used in the United States. Sweetbreads are glands. The elongated sweetbread, the thymus, is at its best in young calves and almost disappears in older animals. The round sweetbread, the pancreas, is considered the better of the two. In old animals, it becomes mushy and pasty, but is still used by some cooks in stew. There are infinite ways of serving sweetbreads: breaded and sautéed *maréchal,* braised with a Madeira sauce, in champagne sauce, in puff paste, in pâté and so on.

1. Sweetbreads: pancreas *(la noix)* on the left; thymus *(ris de gorge)* on the right. Choose sweetbreads that are white and plump. Place the sweetbreads in cold water for several hours. Transfer to a saucepan, cover with cold water and bring to a boil. Let boil for 1 to 2 minutes. Place under cold running water until the meat is cold.

2. Pull off the sinews—the rubbery pieces that adhere to the meat—

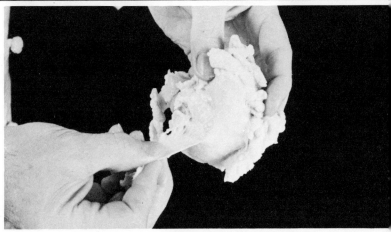

3. on top and around the pieces.

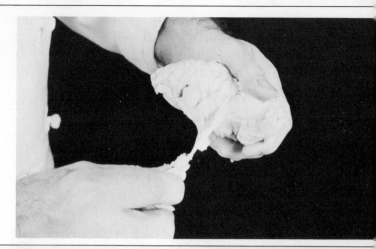

4. Line a cookie sheet with a clean towel, arrange the sweetbreads on top and cover with the towel.

5. Place another cookie sheet on top and place about 6 to 8 pounds of weight on top. Keep pressed for a few hours or overnight. Pressing the sweetbreads extrudes the undesirable pink liquid and gives white, compact and tender sweetbreads. Unpressed sweetbreads are always rubbery. Prepare the sweetbreads following your favorite recipe.

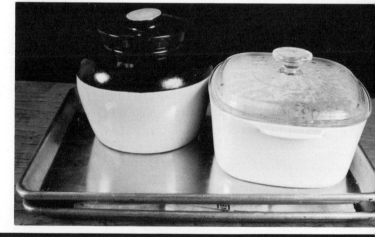

109. Cervelles *(Brains)*

IT IS UNFORTUNATE that brains are rarely featured in restaurants or served in households in the United States. They are excellent, nutritious, easy to prepare and inexpensive. The best brains are veal and lamb brains. (Pork brain is a bit mushy and not as flavorful.) Brains are often poached in a flavorful stock, then fried in butter and served with capers, parsley and lemon. They are also used in pâtés, salads and sauces, and are sometimes simply breaded and fried. Though this technique is illustrated with a veal brain, lamb brain is handled in the same manner.

1. A veal brain weighs approximately 10 to 14 ounces. Soak in cool water for 1 or 2 hours.

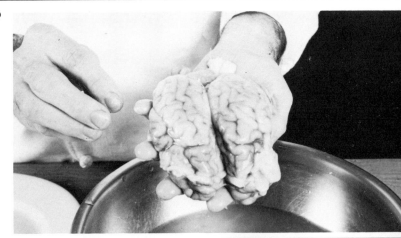

2. Pull off the fine membrane covering the brain. (You can loosen it by sliding the tips of your fingers through the crevices of the brain.) This is not done in all restaurants and is an optional step. I prefer to remove the membrane because it is tough and because the brain will be darker after cooking if the membrane is left on.

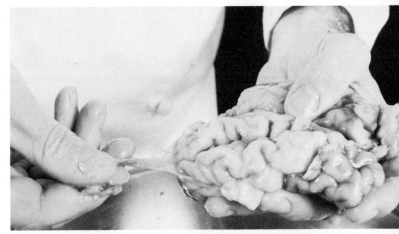

3. Work under water, cleaning up the whole brain. Place 2 cups water, 2 tablespoons good vinegar, 1 bay leaf, ½ cup sliced onion, 1 teaspoon salt and 1 teaspoon crushed peppercorns in a saucepan. Bring to a boil and simmer for 15 minutes. Add the brain to the stock and simmer slowly for 10 minutes. Let the brain cool off in the liquid. Refrigerate in the liquid. It is ready to be used when needed.

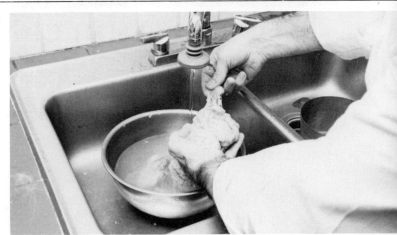

4. Remove the brain from the cooking liquid and separate into halves with a knife.

5. Split each piece open (butterfly).

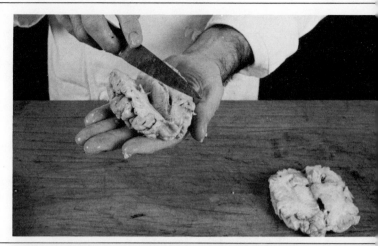

6. One brain ready to be used. For brains in black butter, probably the most common way of serving it, sprinkle with salt and pepper, dredge in flour and sauté in butter and oil until crusted and nicely browned on both sides. Transfer to a serving platter and sprinkle with drained capers and ½ teaspoon vinegar. Melt some butter in a saucepan until black and smoking. Pour over the brain and sprinkle with chopped parsley. Serve immediately.

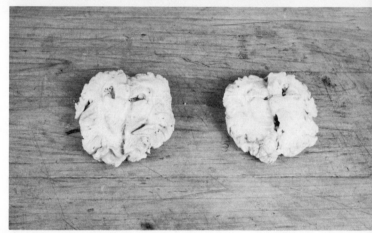

110. Saucisson et Saucisse *(Salami and Sausage)*

THE WORD *saucisson* in French refers to large sausages that are usually dry, like salami. Like smoked salmon, prosciutto, and other cured meats and fish, these sausages are not cooked. *Saucisse* refers to smaller sausages, such as link sausages and even frankfurters and knockwurst. These sausages are cooked and then served. The recipe below can be used to make either sausage—sausage that can be cooked with potatoes, in brioche and the like, or that can be dried to make salami.

In this recipe, the sausage is cured by the addition of regular salt to the ingredients. It could also be salted and cured in brine for a day or two. Saltpeter (potassium nitrate), also called Prague powder, is added to help the sausage achieve a nice pink color. It is used sparingly as it toughens the meat. If you omit it, the difference will be hardly noticeable. Fresh sausage is kept in the refrigerator for a good 2 or 3 days to cure before cooking (dry sausage cures while it dries) and in the process of curing it turns pink even without the saltpeter, though it takes slightly more time.

To dry, the sausage should be hung in a cool cellar or garage. The place should be airy, preferably dark and very dry or the sausage will spoil. The first few days of drying are the most important. The skin of the sausage will become whitish which is a sign that it is curing. After 6 weeks, the sausage can be consumed semi-firm (*demi-sec*). However, dried it will keep for months.

The fresh pork butt, which is part of the shoulder blade roast, is an excellent cut for sausage, as it is readily available, and has the right proportion of lean to fat.

5½ *pounds fresh pork butt*
2¾ *ounces salt (5½ tablespoons); this seems an enormous amount, but it is necessary*
½ *teaspoon saltpeter (optional)*
2 *teaspoons freshly ground white pepper (for fresh sausages, use 2½ teaspoons and omit the peppercorns)*
1½ *teaspoons whole black peppercorns (only for dry sausage)*

1 *large clove garlic, crushed, peeled and chopped fine, technique 2 (1 teaspoon)*
4 *tablespoons dry red wine*

1. For a coarse sausage, the meat can be cut by hand into ¼-inch pieces. If you are using an electric meat grinder, use a large screen with the holes about ⅜ inch wide. Position the vice first, then the knife (flat side out) and the screen. Screw the lid on. Grind the meat. Then mix thoroughly with the other ingredients. (The red wine can be replaced with white wine or omitted, as you prefer. The garlic can also be omitted.)

2. Natural casings come from pig, sheep and beef. Pork casings are 1½ to 2 inches in diameter and are used for Italian sausage. Sheep casings are about 1 inch in diameter and are used for link sausage. The beef casing pictured on the right is about 2½ to 3 inches in diameter and is the best for large sausages. It comes in bundles preserved in salt and can be kept almost indefinitely, packed in salt in a cool place.

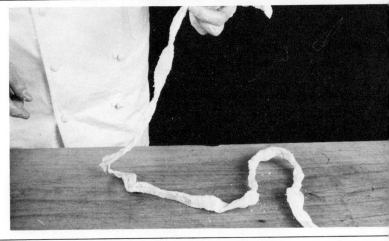

3. Pull the length you need and wash under lukewarm water. Fit the end of the casing to the opening of the faucet and allow tepid water to run through the inside. Then let the casing soak in cold water for 10 minutes. Drain and squeeze the water out.

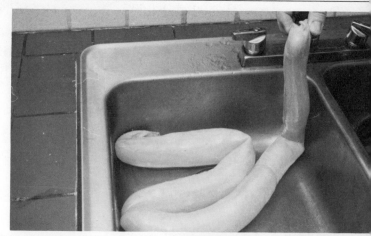

4. To use the meat grinder as a stuffer, you need a sausage attachment. Remove the knife and screen, leaving only the vice. Screw the funnel into place with the lid.

5. Gather the casings on the funnel.

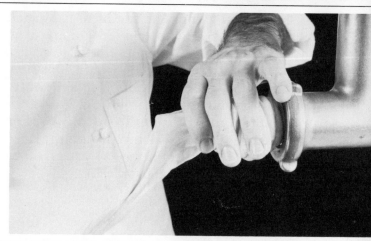

6. Leave a small piece hanging so air can be "pushed" out of the casing. If air pockets form in the sausage, you will find when you slice it that there are "holes" in the meat and the meat will be gray. Fill the casing, holding the tip of the casing lightly so that it does not unroll too fast.

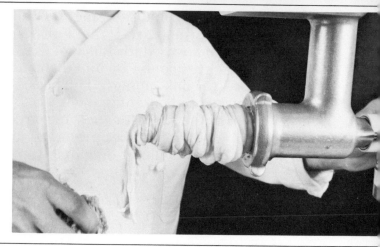

7. To fill the casing by hand, use a large pastry bag with a large plain tube or a funnel with a large opening (at least 1 inch). Slip some of the casing around the tapered part of the funnel to have a good grip. Push the meat into the casing with your fingers.

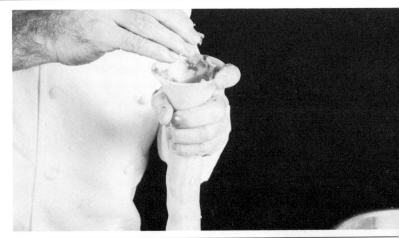

8. Squeeze along the length of the casing to push the meat down.

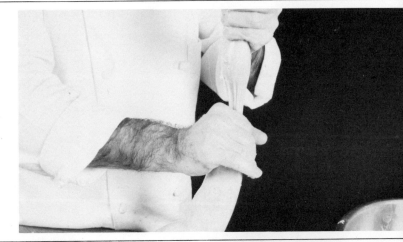

9. To tie the end, make a simple flat knot first.

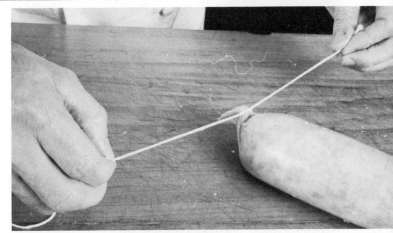

10. Then fold the tip of the casing on top of the knot and

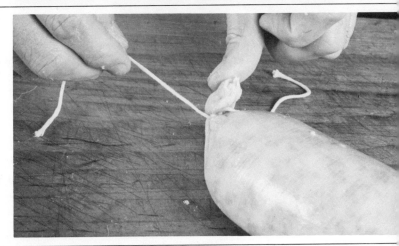

11. tie it again with a double knot.

12. Tie the string so that you have a loop to hang the sausage.

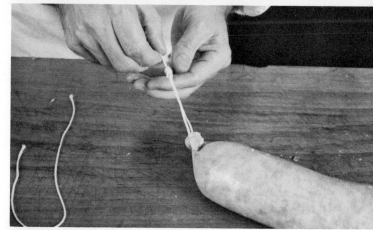

13. With one hand, push the meat toward the tied end. Squeeze the sausage where you want the end to be. Prick with a sharp fork or a skewer wherever you see a little pocket of air. Twist the sausage simultaneously. Be sure that there is no air trapped inside the meat.

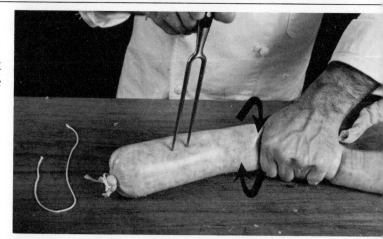

14. Tie the end with a single knot.

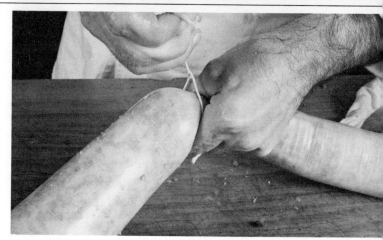

15. Then cut and tie as shown in photographs 10 and 11.

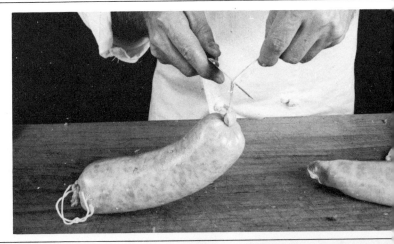

16. Sausage ready to dry. To cook the sausage, let it cure for at least 2 days in the refrigerator. Prick all over with a fork and cook in barely simmering water for 35 minutes. It can also be roasted with potatoes.

17. After 3 weeks of drying, tie the salami, technique 98, to make it more compact. Let dry another 3 to 4 weeks before using.

111. Jambon en Gelée *(Ham in Aspic)*

A WHOLE HAM is the ideal centerpiece for a large party. It can be served lukewarm, studded with cloves, beautifully glazed with apricot or pineapple jam, or hot in a crust with a Madeira sauce. However, on a hot summer night, cold ham, glistening in aspic, makes a stunning presentation. The troublesome matter of having someone carve a whole ham in the dining room in view of all the guests is eliminated by pre-cutting the ham and reforming it in its original shape. Buy the best quality "York" type that you can afford, a fully cooked (so called) and very lightly smoked ham. The one shown here was 19 pounds at purchase. Although called fully cooked, it greatly improves when recooked. You need an extra-large kettle. Cover the ham with cold water and bring to a boil. Lower the heat and simmer very gently, the water barely "shivering," for 3 hours. Let cool in the poaching liquid. This step is better done a day ahead.

1. Remove the cloth, if any, which wraps the ham.

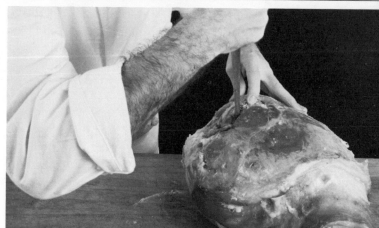

2. Place the ham on its back and cut along the hipbone, or pelvis, to get it loose (see technique 95, steps 2 and 3).

3. Keep cutting, following the outline of the bone and pulling until the hip or pelvis bone comes off. It has to be severed where it is attached at the tip, inside the socket of the hip.

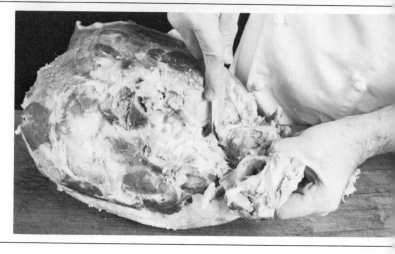

4. Trim, as thin as you possibly can, the dry bottom "skin" of the ham and the top skin all around the ham.

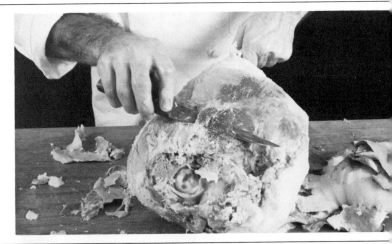

5. Trim around the shank bone (see technique 95, steps 6 and 7).

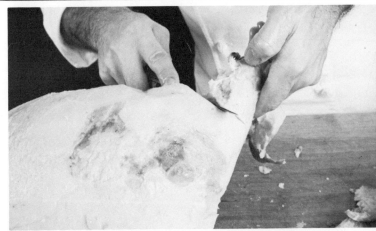

6. Saw the bulky tip of the bone. You will notice that there is a thin bone (part of the fibula) on top of the larger tibia bone.

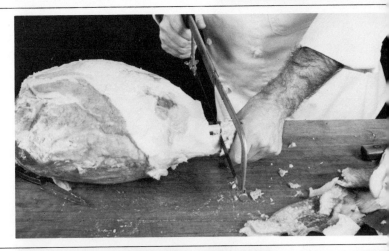

7. Pull the thin bone out. If it comes out easily without tearing the meat, the ham is properly and sufficiently cooked.

8. Trim a layer of the nice, white fat from the top of the ham. (You should have approximately a ¼-inch layer of fat left on the ham at the thickest part of the fat.) Cut the fat into pieces.

9. Place the pieces in a food processor or blender. Blend until pureed smooth. Refrigerate to stiffen it.

10. Cut straight down to the bone, a good inch or so in from the edge of the ham. This will give the slices a clean edge and will protect your hand during the carving in case the knife slips.

11. Start cutting at a slant, not quite parallel to the bone.

12. Be sure to arrange your slices in order as you are cutting.

13. When the ham gets too wide, alternate cutting your slices on the right, then on the left. Keep cutting until you see the long femur bone.

14. Start replacing the slices on top of the ham. They should go back in the same order they came off.

15. Keep building the ham back, trying to reform the original shape as closely as you can.

16. Spread a layer of the puréed fat on top to hide the cut of the slices.

17. Make it as smooth as possible. At this point, the ham should be refrigerated for a few hours (possibly overnight) so that the fat stiffens and sets.

18. Using green of leek, tomatoes, carrots and the like, decorate the ham to your fancy (see technique 11). Cover the cut end near the shank with carrots or leek. Refrigerate.

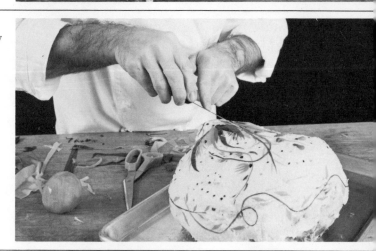

19. Glaze with an aspic, technique 39, making sure the aspic is almost set and the ham very cold.

20. Repeat several times (the aspic does not stick easily on fat), recovering the aspic between glazings and remelting it.

21. Pour enough cold aspic to cover the bottom of a large platter. Let it set until hard. Place the ham on top of the aspic carefully, and fit a frill at the end bone, technique 32.

112. Pâté Maison *(Pork Liver Forcemeat)*

PÂTÉ, WHICH COMES FROM THE LATIN *pasta,* meaning paste or dough, is a forcemeat mixture wrapped and cooked in a crust and served hot or cold. The term pâté *en croûte* (pâté in crust), which is often seen on menus, is a redundancy though its usage is understandable as the word pâté has broadened in meaning to include most ground meat, game, fish and even vegetables cooked with or without a crust and served cold, as well as hot.

Pâté *maison* or pâté *de campagne* (country-style pâté) is usually a coarse, simple loaf made with pork and liver and served cold. It can be excellent or dreadful, depending on the honesty and professionalism of the restaurant. You can think of pâté *maison* as a glorified meat loaf.

There are a few important things to remember about pâté. It should be well-seasoned. The amount of fat should be correct to obtain a moist pâté, and it should cook slowly so that the fat does not melt away too fast, resulting in a dry loaf. Though it is recommended in many recipes, it is not necessary to "press" the pâté after it is cooked. If the proportions were correct, there is no need to press the fat out. For the recipe that follows, you will need two 1½-quart rectangular loaf molds.

2 pounds fresh pork liver
1¾ pounds pork fat
1¾ pounds pork butt or shoulder
Lard leaves, technique 23, or caul fat to line the
    molds
4 bay leaves
1 teaspoon thyme
1½ teaspoons black peppercorns
2 tablespoons salt
2 eggs
¾ cup dry white wine

½ cup chopped onion
1 clove garlic, crushed, peeled and chopped fine,
    technique 2
¾ cup aspic, technique 39 (optional)

1. Trim the fresh pork liver, removing sinews and skin.

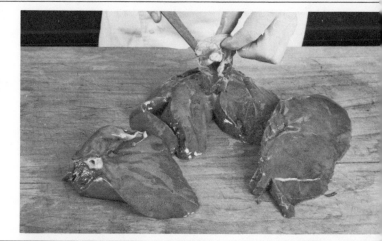

2. Cut into cubes. You should have about 1¾ pounds of trimmed cubes.

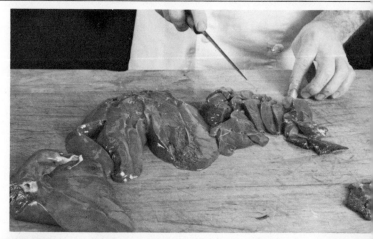

3. Weigh out the fat and pork butt. The liver, fat and meat should be used in equal proportions. Cut into 1-inch cubes. Chop the liver, fat and meat in several batches in a food processor, or have it ground by the butcher. The liver should be liquefied, and the meat and fat chopped like hamburger meat or coarser. Line two loaf molds with lard leaves or caul fat.

4. Using a coffee grinder, pulverize the bay leaves, thyme and peppercorns. Add the pulverized seasonings to the meat with the salt, eggs, white wine, onion and garlic. Mix thoroughly. Divide into two loaves.

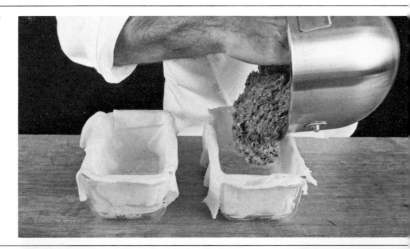

5. Bring the lard leaves back onto the meat and cover with aluminum foil.

6. Place in a roasting pan and add enough cold water to come two-thirds the way up the molds. Place in a 325-degree preheated oven for 1 hour. Reduce the temperature to 300 degrees and bake 2 more hours. The internal temperature should read 150 degrees when the pâté is done. The pâté shrinks while it cooks leaving space all around itself that fills up with fat. The pâté can be cooled and served in its present state or you can pour aspic over the pâté when you remove it from the oven to push the fat up and make it run over the mold.

7. The aspic will get absorbed into the meat during the cooling process and will set and make the meat moist. Either way, the pâté should set at least overnight and preferably for 48 hours. Run a knife around the cold pâté.

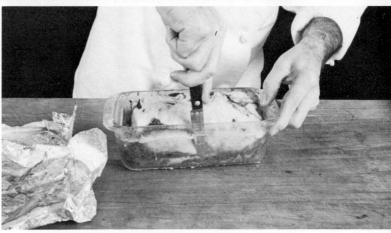

8. Unmold. If the pâté doesn't come out easily, run the bottom of the mold under hot water for a few seconds.

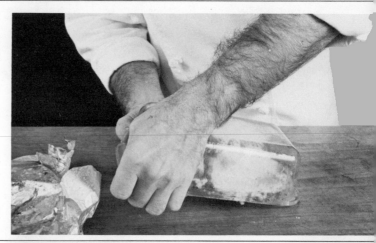

9. Clean the outside of the pâté gently with a wet towel.

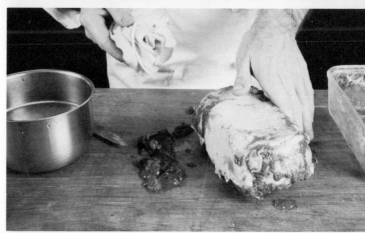

10. Cut into ⅜-inch slices and serve with crusty bread, *cornichons* and a dry white or red wine.

113. Terrine de Ris de Veau

(Sweetbread Terrine)

THE TERRINE, whose name comes from the dish in which it is cooked, is always served cold. The name evokes a more elegant and refined pâté, where the meats are arranged artfully inside the mold. It brings back memories of glistening aspic and the fragrance of cognac and truffles, where pâté *maison* (the preceding technique) brings back the taste of garlic, crusty bread and sour little *cornichons*. For the recipe that follows, you will need an earthenware, enameled or copper terrine or *cocotte*.

2 tablespoons butter
⅓ cup finely chopped shallots or onion
1½ pounds blanched and pressed sweetbreads,
    technique 108
Salt and freshly ground white pepper
Lard leaves to line the terrine, technique 23
1 pound lean veal
¾ pound pork fat
½ pound pork shoulder
2 tablespoons dry sherry

3 tablespoons dry white wine
2 egg yolks
¼ cup shelled pistachio nuts (optional)
1 teaspoon ground parisienne spices (a mixture
    of white pepper, ginger, cinnamon and clove)
1 tablespoon flour
½ teaspoon saltpeter (optional)
2 bay leaves
Thyme
Aspic, technique 39 (optional)

1. Melt the butter in a saucepan. Add the shallots or onion and sauté 1 minute. Add the sweetbreads, ¾ teaspoon salt and ¼ teaspoon white pepper. Roll the pieces in the butter and let cook gently on low heat, covered, for 10 minutes. Line the terrine with lard leaves.

2. The terrine should be well-lined with the leaves hanging on the outside. Using a food processor, chop the veal very fine. Chop the pork fat and shoulder meat in the same manner. Mix with the sherry, white wine, egg yolks, pistachios, 2½ teaspoons salt, 1½ teaspoons white pepper, parisienne spices, flour and saltpeter (see technique 110).

3. Place a layer (about 1 inch thick) of the meat mixture on the bottom of the terrine. Arrange sweetbreads on top. Be sure to stuff some mixture between the pieces of sweetbread. They should not touch but be bound together by the chopped meat.

4. Add more forcemeat, then more sweetbread, and, finally, cover with the forcemeat.

5. Bring the lard leaves onto the mixture. Place the bay leaves on top and sprinkle with thyme. Cover with foil, place in a pan of cold water and bake in a 325-degree preheated oven for 1 hour. Reduce the heat to 300 degrees and bake for another 2 hours. The internal temperature should be approximately 145 to 150 degrees when it comes out of the oven.

6. Remove from the oven when cooked. Pour ¾ cup melted aspic into the terrine (see step 6 in the preceding technique). Cool overnight. When cold, cover with plastic wrap. The terrine is more flavorful after it has set for 48 hours.

7. Cool some more aspic on ice.

8. When syrupy, pour some on the terrine to coat the top. Clean the mold before bringing it to the dining room. Serve from the mold.

114. Pâté de Faisan en Croûte

(Pheasant Pâté in Crust)

PÂTÉ OF PHEASANT in crust is more time consuming and involved than the two preceding techniques—sweetbread terrine and pâté *maison*. The meat marinates with the spices and seasoning for 3 to 5 days. Then, the pâté is cooked and allowed to cool for a day. Next, aspic is poured in and, finally, it can be served the following day. The process takes one week and though it can be accelerated somewhat, it is better when done step by step with the proper amount of time between each step.

THE FORCEMEAT MIXTURE

1 *(2-pound) pheasant*
6 *lard strips (see technique 23)*
1 *piece of caul fat (see photograph 3), or several lard leaves*
1 *pheasant liver plus 1 chicken or duck liver*
1 *black truffle, chopped coarsely (optional)*
1¼ *pounds pork butt or shoulder, chopped fine (it should be half lean, half fat)*
1½ *tablespoons very finely chopped shallots (about 3 or 4)*
¼ *teaspoon thyme leaves, chopped into a powder*
1 *large bay leaf, crumbled and chopped into a powder (the thyme and bay leaf can be pulverized in an electric coffee mill)*
2½ *teaspoons salt*
1½ *teaspoons freshly ground black pepper*
1 *tablespoon good cognac*
3 *tablespoons dry white wine*
1 *tablespoon truffle juice (optional)*
½ *teaspoon saltpeter (optional)*

Bone out a fresh pheasant following the directions for *poulet en saucisse*, technique 90, but remove all the bones. You do not have to worry about keeping the skin in one piece. You should have about 18 ounces of meat. Put aside the two fillets from the breast. Cut each breast into two strips and add to the fillets. You should have ¾ pound clean meat left. Finely chop the remaining meat in a food processor. Reserve the bones, skin, neck and gizzard for the stock.

Put aside the lard strips, the caul fat, the pieces of breast, the livers and the truffle. Mix all the other ingredients thoroughly. Place the reserved ingredients on top. Cover with plastic wrap and refrigerate for about 4 days.

THE STOCK

Place the bones, skin, neck and gizzard in a kettle with cold water. Add some salt, peppercorns, celery leaves, thyme and 1 carrot. Bring to a boil and cook for 2 hours. Strain. You should have approximately 5 cups of liquid. If not, adjust to 5 cups by adding water. Let cool and remove the fat from the surface.

THE ASPIC

Mix 1 cup of green of leek, celery and parsley (see techniques 38 and 39) with 2 envelopes of plain gelatin and 3 egg whites. Add the cold stock. Bring to a boil, stirring once in a while to prevent scorching. As soon as it boils, reduce the heat to a simmer and let simmer 5 minutes. Remove from heat, let stand for 15 minutes, and strain through a sieve lined with wet paper towels. You should have 4 cups of aspic.

THE DOUGH

2½ cups flour
¾ stick (6 tablespoons) butter
2 tablespoons vegetable shortening
½ teaspoon salt
2 egg yolks mixed with 4 tablespoons cold water

Following the technique for pâte *sucrée,* technique 142, make a dough using the ingredients listed above. (You can replace the butter and shortening with lard.) Knead the dough three times (*fraiser*). The dough should be made one day ahead and kept refrigerated.

FINAL ASSEMBLY

1. The mold used in this technique has hinges and comes without a bottom. You could cook the pâté free form or choose another mold.

2. Roll the dough between ⅛ and ¼ inch thick. Cut it to the center and overlap the edges to make a "jacket." This makes the mold easier to line. Line the mold with the dough, pressing it into the corners so the dough will adhere well.

3. A piece of caul fat *(crépine)*—the lacy and fatty membrane which encases the stomach of the pig—is used to line the dough. Lard leaves can be used in its place.

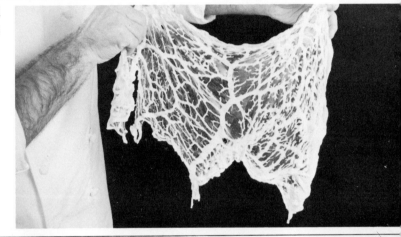

4. Line the dough with the caul fat. Place some of the forcemeat in the bottom of the mold.

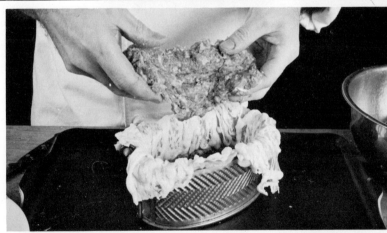

5. Arrange half the lard strips, half the breast meat and the livers in the middle. The livers could also be wrapped in caul fat before being placed in the pâté as pictured here. Cover the livers with the truffle pieces.

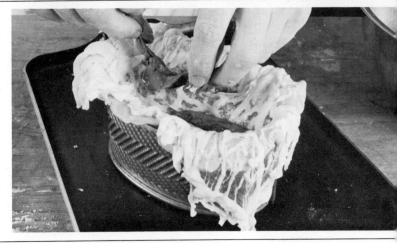

6. Cover with more forcemeat, then more lard and meat strips and finally with the remaining forcemeat.

7. Bring the caul fat back onto the meat.

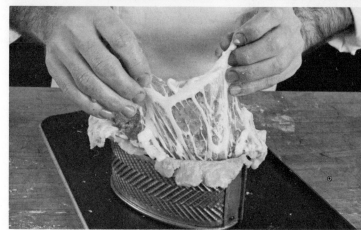

8. Bring the dough back onto the pâté and dampen with water.

9. Roll a piece of dough and place on top of the pâté. Press the side so that it sticks to the wet dough.

10. Trim around the edges.

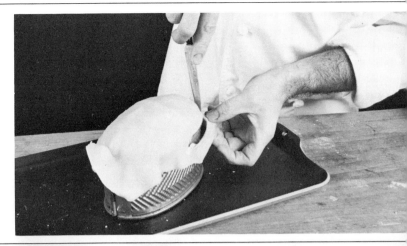

11. Roll more dough and cut shapes with a cookie cutter and a knife.

12. Wet the dough on the pâté and start building the pieces of dough as if you were laying a roof with tiles.

13. Overlap slightly, wetting the dough between each layer. When you finish, make a hole through the top of the dough so that the steam can escape during baking.

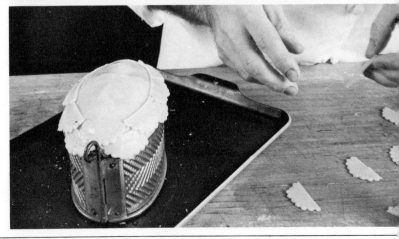

14. Cut lozenges of dough and mark with a knife to simulate the markings of the leaves.

15. Fold and position them around the hole, leaving the opening free.

16. Place a rolled piece of foil through the hole and into the meat. This will act as a chimney for the steam. Brush the pâté with egg wash (1 egg, beaten). Let the pâté "rest" for a few hours, then bake in a 330-degree preheated oven for 2 hours (the internal temperature should read 150 degrees when done).

17. Remove from the oven and, when cool enough to handle, remove the mold by opening the hinges. Cool overnight.

18. Melt the aspic and cool in ice water until syrupy. Pour into the opening. If a "leak" develops through the crust, seal the hole with soft butter. Keep pouring aspic until all the holes inside the pâté are filled. The aspic should stay at the level of the opening without going down. Let set.

19. Brush the outsides of the pâté with syrupy aspic.

20. When slicing, use a serrated knife, holding the crust with the tips of your fingers.

Carving

115. Découpage du Gravlax

(Carving Gravlax)

AFTER THE FILLETS have been cured, technique 56, they are ready to be served. They should be used within a few days or they may turn sour. Keep them refrigerated until ready to carve as it is much easier to carve when the fish is very cold.

1. Unwrap the fillets. Place the fillet flat on the table and, holding it stable with the flat side of a fork, start carving long, paper-thin slices. Cut on a slant.

2. This requires some practice.

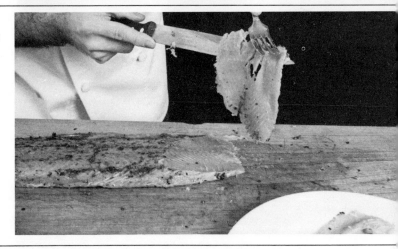

3. Try to cut slices as thin as you possibly can. Spread and arrange about 3 to 4 slices to a plate.

4. Sprinkle 1 teaspoon drained capers on top of each portion.

5. Sprinkle 1 teaspoon of the finest virgin walnut or olive oil and ½ teaspoon good red wine vinegar on each portion. Serve with buttered toast or black bread.

116. Découpage du Saumon Poché
(Carving Poached Salmon)

1. Poach and decorate the salmon, technique 57. The salmon should be cold and well "set" to carve easily. Using a thin sharp blade and holding the fish with the flat side of a fork, cut down to the central bone and across to the center line. Prepare a cold plate with lettuce leaves and some of the garnishes.

2. Cut across in the same manner, approximately 3½ to 4 inches below the first cut.

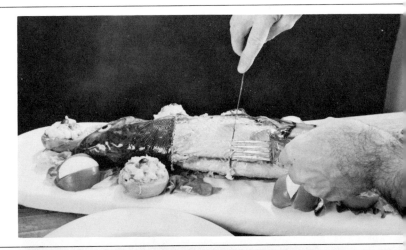

3. Cutting down the center line, loosen and lift a neat little "block" of salmon in one piece. Place on the lettuce.

4. A more elegant method is to carve the block into ⅜-inch slices and arrange them overlapping on the lettuce.

5. Repeat with another "chunk," pushing off the decoration as you carve and removing the bones, if any.

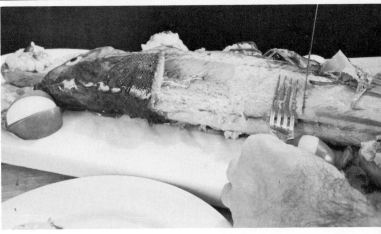

6. This procedure can be used only for a fish like salmon which has a tight, very compact flesh. For fish like striped bass, pike or large trout, serve the whole portion in one piece.

117. Découpage du Poulet Rôti
(Carving Roast Chicken)

1. There is nothing as simple and as delicious as a well-cooked roast chicken. Unfortunately, to get it properly done in a restaurant is as rare as it is simple. Truss the chicken, technique 87. Season the chicken with salt and pepper inside the cavity and outside. Melt 3 tablespoons butter in a large skillet and roll the chicken all around in the melted butter. Place on its side and bake in a 400-degree preheated oven for 15 minutes. Turn on the other side and bake another 15 minutes. Place on its back and baste well with drippings.

2. Bake for another 30 to 35 minutes, basting every 5 minutes. To baste, incline the saucepan on one side and scrape out the juices and drippings. Pour over the chicken. This will give moisture to the meat and crustiness to the skin. Five minutes before removing from the oven, pour ⅓ cup water into the pan to melt the solidified juices and make a natural gravy.

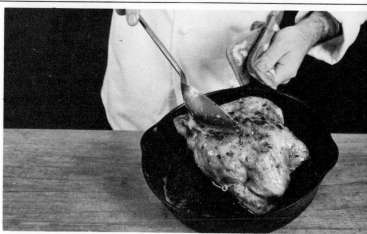

3. Remove the string. Place the chicken on its side. Insert a fork in the leg and pull lightly while cutting the skin all around.

4. Pull the leg up and separate from the body. It should come off easily. If you have difficulty, cut the sinews at the joint as you pull.

5. Holding the chicken with the fork, cut through the shoulder joint.

6. Cut along and all the way down to the bone of the breast.

7. Pull the wing and breast off, keeping the chicken from moving by holding the body with the flat side of the knife.

8. Turn the chicken on the other side and lift up the other leg.

9. Cut the shoulder at the joint.

10. Continue cutting down along the breastbone.

11. Then lift up the wing and breast piece.

12. The only piece left is the central portion of the breast, the sternum *(bréchet)*. Sever at the joint to separate from the backbone.

13. You now have the backbone plus five pieces of chicken.

14. Place the pieces back on the bone in their original position.

15. Chicken carved and reconstituted. Serve with natural gravy.

118. Découpage de la Dinde
(Carving Turkey)

1. Truss the turkey, technique 87. Rub with salt, pepper and ½ stick soft butter. Place in a roasting pan and bake in a 330-degree preheated oven. A 10-pound turkey will take 2¼ hours. Baste every 20 minutes after the first hour. Thirty minutes before the baking time is over, add 1 cup hot water to the pan. Place the turkey on a large serving platter. Insert a kitchen fork into the leg. Cut the skin all around the leg.

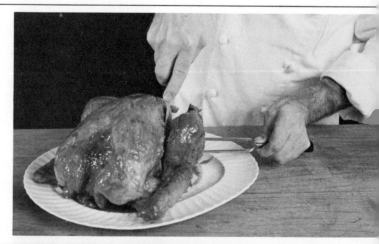

2. Pull off the leg, holding the turkey steady with the knife.

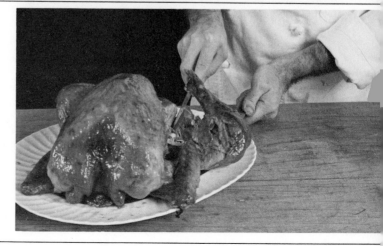

3. Place the leg on a plate and separate the thigh from the drumstick at the joint.

4. Slice the thigh around the bone.

5. Slice the drumstick, arranging the dark meat on a hot plate.

6. With a long, thin knife, cut the breast straight down into very thin slices.

7. Hold the turkey with the fork while cutting.

8. Arrange the slices in order on a hot plate.

9. Separate the wing at the joint.

10. Dark and white meat from one side of the turkey. Repeat on the other side and serve with the natural gravy.

119. Découpage de la Selle d'Agneau *(Carving Saddle of Lamb)*

1. Trim and tie the saddle, technique 92. Sprinkle the saddle with salt and pepper. Melt 2 tablespoons butter in a saucepan and brown the saddle all around on medium to high heat (about 7 to 8 minutes).

2. With the skirts tucked underneath, remove the strings. For a *selle d'agneau provençale,* mix together: ½ stick melted butter, 1 tablespoon chopped shallots, 1 teaspoon chopped garlic, ¼ cup chopped parsley and ½ cup fresh bread crumbs.

3. Gently pack and press the bread mixture onto the surface of the saddle. Place in a 425-degree preheated oven and bake for approximately 20 minutes, depending on the size of the saddle. It should be served pink. Let the meat "rest" at least 10 minutes in a lukewarm oven before carving. Serve with the drippings.

4. Cut off the pieces of skirt tucked under the saddle.

5. Slice on an angle into small pieces if you decide to serve it to your guests. (These pieces are not usually served in restaurants.)

6. There are two different ways to carve the saddle. First method: Holding your knife flat, cut along the flat T-bone which is between the loin and the tenderloin.

7. Slice the loin vertically into very thin slices.

8. Arrange slices on a warm plate as you carve.

9. Keep carving until you reach the backbone. Repeat on the other side, or try the second method.

10. Second method: I do not find this method as desirable as the first because it yields fewer slices, and the crusty herb mixture on top is only on the first slice. Nonetheless it is carved this way in many well-respected establishments. Cut alongside the backbone straight down to the flat T-bone.

11. Holding your knife flat, slice the loin into wide, thin slices.

12. Keep slicing until the flat T-bone is clean of meat. Arrange the slices on plates as you go along.

13. Turn the saddle upside down. Slice the tenderloin off in one piece.

14. Follow the bone as closely as you possibly can so that you get most of the meat off.

15. Remove the other tenderloin. Slice into smaller pieces so that each guest gets a small bit of the tenderloin. The T-bone should be "cleaned" on both sides. (The day after, pick off the bone and eat cold with a garlicky salad.)

16. Carved saddle. The plate in front shows two slices, one from each method. Be sure to have very hot plates and to carve the meat as swiftly as you possibly can because lamb cools off very fast. Serve with the drippings and a creamy potato such as *gratin dauphinois* (potato slices in garlic and cream sauce).

120. Découpage du Carré d'Agneau
(Carving Rack of Lamb)

1. After you have trimmed the rack of lamb, technique 93, sprinkle it with salt and pepper. Melt 2 tablespoons of butter in a skillet and brown the meat all around on medium to high heat (about 5 to 6 minutes). Place in a 425-degree preheated oven for about 10 minutes (depending on size). Let the rack "rest" 5 to 10 minutes before carving. (For *provençale*, see steps 2 and 3 in technique 119.) Holding the meat with the flat side of a fork, cut chops by slicing between ribs. For thinner slices cut one chop with the rib and one between the ribs.

2. Another method of carving is similar to the method used for the saddle in the preceding technique. Holding the rack up with a fork, cut down along the bones but do not separate the meat from the ribs.

3. Holding your knife flat, carve very thin, wide slices from the loin. When serving lamb, the plates should be extra hot, and the carving should be done quickly because the meat cools off very fast. Coat the slices with the natural juices and serve with a puree of carrot, technique 68, and/or a puree of celeriac.

121. Découpage de la Côte de Boeuf *(Carving Rib Roast)*

1. Trim, tie and cook the roast, technique 100. The meat should be rare. Remove the large piece of fat tied on top of the roast. Place the roast under the broiler for 5 to 6 minutes to lightly brown the top. Let the roast "rest" for 20 minutes before carving.

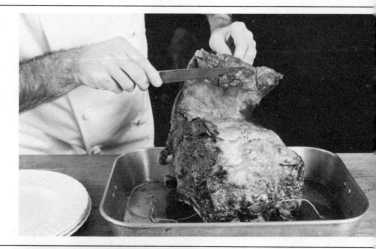

2. "Sit" the roast on its larger side. Using a sharp paring knife, cut straight down a few inches, following the ribs. This cut will give a nice clean edge to the slices of meat.

3. Holding the roast in place with the flat side of a fork, carve holding your knife flat.

4. Cut thin slices and

5. arrange several pieces per person on a warm plate. Serve with the natural gravy.

122. Découpage du Chateaubriand

(Carving Large Fillet or Tenderloin Steak)

THE CHATEAUBRIAND is the largest cut from the fillet (see technique 104). It should be broiled or sautéed rare. Let it "rest" 5 minutes before carving.

Carve on a slant with a thin, sharp knife. Arrange slices on a warm plate, pour some drippings over the top and serve immediately.

123. Découpage de la Bavette

(Carving Flank Steak)

FLANK STEAK makes an excellent lunch. It is not too expensive and it cooks very fast. Sprinkle a 2¼- to 2½-pound trimmed flank steak (see technique 105) with salt and pepper. Place under the broiler for about 7 to 8 minutes on each side. Let the meat "rest" 5 minutes before carving.

1. Holding the meat with the flat side of a fork,

2. cut thin slices on a slant. The thinner the slices the more tender the meat will be. It is important that the meat is cut against the grain or it will be stringy and tough. Arrange the thin slices on a platter. Serve immediately with its natural juice.

Desserts and Pastry

151.	Gâteau St.-Honoré	*Cream Puff Cake*
152.	Pâte à Brioche	*Brioche Dough*
153.	Feuilletage Classique	*Classic Puff Paste*
154.	Feuilletage Rapide	*Fast Puff Paste*
155.	Vol-au-Vent à l'Ancienne	*Large Patty Shell*
156.	Vol-au-Vent à la Moderne	*Large Patty Shell*
157.	Bouchées	*Individual Patty Shells*
158.	Paillettes, Diablotins, Fleurons	*Puff Paste Cheese Straws and Crescents*
159.	Allumettes aux Anchois	*Anchovy Sticks*
160.	Bandes pour Tartes aux Fruits	*Fruit Tart Strips*
161.	Tarte Carrée	*Square Fruit Tart*
162.	Palmiers	*Palm Cookies*
163.	Charlotte de Pommes	*Apple Charlotte*
164.	Charlotte au Chocolat	*Chocolate Charlotte*
165.	Charlotte Royale	*Bavarian Kirsch Cake*
166.	"Gâteau" de Semoule St. Valentin	*St. Valentine Custard Cake*
167.	Bananes Flambées	*Flamed Bananas*
168.	Crêpes Suzettes	*Crêpes Suzettes*
169.	Cigarettes en Chocolat	*Chocolate Cigarettes*
170.	Cheveux d'Ange	*Angel Hair*

124. Crème Anglaise *(English Custard Cream)*

CRÈME ANGLAISE is a basic and essential cream. It is served with innumerable desserts, flavored in different ways. With the addition of sweet butter, it can become a fine butter cream *(crème au beurre);* and with the addition of whipped cream and chocolate it can become a chocolate mousse; frozen it becomes ice cream. It is the base of such desserts as *bavarois,* charlotte and the like. The recipe below will yield 1 quart of *crème anglaise.*

3 cups milk
8 egg yolks
1 cup sugar
1 teaspoon pure vanilla extract
½ cup cold milk or cream

1. Bring the 3 cups milk to a boil. Set aside. Place the yolks, sugar and vanilla in a bowl and beat with a wire whisk for 3 to 4 minutes until it forms a "ribbon." The mixture should be pale yellow in color, and when lifted with the whisk, it should fall back into the bowl like a ribbon folded on itself. When the ribbon is "stretched," it should not break.

2. Combine the hot milk and the yolk mixture in a saucepan. Cook for a few minutes on medium heat, stirring with a wooden spatula, until the mixture coats the spatula. Test by sliding your finger across the cream. The mixture should not run back together immediately; the mark should remain for a few seconds. Do not overcook or the eggs will scramble. As soon as it reaches the right consistency, add the cold milk. Strain through a fine sieve into a cold bowl. Cool, stirring once in a while. Refrigerate until ready to serve.

125. Crème Pâtissière *(Vanilla Custard Cream)*

CRÈME PÂTISSIÈRE is a versatile and important basic cream. It can be used as a filling for éclairs, cream puffs, cakes and napoléons, or as a base for sweet soufflés. It can be made richer by replacing some of the milk with heavy cream. It can be varied with the addition of whipped cream, or flavored with chocolate, coffee, liqueurs and the like. With the addition of fresh sweet butter, it becomes a "lean" butter cream *(crème au beurre).*

2 *cups milk*
6 *egg yolks*
⅔ *cup sugar*
1 *teaspoon pure vanilla extract*
½ *cup flour*

Bring the milk to a boil. Set aside. Place the yolks, sugar and vanilla in a bowl and work with a wire whisk until it forms a "ribbon" (see step 1 in the preceding technique); this should take 3 to 4 minutes. Add the flour and mix well.

1. Add half of the hot milk to the yolk mixture and mix well.

2. Pour the yolk mixture into the remaining milk, mixing as you go along.

3. Bring to a boil on medium heat, stirring constantly with the whisk. The sauce will thicken as soon as it reaches the boiling point. Reduce heat and cook for 2 to 3 minutes, stirring constantly to avoid scorching.

4. Be sure to get into the "corners" of the saucepan. Place your hand on top of the whisk and push the whisk all around, scraping all the corners. Place the cream in a bowl and cover with plastic wrap to avoid a skin forming on top.

Yield: About 3 cups.

126. Crème Pralinée *(Praline Cream)*

Crème pralinée is simply a *crème pâtissière* with the addition of a powdered almond and sugar mixture. It is used as a filler for desserts like *Paris-Brest,* technique 150.

1. To make the *nougatine* (the cooked almond and sugar mixture), place 1 cup confectioners' sugar and ½ cup almonds in a heavy saucepan. Stir with a wooden spoon. Place on medium heat and cook, stirring constantly, until the sugar starts to melt. Since there is no liquid in the mixture, it will take a few minutes. However, as soon as it melts, it will turn rapidly into caramel. This method produces a very hard and tight caramel.

2. As soon as it turns into caramel, pour the mixture onto an oiled marble or an oiled tray. When cold, break into pieces and blend into powder in a food processor or blender.

3. Fold the mixture into the *crème pâtissière*, technique 125.

127. Oeufs à la Neige *(Floating Islands)*

1. To make tender floating islands, the egg whites should be poached in water that doesn't exceed a temperature of 170 degrees. Beat 6 egg whites with a dash of salt in the electric mixer or by hand. When the egg whites are firm, add ¾ cup sugar and continue beating for 30 seconds. Stop the beating and fold in another ¼ cup sugar (see technique 128, step 1).

2. Using an ice-cream scoop, dish the whites out. Round the top of the scoop with your finger to get an "egg" as round as possible.

3. Drop the eggs into the hot (170 degrees) water.

4. Poach for 1½ to 2 minutes on one side, then turn the eggs on the other side.

5. Poach for another 1½ to 2 minutes; then lift the eggs onto a paper-lined tray.

6. Prepare a *crème anglaise,* technique 124, let it cool and place in the bottom of an oval or round dish. Arrange the cold eggs on top of the cream.

7. Mix ¼ cup sugar with ¼ cup corn syrup. Cook until it turns into caramel. Let cool for a few minutes so the mixture thickens. Using a fork, drip the hot caramel over the eggs. The threads should be scattered all over the eggs. Do not refrigerate but keep in a cool place until serving time. Serve cool.

This recipe serves 8 to 10.

128. Meringue

THIS BASIC EGG WHITE and sugar mixture is employed in different ways to produce innumerable desserts. It can be dried and called meringue; it can be poached and called *oeufs à la neige*, technique 127; it can be piped into a shell and called *vacherin;* it can be mixed with nuts and called a *dacquoise;* it can be used to make cookies like ladyfingers and as a base for an *omelette soufflée.* With the addition of fresh butter it becomes a butter cream *(crème au beurre).* I begin here with the simple dried meringue "cookies" and proceed in the next few techniques through the more elaborate meringue confections.

1. For the whites of 6 large eggs, use 1½ cups superfine sugar. Whip the whites by hand or machine, adding a small dash of salt or a few drops of lemon juice before you start to whip. Whip on medium to high speed. When the whites are holding a nice shape, gradually add 1 cup of the sugar and keep beating for 1 minute. The mixture should be stiff and shiny. Fold in the remaining ½ cup sugar, technique 42. Folding in a part of the sugar at the end makes for a tender meringue.

2. Coat a cookie sheet with butter and flour, technique 40. Fill up a pastry bag, technique 41, and pipe out plain and fluted meringues. Lift the tip of the bag in a quick, swift motion to avoid a long tail (see technique 133, step 4).

3. Dip your fingers in cold water and push the tails down. Bake for 1¾ hours in a 180- to 190-degree preheated oven. (In restaurants, the meringues are often dried in a plate warmer at about 135 degrees for 24 hours.) They should be well dried. Though some people insist that meringues should be absolutely white, I fail to see the reason and do not mind if they become slightly beige during baking. Stored dry in a covered container, meringues will keep for months.

4. Meringues can be served on top of ice cream, with chestnut puree, puree of fruits, or plain whipped cream. Place some whipped cream on the flat side of one fluted meringue and

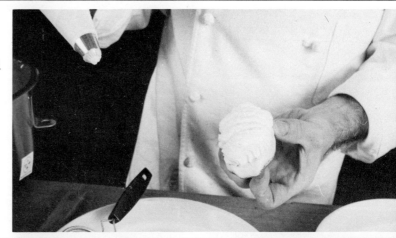

5. place another meringue against the cream. Place the double meringue on its side and decorate the top with more whipped cream.

6. Add grated chocolate.

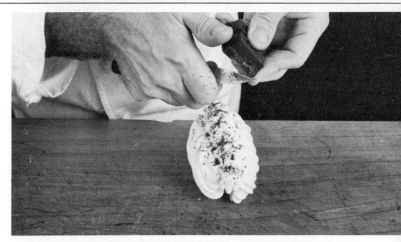

7. To dress up plain meringues sprinkle with bitter cocoa and place two together with whipped cream in between.

8. Decorate the top with whipped cream and sliced almonds.

129. Champignons en Meringue
(Meringue Mushrooms)

THESE LITTLE MUSHROOMS made out of meringue are very decorative. They are occasionally served by themselves as finger food for cocktail parties or buffets. Most often they are used to decorate large cakes such as a *bûche de Noël*. Make the basic meringue mixture following the instructions in the preceding technique. Coat a cookie sheet with butter and flour, technique 40.

1. Fill up a pastry bag, technique 41, with the meringue, using a small plain tube. Squeeze some rounded small meringues and some pointed ones to be used for the "stems" of the "mushrooms." Make them pointed by pulling the meringue mixture up after some of it has been squeezed out of the bag.

2. Flatten the "tails" of the "caps" using a little cold water on your fingers. Bake in a 180- to 190-degree preheated oven for 75 minutes. Let cool for 15 minutes. (The small *vacherin* pictured in the background are described in the next technique.)

3. Holding the cap of the mushroom in one hand, dig a small opening on the flat side with the point of a knife.

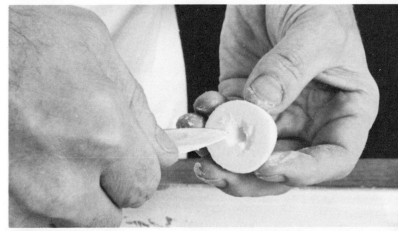

4. Using a paper cornet, technique 33, fill the opening with meringue mixture and

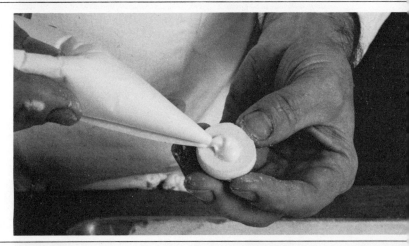

5. stick a stem into place. Bake in a 180- to 190-degree preheated oven for 45 minutes.

6. You should have perfect little mush-rooms.

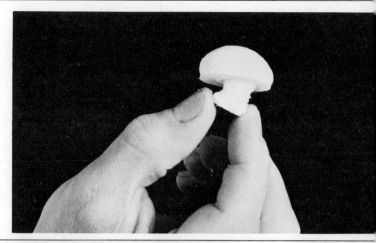

7. You can sprinkle them with bitter cocoa before using them for decoration.

130. Petit Vacherin *(Small Meringue Shells)*

PETIT VACHERIN are the small shells made of meringue that are customarily filled with ice cream, chestnut purée, flavored whipped cream and the like. Make the basic meringue mixture following the instructions in technique 128. Coat a cookie sheet with butter and flour, technique 40.

1. Fit a pastry bag with a fluted tube and fill with the meringue mixture, technique 41. Form small *vacherin* by squeezing out the bottom and piping a circle on the outside to make a "nest."

2. Bake in a 180- to 190-degree preheated oven for 1¾ hours and let cool. Fill with a scoop of ice cream and cover with a peach half. Coat with melba or raspberry sauce.

3. Decorate the top with sliced almonds and whipped cream. Serve immediately.

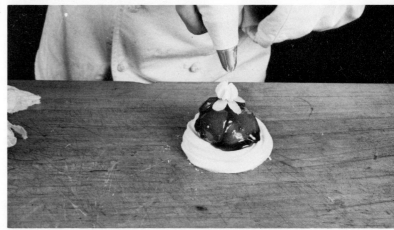

131. Vacherin *(Large Meringue Shell)*

A LARGE VACHERIN makes an impressive dessert for a party. It is not as complicated as it seems, and most of the work can be done ahead of time with little last-minute preparation. Prepare the basic meringue mixture, technique 128. You need 1½ times the amount given which means you'll be working with 9 egg whites instead of 6.

1. Coat several large cookie sheets with butter and flour, technique 40, and make outlines with a flan ring or any round object about 10 to 11 inches in diameter.

2. Place some meringue mixture in a pastry bag fitted with a plain tube, technique 41. Fill in one of the outlines to make a solid base.

3. Make plain rings on the other trays,

4. or double rings if you want to go a bit faster. You will need 6 single rings or 3 double ones. Bake the base and rings in a 180- to 190-degree preheated oven for 1¾ hours. Let cool in the oven for 15 minutes. Keep in a dry place.

5. Using a paper cornet, technique 33, place dots of meringue mixture on the baked base.

6. Place a baked ring on top and

7. keep building the *vacherin* with rings "cemented" with the meringue mixture.

8. Continue until all the rings have been used.

9. Using a metal spatula, coat the outside of the rings with meringue, filling up holes and making it smooth all around.

10. Decorate the top and bottom with a border of meringue.

11. Make strips, or any other motif which suits your fancy, all around the *vacherin*.

12. Embed small pieces of candied violets in the meringue. Return to a 180- to 190-degree preheated oven and bake for 1 hour. Cool in a dry place.

13. At serving time, fill the *vacherin* with slightly softened ice cream. Arrange strained peach or apricot halves on top of the ice cream and cover the fruit with a thick melba or raspberry sauce.

14. Decorate with whipped cream and candied violets.

132. Dacquoise au Chocolat *(Chocolate Meringue and Nut Cake)*

T HE DACQUOISE mixture is akin to meringue but it is made with the addition of nuts and cornstarch, and it is cooked at a much higher temperature than a meringue. The cake is comprised of two flat disks filled with a chocolate butter cream and a rum-flavored whipped cream. The disks should be dry and brittle like a meringue.

¾ cup sugar
1¼ cups nuts (half almond, half filbert), browned in the oven and ground
1 tablespoon cornstarch
6 egg whites
Dash of salt
Chocolate butter cream (technique 137)
1½ cups heavy cream
2 tablespoons confectioners' sugar
1 tablespoon dark rum

1. Coat two cookie sheets with butter and flour, technique 40. Mark the coating with 10-inch rings (see technique 131, step 1).

2. Mix together the sugar, nuts and cornstarch. Whip the whites by machine or hand adding a small dash of salt before you begin. Beat until firm. Fold in the sugar and nut mixture, technique 42. Work fast to keep the whites from becoming grainy.

3. Fill a pastry bag fitted with a plain tube, technique 41, with the meringue mixture. Pipe a ring on each tray, following the outline of the 10-inch ring.

4. Divide the remaining meringue mixture between the two rings.

5. Spread evenly with a spatula.

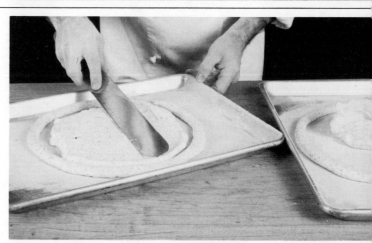

6. The disks should be the same thickness all over. Bake in a 350-degree preheated oven for 20 to 25 minutes, or until nicely browned.

7. Let the disks set for a few minutes, then slide off the tray to a wire rack.

8. After a half hour or so, the meringue should be dry and brittle.

9. Trim the edges to have perfect wheels. Save the trimmings.

10. Make a chocolate butter cream. Place one wheel on a serving platter and, using a pastry bag fitted with a fluted tube, pipe a border all around the wheel.

11. Place a small amount of the butter cream in the middle of the wheel and sprinkle with the trimmings of the cake.

12. Combine the cream, confectioners' sugar and rum. Whip until firm. Arrange the cream in the middle of the wheel.

13. Place the other wheel, smooth side up, on top.

14. Sprinkle with confectioners' sugar, coating the entire top.

15. Decorate the edges and the middle with the chocolate butter cream.

16. Cake ready to be served. Place in the refrigerator and serve cold, a small wedge per person. Use a serrated knife to cut the cake.

This recipe serves 8 to 10.

133. Biscuits à la Cuillère *(Ladyfingers)*

In FRANCE, ladyfingers are traditionally served as a cookie with champagne. They are also used to line molds, such as for a charlotte, technique 164, or in an *omelette soufflée*, technique 134. The following recipe will make 20 to 25 ladyfingers. The raw ingredients should be at room temperature.

3 large eggs
½ cup superfine sugar
½ teaspoon pure vanilla extract
⅔ cup all-purpose flour
Confectioners' sugar

1. Separate eggs, technique 43, and beat the egg whites by machine or by hand. When beating egg whites, be sure the bowl is clean and that there is no egg yolk mixed with the white. If you are not using a copper bowl, a dash of salt or cream of tartar or a few drops of lemon juice can be added to the whites to help the whipping process.

2. When the whites are firm, add the superfine sugar and continue beating for about 1 minute. Using a spatula, fold the vanilla, then the egg yolks into the meringue, technique 42.

3. Sieve the flour on top of the mixture, folding it in as you go along.

4. Coat two cookie sheets with butter and flour, technique 40. Fit a pastry bag with a plain tube, and fill with the mixture, technique 41. Pipe the ladyfingers onto the sheets. They should be approximately 4 inches long by 1 inch wide. Lift up the tip of the bag in a swift stroke against the end of the ladyfinger to avoid a long tail.

5. To make tear-shaped cookies, squeeze some mixture out of the bag; then, stop squeezing the bag and "pull" the mixture to a pointed tail.

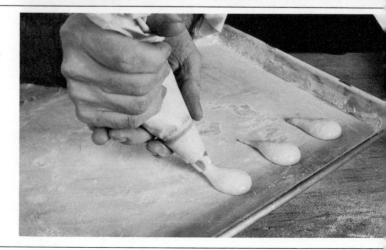

6. Sprinkle the ladyfingers heavily with confectioners' sugar. They should be sprinkled twice. Let them absorb the sugar for 5 minutes between sprinklings.

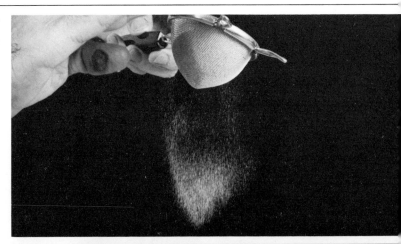

7. Turn the filled sheet upside down and give it a little bang with a knife to make the excess sugar fall on the table. This operation should be done rapidly and swiftly. If the mixture is the right consistency, the ladyfingers will not change shape at all.

8. Bake in a 325-degree preheated oven for 12 to 15 minutes. Let cool for 15 minutes. They should slide easily from the sheet. The color should be pale beige. To avoid drying, stick one against the other and store in a covered container.

134. Omelette Soufflée *(Soufflé Omelet)*

THE OMELETTE SOUFFLÉE is closer to a soufflé than an omelet. It is lighter than a regular soufflé because it is not made with a starch base (a *béchamel* or *crème pâtissière*). It can be put together quickly and easily but it cannot be prepared in advance as regular soufflés can. It will also deflate faster than a regular soufflé. To bake an *omelette soufflée,* you need an ovenproof platter—silver, stainless steel or porcelain—at least 16 × 12 inches. The same mixture can be used in a baked Alaska (*omelette surprise* in French). It is much finer than the boiled frosting normally used. This recipe will serve 10.

8 *egg whites*
1 *cup superfine sugar*
6 *egg yolks*
8 *to* 10 *ladyfingers, technique 133, or the same*
    amount of Génoise, technique 135
⅓ *cup Grand Marnier, cognac or kirsch*
1 *tablespoon confectioners' sugar*

Coat the platter generously with butter and sugar, technique 40. Beat the egg whites until they hold a soft peak. Reduce the speed and add the sugar in a steady stream. Return to high speed for 1 minute. Beat the yolks lightly with a fork and fold into the whites, technique 42.

1. Spread about one-fourth of the mixture in the center of the platter.

2. Arrange the ladyfingers or sponge cake on top and moisten with the liqueur or brandy.

3. Cover with more mixture.

4. Smooth with a spatula.

5. Be sure that the ladyfingers are equally covered all over.

6. Fit a pastry bag with a fluted tube and fill with the remaining mixture, technique 41. Pipe out a decorative border around the edge.

7. Decorate the top and sides to your fancy.

8. Sprinkle with confectioners' sugar and bake in a 425-degree preheated oven for 10 to 12 minutes, or until well glazed.

9. Baked *omelette soufflée.* You may sprinkle it with more confectioners' sugar when it comes out of the oven. Serve immediately.

135. Génoise *(Basic Sponge Cake)*

THE GÉNOISE—a basic sponge cake—is the base of countless cakes. It is also used for *croûtes aux fruits,* petits fours glacés and to line molds. The batter can be made with an electric mixer, as shown in the photographs that illustrate this technique, as well as by hand. The recipe makes two 8-inch cakes. The flour is sifted into the batter rather than folded in, because if poorly incorporated the cake will be grayish and heavy and will have lumps. The melted butter, added at the end, is very heavy and brings the mixture down. To correct this problem, "overwork" the batter slightly. If the butter is omitted or reduced (many cooks use none or only a tiny amount of butter), the mixture should not be whipped more than 5 to 6 minutes. If it is beaten too much, the cake will run over and go up and down like a soufflé, and the result will be a flat and crumbly cake.

6 large eggs, at room temperature
¾ cup sugar
½ teaspoon pure vanilla extract
1 cup flour (use all-purpose, or ⅔ cup all-
    purpose and ⅓ cup cake flour)
¾ stick (6 tablespoons) sweet butter, melted

1. Butter and flour two 8- by 1½-inch cake pans, technique 40. Place the eggs, sugar and vanilla in the bowl of the electric mixer. Mix well to combine the ingredients and stir over boiling water, or the burner, for about 30 seconds, so that the mixture is barely lukewarm. Place on medium to high speed and beat for 10 minutes. The mixture should make a thick ribbon. It should be pale yellow, and it should have at least tripled in volume.

2. Using a wide spatula, fold the mixture with one hand, technique 42, and sift in the flour with the other.

3. Add the butter, using the same procedure.

4. Fill the prepared cake pans about three-fourths full. Place pans on a cookie sheet and bake in a 350-degree preheated oven for 22 to 25 minutes.

5. Remove from the oven and, after 5 minutes, turn

6. upside down on racks.

7. The bottom and sides should be pale golden in color. The cakes should be flat (no sagging) and soft and springy to the touch. When cool, place the cakes in plastic bags to keep them from drying. They will keep for a few days without refrigeration.

136. Biscuit Roulé *(Rolled Cake)*

THIS BATTER IS FOR CAKES such as jelly rolls and the like. It is essentially the same as the *génoise* described in the preceding technique with the addition of an egg yolk. The egg yolk makes the cake moist and easier to roll. (*Biscuit roulé* is used to make *bûche de Noël.*

3 *large eggs, at room temperature*
1 *egg yolk*
½ *cup sugar*
¼ *teaspoon pure vanilla extract*
½ *cup all-purpose flour*
¼ *stick (2 tablespoons) butter, melted*

Place the eggs, egg yolk, sugar and vanilla in a mixing bowl and let the mixture get lukewarm by placing the bowl over boiling water for a few seconds. Remove from the heat and beat on medium to high speed for 5 to 6 minutes. Add the flour, then butter (see steps 2 and 3 in the preceding technique).

1. Butter lightly, in 2 or 3 spots, a 16-×-12-inch cookie sheet and line with a piece of parchment or wax paper. (The butter anchors the paper to the tray.) Butter and flour the paper, technique 40. Spread the mixture evenly in the tray and bake in a 330-degree preheated oven for 11 to 13 minutes.

2. Let the cake set for 5 minutes. Place a piece of wax paper on the table and turn the cake upside down on top of it. Remove the paper which covered the bottom of the cake and loosely place it back on the cake.

3. Let the cake cool to barely lukewarm; then, roll between the two sheets of paper.

4. Fold both ends to enclose the cake and keep refrigerated or in a plastic bag until you are ready to use.

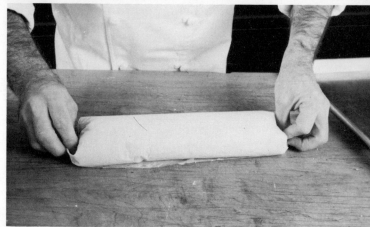

137. Bûche de Noël *(Christmas Yule Log)*

Y EARS AGO IN FRANCE, it was a custom to keep a log burning throughout the Christmas supper. Apparently, this log was the inspiration for the *bûche de Noël,* the traditional French Christmas holiday cake.

Biscuit roulé, *technique 136*
3 *tablespoons lukewarm water*
1 *tablespoon dark rum*
1 *teaspoon sugar*
1 *cup* crème pâtissière, *technique 125*
1 *cup heavy cream*

Make the *biscuit roulé* and set aside until ready to use. Mix the lukewarm water, rum and sugar together to make a syrup. Set aside. Whip the cream until stiff and combine with the *crème pâtissière.* Set aside. Make the chocolate butter cream.

CHOCOLATE BUTTER CREAM

3 *ounces chocolate (1 semisweet, 2 bitter)*
⅓ *cup sugar*
¼ *cup water*
3 *egg yolks*
2 *sticks (½ pound) sweet butter, softened*
2 *to 3 drops green food coloring*

Melt the chocolate in a small bowl (technique 169). Mix the sugar and water in a saucepan. Bring to a boil, and boil for 2 minutes over medium heat.

Meanwhile, place the egg yolks in the bowl of an electric mixer. Pour the sugar syrup on top of the yolks, mixing at medium speed. Put on high speed and keep beating for 5 minutes until the mixture is thick and pale yellow. Add the butter bit by bit, mixing at medium to low speed until the cream is smooth. Take 1 tablespoon of the butter cream, mix in 2 or 3 drops of green food coloring and set aside. Take 2 tablespoons of the butter cream and set aside. Now, add the melted chocolate to the remaining butter cream and beat until smooth. Set aside.

1. Unroll the *biscuit roulé*. Remove the wax paper on top. Sprinkle with rum syrup. Spread the *crème pâtissière* mixture on top.

2. Roll the cake up, removing the bottom sheet of wax paper as you go along. Place on a serving board or a platter.

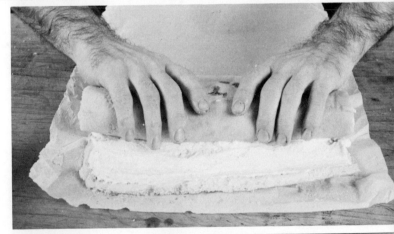

3. Trim one end of the cake.

4. With the trimmings, form a little stump on top of the log.

5. With a spatula, spread the chocolate butter cream all over the log. Spread the reserved white butter cream over both ends and on top of the stump.

6. Pull the tines of a fork down the full length of the roll to simulate bark.

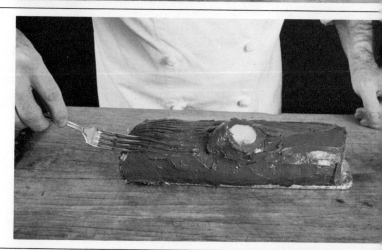

7. You can use a bit of the chocolate cream to decorate the cut stump and the ends of the cake to imitate the veins in the wood. Use a paper cornet, technique 33.

8. Place the reserved green butter cream in another paper cornet. Cut a straight end and make a thin, long strip to simulate an ivy vine.

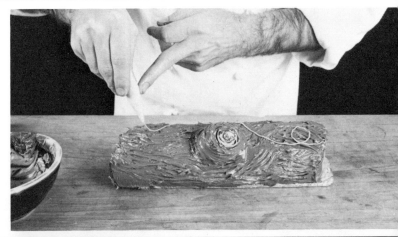

9. Cut the tip of the same cornet on both sides (see technique 33, steps 12 and 13) and pipe small leaves along the vine. Refrigerate until serving time, then decorate with meringue mushrooms, technique 129.

138. Gâteau Moka *(Multilayered Mocha Cake)*

To make this six-layer mocha cake, bake 2 *génoises*, technique 135, a few hours in advance or the day before so the cake is set and will not crumble when sliced. In addition to the cake, you need melted apricot jam, a rum syrup and a coffee-flavored butter cream.

APRICOT JAM

Empty a 10-ounce jar apricot jam into a heavy saucepan. Melt slowly over low heat to avoid scorching. When liquefied, strain through a metal sieve and reserve.

RUM SYRUP

1 *cup strong coffee, lukewarm*
3 *tablespoons sugar*
2 *tablespoons dark rum*

Mix together and reserve.

COFFEE BUTTER CREAM

½ cup sugar
½ cup very strong espresso coffee
3 egg yolks
2 sticks (½ pound) sweet butter, softened

Combine the sugar and coffee in a saucepan, bring to a boil and boil for 2½ to 3 minutes. Set aside. Place the yolks in the bowl of an electric mixer. Beat at medium speed, adding the sugar syrup slowly. Then beat on high speed until the mixture is the consistency of light mayonnaise (this should take about 5 to 6 minutes). Return to medium speed and add the softened butter, piece by piece, until the whole mixture is smooth and homogenous.

1. Cut a piece of cardboard the exact size or slightly larger than the cake so that it will come level with the cream topping. Using a long-bladed serrated knife, cut each *génoise* into three horizontal slices.

2. Keep one hand flat on the cake and hold your knife perfectly flat so the slices are the same thickness throughout. This requires some practice.

3. Rearrange the slices in order as you cut.

4. Place one layer, crusty side down, on the cardboard (it must be a top or bottom layer) and moisten with some rum syrup.

5. Spread a ¼-inch layer of butter cream all over with a thin, flexible metal spatula.

6. Place another layer on top.

7. Moisten it with more rum syrup and spread about 3 tablespoons of melted apricot jam on top.

8. Continue with a layer of syrup-moistened cake topped with butter cream.

9. Alternate fillings, finishing with a layer of butter cream. Smooth the top as flat as you can.

10. Holding the cake flat on one hand, ice all around. Turn the cake on your hand against the direction of the spatula.

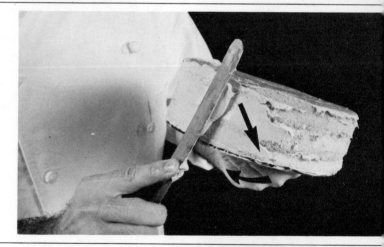

11. Smear some cream on one side. Starting at the top of the cake, go down and forward with the spatula in a smooth, direct motion. The butter cream should not be too cold.

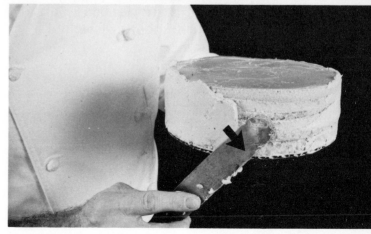

12. Let the cake cool for at least 1 hour in the refrigerator. Using the serrated edge, hold the knife on an angle and slide left to right in a swivel motion to decorate the top.

13. Place some reserved cream in a pastry bag fitted with a plain tube, technique 41, and decorate the top to your fancy.

14. With a fluted tube, make a border all around.

15. Place some melted chocolate in a paper cornet, technique 33, and "draw" on top of the cream.

16. Holding the cake in one hand, take a handful of cake or cookie crumbs and coat around the bottom of the cake (about 1½ inches high), turning the cake as you go along. Refrigerate until ready to serve. Do not cut your wedges too fat.

139. Gâteau au Kirsch *(Kirsch-Flavored Cake)*

PREPARE ONE *génoise* (half the recipe in technique 135) and cut it into three layers (see steps 1–3 in the preceding technique). Make a syrup with ⅓ cup strong coffee, 1 tablespoon sugar and 1 tablespoon kirsch of the best possible quality. You will need ½ cup of cake crumbs. (Grind stale cake or cookies if you don't have cake trimmings on hand.)

KIRSCH BUTTER CREAM

½ cup sugar
¼ cup water
3 egg yolks
2 sticks (½ pound) sweet butter, softened
3 tablespoons kirsch

Combine the sugar and water in a saucepan, bring to a boil and boil for 2 minutes. Set aside. Place the yolks in the bowl of an electric mixer. Beat at medium speed, adding the sugar syrup slowly. Then beat on high speed until the mixture is pale yellow and the consistency of a light mayonnaise (this should take about 5 to 6 minutes). Return to medium speed and add the softened butter, piece by piece, adding the kirsch a little at a time in between the pieces of butter. Set aside until ready to use.

1. Place a cake layer, crust side down, on a round piece of cardboard covered with foil. Sprinkle with the kirsch syrup. Spread some of the butter cream on top. Repeat with the next two layers.

2. Holding the cake in one hand, press the crumbs all around the cake.

3. Arrange chocolate cigarettes, technique 169, on top, the longest ones in the middle of the cake.

4. Trim the chocolate all around.

5. Lay strips of wax paper on top of the cake and sprinkle with confectioners' sugar.

6. Remove the wax paper carefully.

140. Gâteau au Chocolat *(Chocolate Cake)*

Tʜɪs ʀᴇᴄɪᴘᴇ makes two 3-layer chocolate cakes. The cakes use a *génoise* as the base and are filled with *ganache soufflé*, topped with *ganache* and decorated with *glace royale*.

The *ganache* is a delicate, glossy chocolate icing that is made from quality chocolate and heavy cream brought to a boil. The mixture is poured on the cake while still slightly tepid. If the *ganache* is allowed to cool, it will become too thick and won't run down the sides of the cake properly. If it is too hot, it will melt the filling and won't stick to the cake.

The *ganache soufflé*—the filling for the cake—is simply a *ganache* that has been cooled and then worked with a whisk. It lightens in color, gains in volume and becomes fluffy due to the addition of air.

The *glace royale* is a simple sugar and egg white icing that is piped onto the chocolate icing in a decorative motif. I have used a motif for each cake.

Begin by baking 2 *génoises* (the whole recipe in technique 135). If you want the cakes themselves to be chocolate, you can substitute ⅓ cup bitter cocoa for ⅓ cup of the flour in the basic recipe. Make cardboard bases for the cakes and cut each cake into 3 layers (see technique 138, steps 1–3).

GANACHE SOUFFLÉ *(Whipped Chocolate Filling)*

1 *cup heavy cream*
8 *ounces (squares) chocolate (4 ounces bitter,
    4 ounces semisweet)*
1 *tablespoon dark rum*

Combine the cream and chocolate in a saucepan. Place on low to medium heat and bring to a boil, stirring to melt the chocolate and avoid scorching. As soon as it boils, cool, mixing once in a while, until it starts to thicken and set. When cool, place in the bowl of an electric mixer. Add the rum and beat on high speed for 4 to 5 minutes. It will lighten in color and approximately double in volume. Use immediately; it will quickly become hard and unspreadable.

GANACHE *(Chocolate Icing)*

12 ounces (squares) good chocolate (6 ounces bitter, 6 ounces semisweet)
1½ cups heavy cream
2 to 3 tablespoons water (optional)

Melt the chocolate in the cream, stirring with a wooden spoon. Bring to a boil. Set aside. Let cool to barely lukewarm. If too thick or too oily, add 2 to 3 tablespoons water.

GLACE ROYALE *(Royal Icing)*

½ cup confectioners' sugar
⅓ of 1 egg white
3 to 4 drops lemon juice

Combine the sugar, egg white (do not use more than ⅓ of 1 egg white) and lemon juice in a bowl. Work the mixture with a wooden spatula for about 2 minutes until it is nice and creamy and thick enough to form a ribbon.

1. Place one layer, crusty side down, on each cardboard base and spread the surfaces with some *ganache soufflé,* using a thin, flexible metal spatula. Place the next layer on, add more *ganache soufflé,* and then the last layer. Smooth out the coating on top, leaving a little lip of cream all around.

2. Holding the cake in one hand, use your spatula to smooth out the sides. Go in a down-forward motion, getting rid of the lip as you go along (follow technique 138, steps 10 and 11). Refrigerate the cakes for at least 1 to 2 hours. They should be cold and well-set. While the cakes are cooling prepare the *ganache* and the *glace royale.*

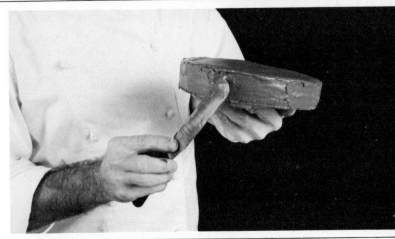

3. You will have at least one-third too much chocolate icing for both cakes, but you need a great amount to coat the cake correctly. The leftover can be kept for at least one month in the refrigerator. Don't be skimpy; pour half of the chocolate icing on top of one cake.

4. Spread rapidly with a long metal spatula.

5. Make sure all the sides are coated and the layer is about ¼ inch on top and around. If you take too long, the chocolate will cool off and become very thick.

6. Lift up the wire rack and tap it gently on the table to help smooth the sides and the excess chocolate at the bottom. Run your fingers or a spatula under the cake rack to smooth out the droppings of chocolate.

7. The cakes should be decorated with the *glace royale* while the chocolate on top of the cake is still slightly soft. It should not be too set and too hard. Place some icing in a paper cornet, technique 33. Cut the tip and, for the first cake, pipe out lines about 1 inch apart.

8. Turn the cake and run a long, thin-bladed knife through the lines. The knife should just barely touch the chocolate. Pull toward you so the white lines are "dragged" through the chocolate.

9. Cleaning the blade of the knife with a wet rag after each stroke, repeat about every 1½ inches.

10. Turn the cake around and drag the knife between each stroke in the same manner, but pulling the icing in the opposite direction. This design is called *décor Mexicain*. Refrigerate to have it cold before serving.

11. Using the paper cornet and the *glace royale,* decorate the second cake by drawing a coil. It requires practice to draw it uniformly.

12. Keep going without pausing to avoid breaking the line. You need a steady hand.

13. Using your knife, draw 8 equidistant lines from the center to the outside of the cake.

14. Repeat between each line but this time dragging the knife from the outside to the center. Refrigerate before serving.

141. Pâte Brisée et Croûte *(Pie Dough and Pie Shell)*

THE PIE DOUGH, *pâte brisée*, is certainly the most useful all-purpose dough in French cooking. Though the dough is easier to make with a combination of butter and shortening, an all-butter dough is finer. However, for quiche, *tourte* (meat pies) and the like, the difference is difficult to detect. The reasons are that the quiche is served hot or lukewarm, and the filling (bacon, mushrooms, onions and the like) has a strong taste of its own. The difference would be quite apparent in a shell for a raspberry tart because it is served cold and the filling is very delicate.

When working with dough, remember that the more you knead and the more water you use, the more elasticity and shrinkage you get. The less water and the more fat you use, the more crumbly and lax the dough will be. At one end of the spectrum you have the bread dough (flour and water) which is elastic, springy and unrollable. At the other end of the spectrum, the cookie dough (mainly flour and fat) is soft, crumbly and hard to roll. The pie dough is in the middle and will lean toward one side or the other, depending on your ingredients and method. This recipe makes enough dough for one 9-inch pie.

2 *cups all-purpose flour*
1½ *sticks (6 ounces) sweet butter, very cold and*
    cut into ¼-inch cubes
¼ *teaspoon salt*
½ *teaspoon sugar*
⅓ *cup cold water (approximately)*

1. Place the flour, butter, salt and sugar in a large bowl. Mix the ingredients enough so that all the butter pieces are coated with flour.

2. Add water and start kneading the ingredients to gather the dough into a ball. Do not worry if there are little pieces of plain butter here and there. This will give flakiness to the dough, making it slightly similar to a puff paste. The dough should be malleable and usable right away. If overworked, it will become elastic, in which case you should let it "rest" in the refrigerator for 1 hour before using.

3. Place on a floured board and roll uniformly, turning the dough a quarter of a turn as you are rolling so that it forms a nice "wheel." Be sure the board is well floured underneath. The dough should be approximately ⅛ inch thick, although many cooks like it thicker.

4. Roll the dough back

5. on the rolling pin.

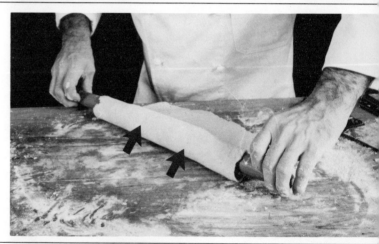

6. Lift up and

7. unroll on a flan ring or other mold.

8. With the tips of your fingers, push in the corners so that the dough does not get stretched, which would cause it to shrink during the baking.

9. Squeeze a lip all around the inside of the flan ring, working the dough between your thumb and forefinger.

10. Use a knife, or roll your pin on top of the ring to trim the excess dough.

11. Remove. (The excess dough can be stored in the refrigerator for a few days, or frozen.)

12. Re-form the edge between your thumb and forefinger.

13. Mark the edges with a dough crimper or the tines of a fork, or by squeezing it between your fingers.

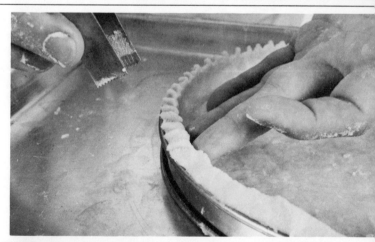

14. Shell, ready to be used. If your recipe calls for a precooked shell, line the shell with wax paper and weight it down with beans or the like (see steps 4 and 5 in the next technique) to prevent the dough from shrinking during the first 15 minutes of baking.

142. Pâte Sucrée et Croûte

(Sweet Pie Dough and Pastry Shell)

THE SWEET PIE DOUGH, *pâte sucrée*, is quite different from the *pâte brisée* described in the preceding technique. The texture is not flaky or tender, but rather is close to that of a cookie dough. The dough is not at all elastic or springy. It rolls easily but is a little difficult to pick up. It makes an excellent shell for runny ingredients because it does not get soggy as easily as regular pie dough. This recipe makes enough dough for two 9-inch pies.

3 *cups all-purpose flour*
2½ *sticks (10 ounces) sweet butter, softened and*
cut into pieces
½ *cup superfine sugar*
¼ *teaspoon salt*
1 *egg, beaten lightly with a fork*
1 *egg yolk*

1. Place the flour in the middle of the working table. Make a well in the center and add the remaining ingredients. Gather the dough, with a pastry scraper or your fingers, into a compact mass.

2. Place the dough close to you and, with the heel of your hand, take a mass about the size of a golf ball and "smear" it about 10 inches forward. Keep your fingers pointed upwards. Repeat, smearing more and more of the dough forward, until it has all been processed. Gather the dough into a ball and repeat the operation once more. The two smearings (*fraiser* in French) help homogenize the ingredients, making a well-blended dough.

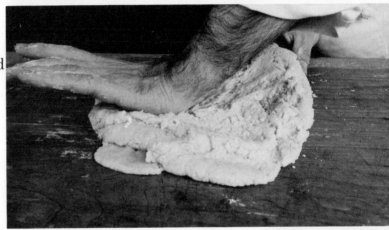

3. Roll the dough and fit it into a mold as described in steps 3–13 of the preceding technique. You can use a flan ring or a tart mold with a removable bottom, as pictured here.

4. Cut a round disk of wax paper, technique 30, and fringe the edge with a pair of scissors.

5. Line up the dough with the paper. Fill the shell with dry beans, rice, pebbles or any heavy, dry ingredient, to hold the dough in place during the baking.

6. Place on a cookie sheet and bake in a 400-degree preheated oven for approximately 45 minutes. Remove the paper and beans and keep for later use.

7. Brush the inside of the shell with an egg wash (1 whole egg, beaten). Return to the 400-degree oven for 5 to 8 minutes.

8. Remove from mold. The egg coating forms a waterproof layer and prevents the dough from getting soggy when filled with cream or juicy fruits. The same technique is used with *pâte brisée* on those occasions when you precook a shell for quiche or custard.

9. The dough should always be well cooked and crunchy (better overcooked than underdone). If, by a stroke of bad luck, the dough burns underneath, turn upside down when cool, and rub with a grater to remove the blackened part.

143. Croûte en Pâte à l'Envers

(Upside-Down Pastry Shell)

PASTRY SHELLS are often baked upside down. The gravity pulls the dough down, and the weight on top keeps the dough in shape, avoiding any shrinkage during baking.

1. Roll the dough to a ⅛-inch thickness (see technique 141, steps 3–7).

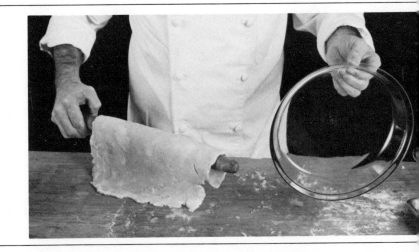

2. Place directly on top of an upside-down pie plate.

3. Fit another pie plate on top of the dough.

4. Turn the plates right side up and trim the dough.

5. Place upside down on a cookie sheet and bake in a 400-degree preheated oven for approximately 35 minutes, or until well browned.

6. Remove the shell and use, according to your recipe.

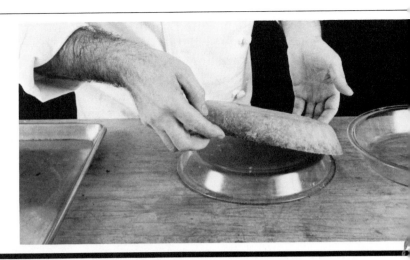

144. Coquille en Pâte *(Scalloped Pastry Shells)*

Lᴵᴛᴛʟᴇ ɪɴᴅɪᴠɪᴅᴜᴀʟ ᴘᴀsᴛʀʏ sʜᴇʟʟs can be used as a first course (stuffed with eggs or avocado), as a main course (stuffed with fish, lobster, chicken livers and the like) or as dessert (with berries and whipped cream). Use *pâte brisée,* technique 141, for salted dishes, or *pâte sucrée,* technique 142, for desserts.

1. Roll the dough about ⅛ inch thick. Butter the outside of the shells. Slide the shell under the dough.

2. Press the dough on the buttered side of the shell. Trim by pushing the dough on the edges with your fingers.

3. Holding the lined shell in one hand, push the dough slightly around the edge of the shell to anchor it. This prevents too much shrinkage during baking. Brush the dough with an egg wash (1 whole egg, beaten), place on a cookie sheet and bake in a 400-degree preheated oven for 25 to 30 minutes, or until nicely browned.

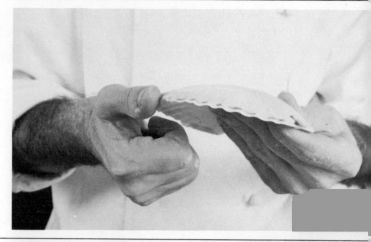

4. Pick the pastry off of the shell (it should slide easily) and garnish to your liking.

145. Tarte aux Pommes (Apple Tart)

OPEN-FACED TARTS are as distinctly French as apple pie is American. The dough can be arranged in a flan ring as shown below, or in a removable bottom mold or in a regular pie plate. It can also be cooked free form on a cookie sheet with the edges rolled to hold in the filling. I like the dough rolled very thin and the shell well-cooked. Any apple can be used, keeping in mind that some are more tart than others, and some hold their shape better than others while cooking (see technique 146).

1. Make your pie dough, technique 141, and fit it into a 9-inch ring or mold. Trim both the stem and flower ends of 4 to 5 good-sized apples. Holding a paring knife by the blade, use only the point of the knife and your thumb as a pivot to cut the stem off. (This technique can also be used for pears, tomatoes and the like.)

2. Using a vegetable peeler or a sharp paring knife, peel the apples. Cut into halves through the stem and remove the seeds with the point of the knife, using the method described in step 1.

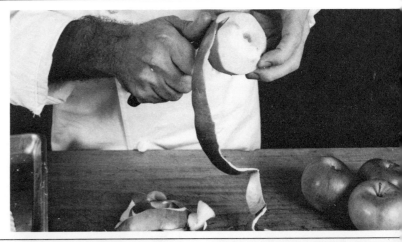

3. Cut into about ¼-inch slices. Chop the end slices coarsely, reserving the uniform center slices.

4. Arrange the chopped apples on the bottom of the pie shell.

5. Fan out the center slices as you would a deck of cards and

6. arrange on top of the chopped apples. (You may arrange the slices one by one if you feel it is easier.)

7. Arrange apple slices in the center of shell

8. to simulate the petals of a rose.

9. Sprinkle 3 tablespoons sugar on top and 2 tablespoons sweet butter, cut into pieces.

10. Bake in a 400-degree preheated oven for approximately 75 minutes. It should be well browned and the crust golden. Remove the flan ring. The pie shrinks slightly during baking making the ring easy to remove.

11. Using a large metal spatula, remove the pie from the cookie sheet and glaze (optional) with an apricot or apple jam. (Strain apricot jam through a fine sieve and dilute slightly with calvados, cognac, kirsch or even water, if you object to alcohol.) Serve at room temperature; refrigeration is not recommended.

This recipe serves 8 to 10.

146. Tarte Tatin *(Upside-Down Apple Tart)*

THE UPSIDE-DOWN OPEN TART, first made by the old "demoiselles Tatin," has become a classic of the French repertoire. There are many interpretations of it which are quite simple and satisfactory. The one below is a little more involved, but the result is quite distinctive.

Prepare half of the recipe for *pâte brisée,* technique 141. Trim, peel and slice 8 apples (see steps 1–3 in the preceding technique). Use firm apples that will hold their shape during cooking—Calville, Rennet, Granny Smith or the all-purpose green or Golden Delicious. You should have 6 cups of sliced apples. For a 10-inch pie plate, place ⅓ cup sugar and ¼ cup water in a saucepan, bring to a boil and keep boiling until it turns a nice caramel color.

1. Pour the caramel into the pie plate.

2. Tilt it so that the whole bottom and half of the sides are coated. Do this quickly before the caramel cools off and hardens.

3. Grate the rind of 1 lemon, technique 17. Use only the yellow part of the skin. You should have about 1 teaspoon of grated rind.

4. Place ½ stick (4 tablespoons) sweet butter in a large saucepan and melt until foaming. Add the apples, ⅓ cup sugar and the lemon rind. Sauté for 5 to 6 minutes, being careful not to break the slices too much. Pour onto a large cookie sheet to cool.

5. When cool enough to handle, start arranging the nicest slices from the middle of the pie plate out. Overlap the slices so the rounded sides are hidden. The nicest side shows after unmolding when the bottom of the pie plate becomes the top.

6. Continue to arrange in layers until the whole bottom and part of the sides are covered.

7. Fill the cavity with the remaining apples.

8. Unroll the dough on top of the apples.

9. Trim the dough so that it comes to the edge of the apples, brush the dough with an egg wash (1 whole egg, beaten) and prick with a fork or a knife.

10. Bake on a cookie sheet in a 400-degree preheated oven for 45 minutes, or until the dough is nicely browned. Run a knife all around to loosen the crust. Let the pie set for 5 minutes.

11. Place a platter on top of the pie plate and

12. turn upside down.

13. The pie plate should come off easily. If some slices stick to the bottom, pick them up and arrange them in the design. If the pie is taken out of the oven and turned upside down immediately, it may collapse during unmolding. However, if left to set too long, the caramel will harden and half of the bottom will stick. If this happens, heat the pie plate for a few seconds directly on the gas burner before unmolding.

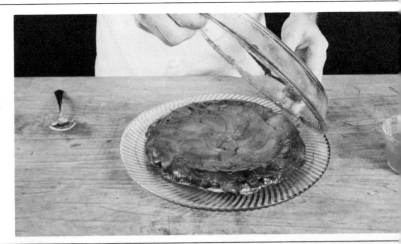

14. You may brush the top with an apricot glaze (see step 11 in the preceding technique), and decorate with sliced almonds. Eat barely cool; do not refrigerate.

This recipe serves 8 to 10.

147. Pâte à Choux *(Cream Puff Dough)*

ALONG WITH the *pâte brisée*, technique 141, and *feuilletage*, technique 153, *pâte à choux* is one of the mother doughs of French pastry making. It is used to make countless desserts such as éclairs and *choux, gâteau St.-Honoré* and *Paris-Brest* as well as such dishes as *pommes dauphine* and even quenelles. It is always made with what is called a *panade*—a combination of water, butter and flour—to which eggs are added.

1 *cup water*
½ *stick (4 tablespoons) sweet butter*
¼ *teaspoon salt*
1 *cup all-purpose flour*
4 *large eggs*

1. Place the water, butter (cut into pieces) and salt in a heavy saucepan. Bring to a boil. When the butter is completely melted, remove from the heat and add the flour all at once. Mix rapidly with a wooden spatula.

2. Place the mixture on top of a low flame and "dry" for 5 to 6 minutes, mixing with the wooden spatula. The dough should be soft and should not stick to your fingers when pinched. This mixture is called the *panade*.

3. Transfer the *panade* to a clean bowl. You will notice that the bottom of the pan is covered with a thin crust (an indication that the dough has been sufficiently dried). The eggs are mixed into the *panade* in the bowl because if they were added in the pan, the white crust at the bottom would break into dried little pieces that would stick in the dough.

4. Let the dough cool for at least 5 minutes. Add the eggs one at a time, beating carefully after each addition so that the mixture is smooth before the next egg is added.

5. The dough should be smooth, shiny, and as thick and as heavy as mayonnaise. This makes enough dough for 14 to 16 *choux* or éclairs which are described in the following technique.

148. Choux et Eclairs *(Cream Puffs)*

THE ONLY DIFFERENCE BETWEEN a *choux* and an éclair is that the former is round and the latter is long. Both can be filled with flavored whipped cream, *crème pâtissière*, ice cream, jam and the like. The smallest *choux* are known as *profiteroles* and are often filled with vanilla ice cream and served with a lukewarm chocolate sauce. (The *ganache* used for the icing in the *gâteau au chocolat*, technique 140, can be diluted with water and used as a chocolate sauce.)

1. Prepare the *pâte à choux* following the recipe in the preceding technique. Fill a pastry bag with the dough and coat a large cookie sheet with butter and flour, techniques 41 and 40. Squeeze out puffs about the size of a golf ball or elongated éclairs.

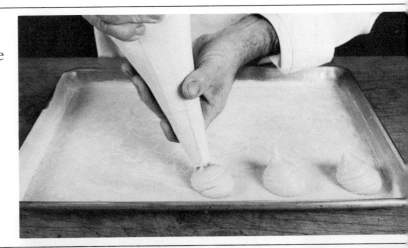

2. Brush the tops with an egg wash (1 whole egg, beaten), pushing down the "tails." The *choux* can also be formed by dropping spoonfuls of dough on the cookie sheet (see technique 82, steps 5 and 6).

3. Drag the tines of a fork to make a design on top of the éclairs. Let the *choux* and éclairs dry for at least 20 minutes before cooking. (The egg wash gives a shiny glaze, providing it is allowed to dry for a while before baking.)

4. Bake in a 370-degree preheated oven for 35 minutes, or until well puffed and golden. Shut off the heat, open the oven door halfway (to get rid of any steam) and let the puffs cool slowly and dry for 1 hour. *Pâte à choux* will soften and collapse if cooled too fast. Cut into halves to fill or, if you want to, keep them whole. (See technique 151, steps 4 and 5.)

149. Cygnes en Pâte à Choux

(Cream Puff Swans)

1. Prepare the *pâte à choux* following the recipe in technique 147. Fill a pastry bag with the dough and coat a large cookie sheet with butter and flour, techniques 41 and 40. Squeeze large teardrops of dough onto the cookie sheet (see technique 133, step 5).

2. Make a paper cornet, technique 33, fill with dough and squeeze out small "question marks." Make a pointed "beak" by "pulling" the cornet up.

3. Brush with an egg wash (1 whole egg, beaten). Bake in a 375-degree preheated oven for 10 to 12 minutes. Remove the small question marks and return the cream puffs to the oven for another 25 minutes, a total baking time for the cream puffs of 35 to 37 minutes. Shut off the heat and open the oven door halfway, allowing the steam to escape. Let cool and dry for 1 hour.

4. Holding the *choux* on the side, slice off the top on a diagonal with a sharp, long-bladed knife.

5. Cut the lid into halves.

6. Fill the *choux* with sweetened whipped cream.

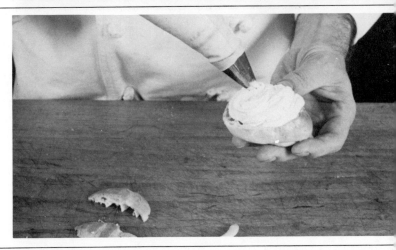

7. Place both pieces of the lid back on the cream to simulate wings.

8. Stick the "neck" into the cream between the point of the wings.

9. Sprinkle with confectioners' sugar.

VARIATION: Place 1 tablespoon of good raspberry jam in the bottom of the opened swan. Top with a small scoop of vanilla ice cream and decorate with whipped cream. Place the wings and neck into place. Just before serving, pour diluted raspberry jam or raspberry sauce into a large platter. It should be about ¼-inch deep. Arrange the swans so they are "swimming" on top of the sauce. Surround with angel hair, technique 170, and serve immediately.

150. Paris-Brest *(Cream Puff Ring)*

THE PARIS-BREST is made from a ring of *pâte à choux* that is baked and filled with praline cream and whipped cream, then topped with sliced almonds and confectioners' sugar. The cake serves 16.

1. Coat a cookie sheet with butter and flour, technique 40. Using a flan ring, or any circular mold, mark an outline about 10 inches in diameter.

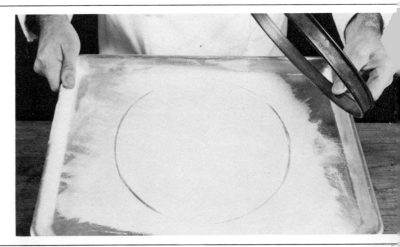

2. Prepare the *pâte à choux,* technique 147. Fit a pastry bag with the dough, technique 41. Squeeze out a ring of *pâte à choux* about 1 inch wide, following the outline.

3. Squeeze another ring inside or outside the first, depending on how large you want the cake to be.

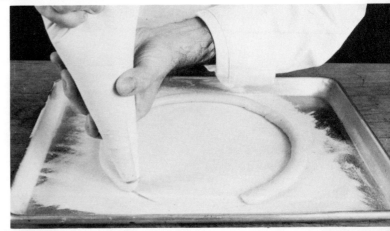

4. Squeeze 1 ring on top of the others.

5. Brush with an egg wash (1 whole egg, beaten).

6. Sprinkle 1 tablespoon sliced almonds on top.

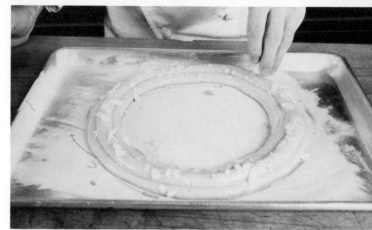

7. Let the cake dry for about 20 minutes. Bake in a 400-degree preheated oven for 45 minutes. Shut off the heat, open the oven door halfway to let the steam escape and leave the cake in the oven for 1 hour so it cools and dries. Using a long-bladed knife, cut a lid off the cake.

8. Fill the bottom part with *crème pralinée*, technique 126.

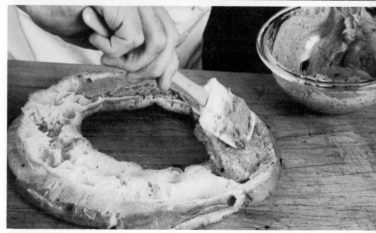

9. Then decorate with slightly sweetened whipped cream.

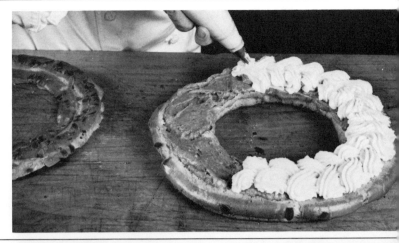

10. Place the lid back on top.

11. Sprinkle with confectioners' sugar. Keep in a cool, not too cold, dry place. Cut into small wedges with a serrated knife.

151. Gâteau St.-Honoré *(Cream Puff Cake)*

THIS CLASSIC FRENCH CAKE was named for the "sometimes" patron saint of bakers. It is made from a *pâte brisée* (or *pâte sucrée*) base that is topped with cream-filled *choux* coated with caramel. I use larger *choux* than are normally used (a personal preference) and instead of the classic St.-Honoré cream, which is made with hot *crème pâtissière* mixed with beaten egg whites, I use a *crème pâtissière* combined with whipped cream.

Make the *crème pâtissière*, technique 125, adding 1 envelope unflavored gelatin to the sugar in the recipe. When the cream is cool, fold in 2½ cups unsweetened heavy cream, whipped firm, technique 42.

Make half the recipe for *pâte brisée,* technique 141, and a batch of *pâte à choux,* technique 147. Bake 10 *choux* and reserve the remaining mixture for use in step 2.

1. Roll the *pâte brisée* dough ⅛-inch thick and place on a cookie sheet. Using a flan ring, or another round object about 10 inches in diameter, trim the dough into a wheel.

2. Fit a pastry bag with a tube with a small opening and fill with the remaining *pâte à choux,* technique 41. Squeeze 3 small rings around the edge of the *pâte brisée.*

3. Prick the center with a fork and bake in a 400-degree preheated oven for 30 minutes. It should be well baked and nicely browned.

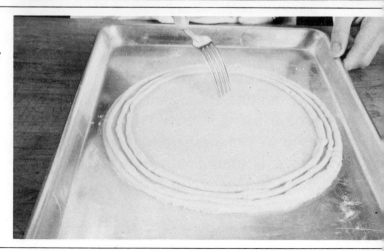

4. Using the tip of a knife, make a hole in the bottom of each *choux*.

5. Fill a pastry bag with the *crème pâtissière* and fill each *choux* by inserting the tube through the opening at the bottom and squeezing the cream inside.

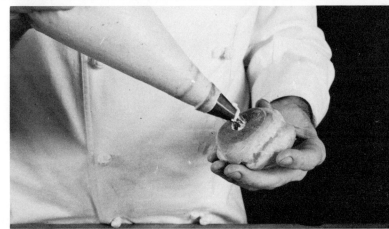

6. Make a caramel using 1 cup sugar mixed with ¾ cup corn syrup. Let the caramel cool off for at least 5 minutes so it thickens. Place the saucepan containing the caramel in a pot of hot water to keep it at the right consistency. Holding the filled *choux* by the bottom, dip the top into the caramel. Be careful not to burn your fingers. Lift up and

7. let the excess drip on the cream puff border. Quickly set the *choux*, glazed side up, on the drips of caramel so that the *choux* is anchored on the border.

8. Repeat all around, arranging the *choux* in an orderly fashion, fastening them with the caramel drips.

9. Scoop some of the remaining *crème pâtissière* into the middle. Place some in a pastry bag with a fluted tube and decorate the top.

10. Place the last puff in the middle of the cake. You may decorate with angel hair, technique 170. Place in a cool, not cold, dry place until serving time.

This cake serves 10 to 12.

152. Pâte à Brioche *(Brioche Dough)*

BRIOCHES ARE THE SMALL, moist and buttery cakes eaten for breakfast throughout France. In parts of the country, like Lyon, this yeast-risen dough is used to encase sausage, goose liver, game and other pâtés. The brioche dough is not as difficult to make as *pâte feuilletée*. It is easiest to use a large mixer rather than beating by hand, but both methods give excellent results. The dough should be very satiny and elastic. A *brioche mousseline,* which is especially good, is a brioche dough loaded with butter. This recipe will make from 18 to 20 small brioches.

½ teaspoon sugar
¼ cup lukewarm water
1 (¼-ounce) package dry yeast, or ½ cake fresh
    yeast
2¼ cups all-purpose flour
4 large eggs
2 sticks (½ pound) sweet butter, at room
    temperature and cut into ½-inch pieces
½ teaspoon salt

In a bowl, mix the sugar, water and yeast until smooth. Set the mixture aside and let it "work" for 5 minutes (the yeast will make it foam or bubble). Place the remaining ingredients in the bowl of an electric mixer. Using the flat beater, start mixing on low, adding the yeast mixture slowly. When all the ingredients hold together, scrape the sides and bottom picking up any loose pieces. Place on medium speed and beat for 8 minutes. Scrape the sides and bottom twice more during the process so the ingredients are well blended. The dough should be elastic, velvety and hold into a lump around the beater. It should separate easily from the beater if pulled.

1. If you are making the dough by hand instead of machine, work it for at least 10 minutes. Grab the dough on both sides,

2. lift it from the table and

3. flip it over, slapping it on the table.

4. It should come up in one lump from an unfloured table. Place the dough in a bowl, set in a draftless, lukewarm place, cover with a towel and let rise until it has doubled in bulk (about 1½ to 2 hours).

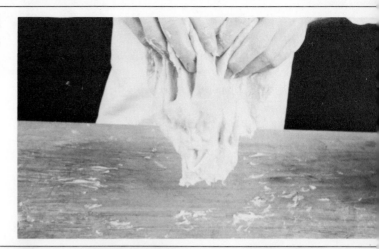

5. Break the dough down by pushing and lifting with your fingers. If you are not going to use the dough immediately, wrap it in a towel and plastic wrap and place it in the refrigerator (the cool meat drawer) to prevent the dough from developing too much. It can be made a day ahead.

6. To make small brioches, generously butter individual brioche molds. Divide the dough into balls the size of a golf ball (about 2½ to 3 ounces) and roll on the table in a circular motion to give body to the brioche.

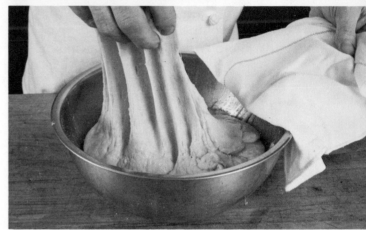

7. With the side of your hand, "saw" a small piece of the brioche in a back and forward motion.

8. This forms a small lump which should remain attached to the body of the brioche.

9. Lift the brioche by the "head" and place in the buttered mold.

10. Push the head down into the brioche.

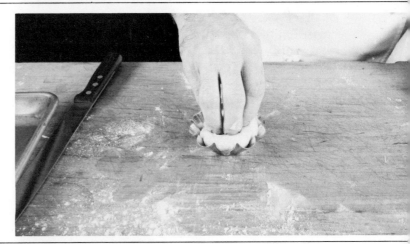

11. Brush with an egg wash (1 whole egg, beaten).

12. A large brioche (*brioche parisienne*) is done similarly, but slits are cut all around to give texture to the finished brioche.

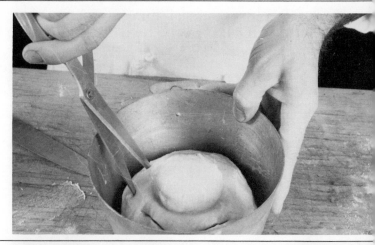

13. Let the brioches rise in a warm place for 1½ to 2 hours.

14. Bake the small brioches in a 400-degree preheated oven for approximately 25 minutes, and the large ones for approximately 45 minutes. They should be golden. Keep in a plastic bag to avoid drying out.

153. Feuilletage Classique *(Classic Puff Paste)*

THE PUFF PASTE, or *feuilletage*, is the hardest dough to make, and it has its pitfalls even for professionals. The dough will be easier to make and will rise fantastically if you use shortening, which melts at a higher temperature than butter. However, nothing can replace the taste and fragrance of butter. The difference is evident, even though some restaurants are naïve enough to believe they are fooling their customers.

The puff paste is made with flour and butter in equal proportions. The flour is bound with a liquid, usually water, into an elastic and shiny dough (*détrempe*). The butter is encased in the dough, and both elements are rolled together. By folding, rolling and folding the dough, a multilayered effect is achieved, with layers of elastic dough and layers of butter. The butter melts during cooking and develops steam which tries to escape, "pushing" the layers up into the "thousand-leaf" effect. American all-purpose flour is high in gluten (the protein part of the flour that makes the dough elastic). You can use about one-fifth cake flour with the regular all-purpose flour to "tone down" the resilience of the dough, or you may use pastry flour which is more akin to the French flour.

The butter and the basic dough should be the same temperature and consistency. If the butter is too cold, it will break and crumble and push through the dough during the rolling. If it is too soft, it will be "squished" and will run between the layers. Beware of hot and humid days; the ingredients are limp and have a tendency to blend together.

Puff paste tends to darken and become quite elastic when stored in the refrigerator. However, well wrapped, it freezes beautifully. You cannot make a recipe for less than 1 pound of flour, or it will not be uniform. It is preferable to weigh the flour because it is not accurate with cup measurement. Three cups of tightly packed flour equals 1 pound. On the other hand, 1 pound of sifted flour may fill up 4½ cups.

Cream can be used instead of water in the basic dough, making an extremely light, tender and delicate pastry. Use the best sweet butter available.

2 *pounds sweet butter*
2 *pounds flour (see above) and 1 cup for rolling*
2 *cups water or 2½ cups heavy cream*
2 *teaspoons salt*

1. Place the butter on the work table, flatten with the roller and sprinkle ¾ cup flour from the preweighed 2 pounds. Using a pastry scraper and your hands, work the mixture together until well mixed and smooth.

2. Form a square "cake" with the mixture and refrigerate.

3. Place the flour in the mixing bowl (if you use an electric mixer) or on the table. Make a well in the center and add the water (or cream) and the salt. Mix carefully into a homogenous and shiny dough. Do not overwork.

4. Make a crisscross cut on top of the dough and roll or spread out with your hands the four sections of the dough, making a large four-leafed clover.

5. Place the butter on top of the dough.

6. Bring the edges back on top of the butter.

7. Seal the leaves to enclose the butter tightly inside.

8. Roll the dough into a thick rectangle. Roll gently, without pressing down too much.

9. Place in the refrigerator for a good 30 minutes. This will give the dough and butter a chance to get to the same temperature, insuring uniform rolling.

10. Roll the dough gently into a long rectangle, about ⅜ inch thick. Roll the dough enough to thin it and spread it out but do not roll it back and forth relentlessly or you will make the dough too resilient. Roll from the center out. Be careful in this first rolling as the dough is at its most delicate and can easily open letting butter squish through. Fold the dough back on itself to a point about two-thirds up the rectangle.

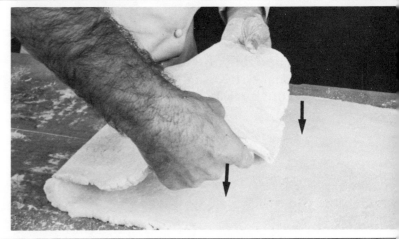

11. Roll the folded part lightly to equalize it.

12. Holding your rolling pin at the edge of the folded dough, strike the single layer with the pin to make a depression in the dough. This will make a "hinge."

13. Fold the single layer back onto the dough. You now have a three-layered package. This is known as one "turn." Place on a large cookie sheet, cover with a towel and refrigerate for 15 to 20 minutes.

14. Place the folded dough, narrow (open) side facing you, on the floured board. Roll the dough uniformly, pushing and rolling at the same time. Remember that excess rolling will make the dough contract and develop too much elasticity.

15. During the rolling, it is important that the board is properly floured so that the dough can slide and spread uniformly. If the dough sticks at any point, pushing with the roller will smear and break the layers, making the butter bleed during cooking.

16. Be sure to dust the dry flour off the dough before folding. Dry flour "imprisoned" between layers will result in a dry and tough pastry. If the dough is not too elastic, you may give two turns consecutively. Otherwise, let the dough "rest" for 15 to 20 minutes before the next turn.

17. Imprint the number of turns into the dough with your fingertips so that you don't forget. The classic puff paste gets six turns. However, if the dough becomes too elastic and hard to work, stop after five turns. Cover and refrigerate before using. When you need a piece of the dough, cut the dough "widthwise." Whatever trimmings you have left, gather in a ball and refrigerate or freeze. The trimmings, called *demi-feuilletage* (half puff paste), are quite adequate for tarts, *fleurons,* sausage or pâté in crust and the like.

154. Feuilletage Rapide *(Fast Puff Paste)*

WHEN IN A HURRY, you can prepare a fast puff paste in one hour at the most, and use it right away. It is quite satisfactory in most instances, except for vol-au-vent (patty shells). The dough does not develop quite as uniformly and is not as flaky as the classic dough described in the preceding technique, but the differences are small and apparent only when the doughs are compared side by side. The dough can be made with regular all-purpose flour, as well as with "instant blending" flour.

4 sticks (1 pound) sweet butter, very cold
1 pound flour (all-purpose or instant blending)
  plus ¾ cup for rolling
1 teaspoon salt
1 cup cold water

1. Dice the cold butter into ⅜-inch cubes. Arrange a well in the flour and place the butter and salt in the center.

2. Using a pastry scraper, "cut" the butter into the flour.

3. Add the water and combine all ingredients into a mass rapidly. Do not knead the dough.

4. At this point, the dough will look very lumpy (the butter is still in pieces), but it should hold together. Flour the working table generously. (This dough requires more flour during the rolling than a conventional dough.) Roll the dough into a ⅜-inch-thick rectangle.

5. Brush the flour from the surface and fold one end in to the center of the rectangle.

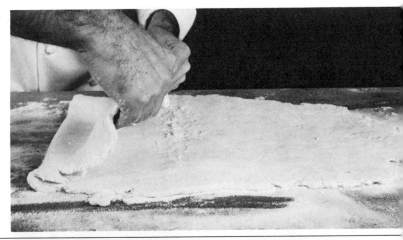

6. Fold the other end in. Both ends should meet in the center. Brush again to remove excess flour.

7. Fold the dough in half.

8. You now have one double turn that gives you 4 layers of dough. Give two more double turns—a total of 3 altogether. This is the equivalent of 4 to 5 single turns and is enough for a fast puff paste. If the dough does not become too elastic, the 3 turns can be given consecutively. Handle and store as you would classic puff paste.

155. Vol-au-Vent à l'Ancienne

(Large Patty Shell)

VOL-AU-VENT ARE CUSTOMARILY FILLED with sweetbreads, chicken, quenelles and mushrooms, lobster meat and the like, usually bound with a sauce. They are one of the most delicate pastries to make and must be made with perfect classic puff paste dough. The shell should be cut from the middle of the dough because the middle develops more uniformly than the edges. Begin by making the classic puff paste dough, technique 153. One pound of flour will make enough dough for 2 vol-au-vent. A filled vol-au-vent serves 8.

1. Roll the dough ⅜ inch thick. Using a round object as a guide (in this case, a cake pan), cut two disks 8 inches in diameter. Be sure to cut the dough with a sharp knife. If the dough is cut with a dull blade, the layers will squish together and will not rise properly.

2. Using a smaller round object, cut a disk from one of the wheels to make a ring. The ring should be at least 1¼ inches wide. Reserve the center of the ring for half puff paste *(demi-feuilletage)*.

3. Place the solid wheel on a cookie sheet lined with parchment paper. Brush the surface with an egg wash (1 whole egg, beaten).

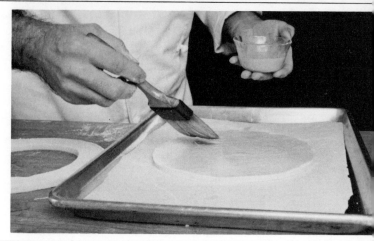

4. Place the ring of dough carefully on top and press all around so that it adheres well to the bottom layer. The dough is now ¾-inch thick at the edge.

5. Brush the ring with the egg wash. It is important that the wash does not run down the sides of the shell. If this happens, the layers will be "glued" together by the wash and will have difficulty rising.

6. Using the dull side of the blade, mark the edge all around.

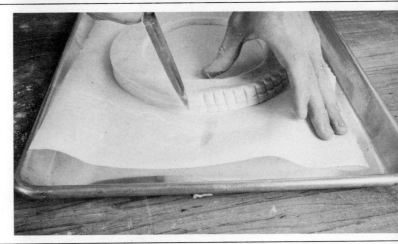

7. Cut about ⅛-inch deep into the bottom layer following the curve of the ring. This incision creates the "lid." Carve a trellis in the center of the lid. Cool the vol-au-vent for 1 hour. Bake in a 425-degree preheated oven for 40 to 45 minutes. If, after the first 10 minutes of baking, the shell is rising unevenly, cut the high side at the lid incision to let the steam escape and allow the other side to level off. When baked, cut off and remove the lid. Discard some of the mushy dough from the inside, fill, cover with the lid and serve.

156. Vol-au-Vent à la Moderne

(Large Patty Shell)

T HIS IS AN EASIER and more dramatic way of making a large patty shell, and it doesn't require a dough as perfect as the one just described. Fast puff paste as well as puff paste trimmings (half puff paste or *demi-feuilletage*) are adequate, and it can also be done with a *pâte brisée*, although it is not as spectacular as when made with puff paste. Make the puff paste, either the classic or the fast, technique 153 or 154.

1. Roll the dough approximately ³⁄₁₆ inch thick. Using a round object as a guide, cut out an 8-inch circle. Place the circle on a wet, or parchment-lined cookie sheet. Place a ball of aluminum foil, about 3½ inches in diameter, in the middle of the circle. Brush the dough all around the ball with water.

2. Roll another sheet of puff paste and place on top of the foil. Push all around to have the top layer adhere well to the bottom. Be sure that the dough is stretched uniformly around the foil ball.

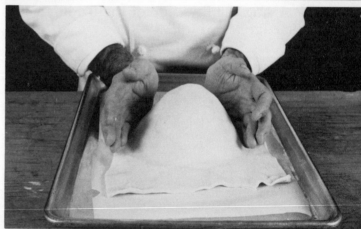

3. Trim the top layer of dough so it is even with the bottom. You can do this freehand or use an 8-inch flan ring as a guide. Cut with a sharp knife (see technique 155, step 1).

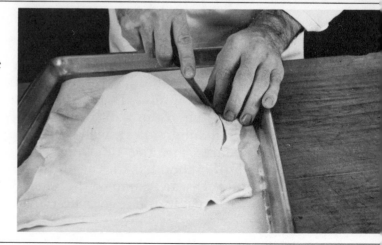

4. Brush the dough with an egg wash (1 whole egg, beaten). Do not let the wash run on the edges. Cut out little triangles from the edges.

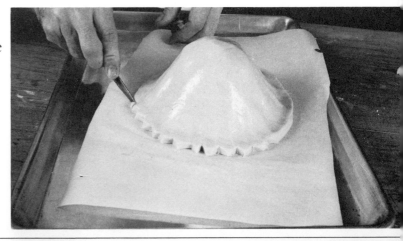

5. Cut long, thin strips of dough and decorate the shell to your fancy.

6. Cut lozenges from the dough to simulate leaves and finish decorating the shell. Brush again with egg wash.

7. Make a hole at the top to let the steam escape during baking. Let the shell "relax" in a cool place for 1 hour. Bake in a 425-degree preheated oven for 30 to 35 minutes.

8. Let the shell cool for 10 to 15 minutes and cut the "lid" off, following the outline of the decoration.

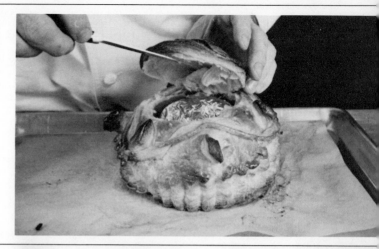

9. Being careful not to damage the shell, slide your thumb and index finger on both sides of the aluminum foil and squeeze to reduce the size of the ball.

10. Pull the foil out. The shell is now ready to be garnished.

157. Bouchées *(Individual Patty Shells)*

MAKE THE CLASSIC PUFF PASTE DOUGH, technique 153. For individual patty shells, as well as for *fleurons*, cheese straws and other puff paste garnishes described in the following technique, it is preferable to roll the dough in long sheets (about ³⁄₁₆ inch thick) the day before, allowing it to "relax" overnight in the refrigerator. This prevents the dough from shrinking when it is cut.

1. Cut rounds about 3 inches in diameter with a plain or fluted edge cutter. Be sure that the cutter is sharp. If the edge is dull, the layers will get squeezed together and will not rise properly.

2. Using a smaller cutter, cut a piece from the center of half of the rounds. The outside rings are used to form the walls of the patty shells. They should be ½ inch wide.

3. Rub your finger underneath the cutting edge of the cutter to be sure that the outside ring of the dough is "free."

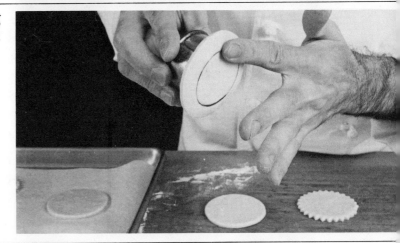

4. Place the rounds on a cookie sheet lined with parchment paper. Brush the top with an egg wash (1 whole egg, beaten). Position the ring (still attached to the cutter) over the round and push it into place. Remove the cutter. Reserve the piece of dough inside the cutter for half puff paste (*demi-feuilletage*).

5. Brush the ring with egg wash. Do not let it run down the sides.

6. To prevent the shells from tilting and falling over while baking, place a wire rack on top. The shells should rise five to six times their original thickness. Hence, the wire rack should not be more than 2 inches high at the most. If the shells rise crookedly, the high side will be stopped when it touches the rack, and the other side will equalize itself. Bake in a 425-degree preheated oven for 20 to 25 minutes. Lift the lid up and fill to your liking. Place the lid back on top of the food before serving.

158. Paillettes, Diablotins, Fleurons
(Puff Paste Cheese Straws and Crescents)

P AILLETTES AND DIABLOTINS are cheese straws; the first are flat strips and the other twisted. You can serve them with consommé for a very elegant first course, or with cheese or drinks. *Fleurons* (crescents) are classically used to decorate whole fish or fish fillets served with a sauce and glazed, such as sole *Bercy*. Both can be made with classic puff paste, fast puff paste or the trimmings of either *(demi-feuilletage)*, techniques 153 and 154.

1. For the cheese straws, roll the dough ⅛ inch thick. If you have the time, it is preferable to roll it out the day before and let it "relax" in the refrigerator overnight. This will reduce shrinkage and irregular puffing. Brush the surface of the dough with an egg wash (1 whole egg, beaten). Mix together ⅔ cup freshly grated Parmesan cheese and ¼ cup good paprika. Sprinkle the mixture on top and rub so that the whole surface is covered.

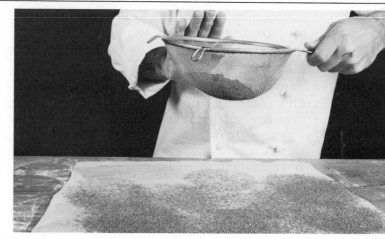

2. Turn the dough upside down and coat the other side with the mixture.

3. Both sides of the dough are now covered with the cheese and paprika mixture. Fold in half.

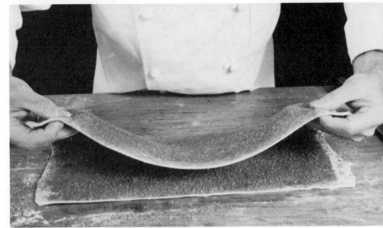

4. Cut strips about ⅜ inch wide.

5. Unfold strips. To make twisted cheese straws, place one hand at each end of the strip. In a swift movement, roll the strip forward with one hand and, at the same time, roll backward with the other. The strip will be twisted into a corkscrew-like spiral.

6. Place the strips, whether they are twisted or flat, on a wet or parchment-lined cookie sheet. To prevent the strips from shrinking during baking, smear the ends onto the cookie sheet so they stick and hold the dough stretched.

7. Bake in a 425-degree preheated oven for 7 to 8 minutes, or until nicely browned and crisp. Trim the ends off and cut into 4-inch sticks. See color plate 13.

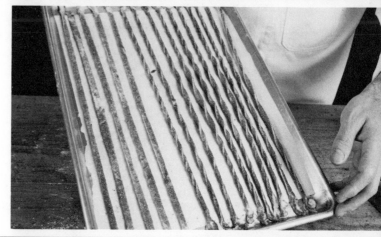

8. To make *fleurons*, roll the dough about ³/₁₆ inch thick and brush with an egg wash. Cut the half-moon crescents with a cookie cutter. Move forward and cut only with the front half of the cookie cutter. Let the *fleurons* "relax" for 20 minutes at least, then bake in a 425-degree preheated oven for 9 to 10 minutes.

159. Allumettes aux Anchois

(Anchovy Sticks)

ANCHOVIES WRAPPED IN PUFF PASTE make attractive finger food for buffets or to serve as an hors d'oeuvre with drinks. They are customarily shaped into sticks (Method 1), but can also be made to look like little fish (Method 2). Make the puff paste, either the classic or fast, techniques 153 and 154, or use leftover trimmings of either *(demi-feuilletage)*. It is preferable to roll the dough the day before, allowing it to "relax" overnight in the refrigerator before using.

METHOD 1

1. Roll the dough into 4-inch-wide strips, about ⅛ inch thick. Brush with an egg wash (1 whole egg, beaten).

2. Arrange anchovy fillets (preserved in olive oil) about 2 inches apart on a sheet of dough. Sprinkle the anchovies with chopped hard-boiled egg and parsley (optional). Place another layer of dough on top.

3. Press the side of your hand between each anchovy so that the top layer of dough adheres well to the bottom.

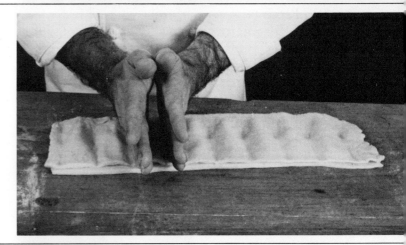

4. Brush again with egg wash and cut into individual pieces.

5. Decorate the top of each piece with the point of a knife. Let "relax" for at least 1 hour before baking. Bake in a 425-degree preheated oven for 20 to 25 minutes.

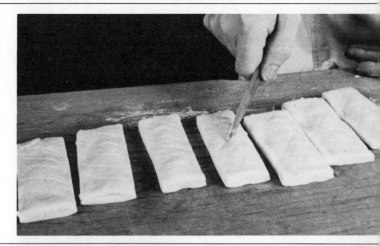

METHOD 2

1. Roll and cut the dough into 2½-inch-wide strips. Brush with an egg wash.

2. Place two rows of anchovies side by side, slightly staggered. Cover with a top layer of dough and press so the layers adhere. Brush again with egg wash.

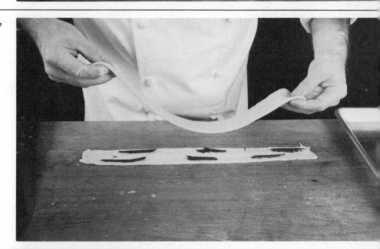

3. Separate the rows of anchovies, cutting in a sinuous pattern to simulate the shape of a fish. Separate into individual pieces.

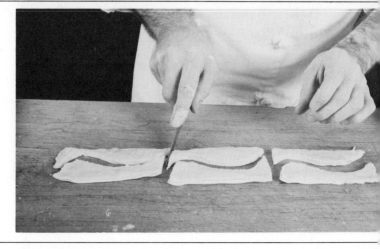

4. Trim the "tail" of the fish.

5. With the point of a knife, "draw" the scales, gills and eyes of a fish. Let the dough "relax" for a good hour.

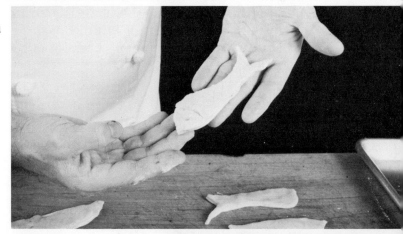

6. Bake in a 425-degree preheated oven for 22 to 25 minutes.

160. Bandes pour Tartes aux Fruits
(Fruit Tart Strips)

THIS RECTANGULAR FRUIT TART is excellent for large gatherings because it is easy to serve. You just carve across at the end of each piece of fruit. The tart is made from a base of dough bordered with strips. The dough is baked, spread with a layer of *crème pâtissière* and then topped with poached fruit. The pastry can be made from fast puff paste or puff paste trimmings (*demi-feuilletage*), technique 154. Sometimes the base is made from *pâte brisée* or *pâte sucrée* and only the border is puff paste.

1. Roll the dough ¼ inch thick. Cut in a strip the length of your cookie sheet and about 5 inches wide. Cut two strips about ½ inch wide for the border. Wet about 1 inch on each side of the base and position the strips in place, pressing to make sure they adhere.

2. Using the dull side of the blade, decorate the edges of the tart with a knife. Brush the border with an egg wash (1 whole egg, beaten).

3. Prick the center with a fork (you don't want the dough to develop too much in the center). Let the dough "relax" for at least 30 minutes. Bake in a 425-degree preheated oven for 20 minutes. It should be well browned. In the photograph on the right, *pâte sucrée* has been used for the base. It is the hardest of the doughs, the most compact and will resist becoming soggy the longest.

4. Place a ¼- to ½-inch layer of *crème pâtissière*, technique 125, on the bottom and arrange poached apricot or peach halves on top. (Be sure the fruits are well drained to prevent the cream from thinning down.) You may use any kind of berries also.

5. Brush the fruits with an apricot glaze (see technique 145, step 11), and sprinkle confectioners' sugar on the border.

161. Tarte Carrée *(Square Fruit Tart)*

MAKE SOME PUFF PASTE, either classic or fast, techniques 153 and 154, or use leftover puff paste *(demi-feuilletage)*. If you can spare the time, roll the dough the day before and let it "relax" in the refrigerator overnight to avoid shrinkage and irregular puffing.

1. Roll the dough ⅛ inch thick. Let it "relax" for at least 1 hour.

2. Fold the dough in half diagonally and trim it to have a folded square. You now have a right-angle triangle.

3. Cut a border on both square sides of the triangle, about ¾ inch wide.

4. Be sure that the borders are still attached in the right-angle corner.

5. Unfold the dough and wet the edges with water.

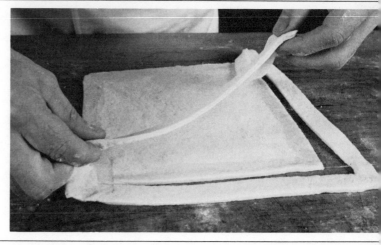

6. Bring half the border over and place on the wet edge of the dough.

7. Then bring over the other half. Press to make the border adhere.

8. Trim the corners where the dough overlaps.

9. Prick the center with a fork. Bake in a 425-degree preheated oven for 20 to 25 minutes. If the dough still develops in the center during baking, just press it down with a fork.

10. Make a caramel with ½ cup sugar and ¼ cup water and pour inside the shell, covering the whole bottom with a thin layer. The caramel gives crunchiness to the tart and keeps the cream from making the dough soggy.

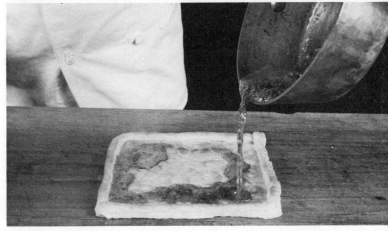

11. Cover with *crème pâtissière,* technique 125.

12. Fill with orange sections, technique 15, banana slices, berries or the like. Glaze the top with an apricot, raspberry or strawberry glaze (see technique 145, step 11).

162. Palmiers *(Palm Cookies)*

1. Prepare the puff paste, technique 153 or 154. Sprinkle the board and dough generously with sugar. Roll the dough in the sugar instead of flour. Roll to about ⅛ inch thick.

2. Do not brush the surface sugar off. Fold both ends of the dough so that they meet in the middle.

3. Roll the pin lightly on top to make it flat.

4. Fold again so that the ends meet again in the middle. Roll lightly with the pin.

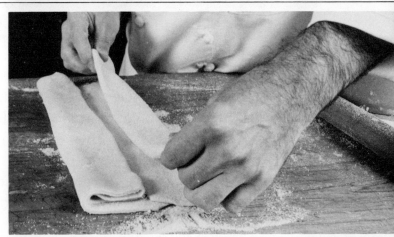

5. Fold both sides together to make a simple loaf. Let the dough "relax" in the refrigerator for at least 1 hour.

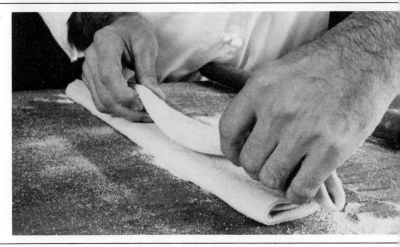

6. Slice into cookies about ⅜ inch thick.

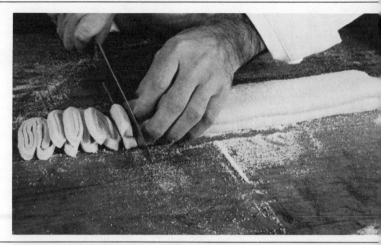

7. Arrange the cookies flat on a cookie sheet. Turn the edges outward slightly to give them a nicer shape. Bake in a 425-degree preheated oven for approximately 25 minutes. After 15 to 20 minutes, turn the cookies on the other side so that both sides are uniformly glazed with the sugar.

163. Charlotte de Pommes
(Apple Charlotte)

T HERE ARE TWO KINDS of desserts called charlotte. The first and the oldest is the hot or lukewarm apple charlotte created by an unsung chef during the reign of George III and named in honor of his Queen. The other charlotte, made with cream and lined with ladyfingers or *génoise* cake, is served cold and was created by Carême. The apple charlotte is the subject of this technique, and the cream-filled charlotte is described in the next.

8 *to* 10 *apples, depending on size*
¾ *stick (6 tablespoons) sweet butter*
Grated rind of 1 lemon
Juice of 1 lemon
2 *to* 3 *tablespoons sugar (depending on sweetness of apples)*
3 *tablespoons apricot jam*
10 *to* 12 *slices firm white bread*

Pare and core the apples and cut into ¼-inch slices. Use a variety of apples. Pick apples that will hold their shape during cooking (Calville, Rennet, Granny Smith or the all-purpose green or Golden Delicious). Melt 4 tablespoons butter in a large skillet. Add the apple slices and sauté until all the juices are released and they start to boil. Add the lemon rind, juice and sugar. Cook on medium heat until all of the liquid has evaporated. Take off the heat and stir in the apricot jam. It is important that the apple mixture be thick and tight; otherwise, the charlotte will collapse when it is unmolded. Set aside. Butter a 1-quart charlotte mold generously with the remaining 2 tablespoons butter.

1. Cut 4 of the bread slices in half diagonally and trim into triangles.

2. Arrange the triangles tightly together in the bottom of the mold.

3. Trim the crusts off the remaining bread slices and cut into halves lengthwise. Arrange overlapping around the side of the mold.

4. Fill the prepared mold with the apple mixture.

5. Pack it as much as you can in the center because the charlotte sinks as it cools. Cover with a round piece of wax paper, technique 30. Bake in a 400-degree preheated oven for approximately 35 minutes.

6. Remove from oven. Press down with a spoon to pack the apple mixture tightly. Trim the pieces of bread which are exposed above the apple mixture and place on top. Cover with wax paper and return to the oven for 15 to 20 minutes. Let cool until lukewarm.

7. Run a knife around the charlotte.

8. Place a platter on top of the charlotte, then turn upside down.

9. Remove the mold. Serve with an apricot sauce.

This charlotte serves 8 to 10.

APRICOT SAUCE

1 *cup thick apricot jam*
1 *tablespoon sugar*
3 *tablespoons water*
3 *tablespoons Armagnac, cognac or kirsch*

Place jam, sugar and water in a saucepan. Bring to a boil and boil for 2 to 3 minutes. Strain through a fine sieve. Cool, stirring occasionally. When lukewarm, add the alcohol. Pour half the mixture on top of the charlotte. Serve lukewarm with the remaining sauce on the side.

164. Charlotte au Chocolat
(Chocolate Charlotte)

Ladyfingers
4 *egg yolks*
½ *cup confectioners' sugar*
1 *tablespoon dark rum plus ¼ cup dark rum or cognac*
8 *ounces chocolate (4 ounces sweet, 4 ounces bitter)*
2 *sticks (½ pound) sweet butter, softened*
1 *tablespoon warm water (optional)*

8 *egg whites*
Whipped cream
Candied violets
Crème anglaise, *technique 124 (optional)*

1. Prepare both long and tear-shaped lady-fingers, technique 133. Trim the tear-shaped ones slightly.

2. Place a round piece of wax paper in the bottom of a 1-quart charlotte mold. Arrange the tear-shaped ladyfingers upside down in a petal effect on the bottom of the mold.

3. Place a fringed strip of wax paper around the inside of the mold. Trim one end of the long ladyfingers and the sides so that they are slightly narrower on one end. Arrange the "fingers," cut end down, with the rounded side touching the wax-paper-lined mold.

4. Be sure they fit tightly, one against the other.

5. Combine the egg yolks, sugar and 1 tablespoon rum in a bowl. Beat with a whisk for 4 to 5 minutes until nice and fluffy. Melt the chocolate (see technique 169). Combine the chocolate and softened butter and whip for 1 minute. Combine with the egg yolk mixture. If it curdles, add 1 tablespoon warm water and whisk until it smooths out. Keep the mixture lukewarm.

6. Whip the egg whites until stiff. Whisk about one-third of the whites with the chocolate mixture. Fold in remaining whites, technique 42. The mixture will lose volume. Try to go as fast as you can to prevent the whites from getting too grainy.

7. Fill the mold alternating the chocolate mixture with a layer of ladyfinger trimmings sprinkled with rum or cognac until all ingredients have been used. End with the chocolate mixture.

8. With a pair of scissors, trim the ladyfingers at the level of the filling and place on the chocolate to cover. Cover and refrigerate for at least 2 hours.

9. Unmold and remove the wax paper. Decorate with whipped cream and candied violets, and serve with *crème anglaise*.

This charlotte serves 8 to 10.

165. Charlotte Royale *(Bavarian Kirsch Cake)*

THIS IS A SOMEWHAT UNCONVENTIONAL charlotte. It is made with a *gènoise*-type *biscuit* colored with different jams and filled with kirsch-flavored fruits and custard. The cake, technique 136, should be made first and be ready to receive the filling.

1. Combine ⅓ cup mixed candied fruits with ¼ cup good kirsch and set aside. This mixture will keep almost indefinitely in the refrigerator. In fact, it is better if it is made a few days ahead. Prepare the *biscuit roulé* and let it cool for 30 minutes, covered. Do not roll. Cut into halves. (Leave the bottom sheet of wax paper in place.)

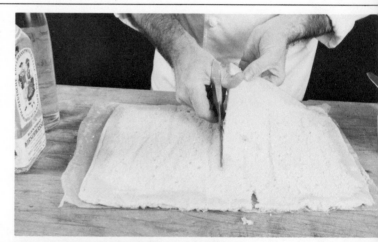

2. Place 1½ (10-ounce) jars good apricot jam into a saucepan. Add 2 tablespoons water and bring to a boil. Boil for 1 minute until the mixture is loose. Strain through a fine sieve into a bowl. Cover with plastic wrap. When cold, add 2 tablespoons good kirsch. The mixture should be thick but spreadable. Spread on one half of the *biscuit*.

3. Take ½ pint fresh raspberries, or 1 (10-ounce) package frozen raspberries, and combine with 1 (10-ounce) jar good raspberry preserves. Blend in a food processor or blender, place in a saucepan, bring to a boil and reduce by half. Strain the mixture through a fine sieve into a bowl. Cover with plastic wrap. When cold, add 2 tablespoons good raspberry liqueur like *framboise blanche*. Spread the raspberry mixture on the other half of the *biscuit*.

4. Cut each piece into halves. A pair of scissors is easier to use than a knife. Cut right through the paper.

5. Place a piece of wax paper on top of one of the coated pieces. Turn the coated cake, jam side down, on your hand and peel the back paper. Place the piece, uncoated side down, on top of a piece coated with the other flavored jam. Repeat, stacking the 4 pieces, alternating layers of raspberry and apricot jam. Remove the paper as you go along. The bottom and top layers are uncoated.

6. Cut the stacked layers into ½-inch slices. Trim one end of the slices into a point.

7. Line a 5- to 6-cup bowl with the strips so they meet in the center.

8. Place smaller "wedges" snugly between the first strips.

9. Make the filling (recipe below) and place one-third of the filling in the bottom of the lined bowl. Sprinkle with one-third of the kirsch and fruit mixture.

10. Cover with more filling and then more fruit mixture.

11. Cover the filling with leftover pieces of cake. Place a piece of wax paper or plastic wrap on the top and refrigerate for at least 3 to 4 hours before unmolding. Decorate with whipped cream, or serve plain or with a *crème anglaise*.

This charlotte serves 12.

THE FILLING

1 *cup milk*
2 *egg yolks*
⅓ *cup sugar*
1 *envelope unflavored gelatin mixed with the sugar*
½ *teaspoon vanilla*
1 *large ice cube*

Prepare a *crème anglaise* using the above ingredients and following the steps in technique 124. Use the ice cube instead of cold milk to stop the cooking. Stir once in a while until room temperature. Do not let the mixture set. Meanwhile, whip 1½ cups heavy cream not too stiff. If the cream is over-whipped, the dessert will taste "buttery," instead of tasting of sweet cream. Fold the whipped cream into the *crème anglaise*. If the custard is too "set," whip it with a whisk for a few seconds to smooth it.

166. "Gâteau" de Semoule St. Valentin *(St. Valentine Custard Cake)*

This unusual creation is not a cake in the traditional sense of the word but rather a molded custard served with poached fruit. It is made with farina, though rice or semolina could be used instead. Serve with any fruit in season—pear, peach, apricot or apple—or serve plain, without fruit, like a rice pudding.

8 *medium-sized pears (William, Comice or Bartlett)*
1 *stick vanilla*
Peel of 1 lemon and 1 orange
1½ *cups sugar*
Grated rind of 1 orange, technique 17
5 *egg yolks*
1 *teaspoon vanilla extract*
1½ *envelopes unflavored gelatin*
2 *cups milk*
¼ *cup farina*
2 *cups heavy cream*

3 *tablespoons confectioners' sugar*
Almond or peanut oil to coat mold
1 *(10-ounce) jar apricot jam*
Food coloring
1 *ounce chocolate (½ ounce bitter, ½ ounce semisweet)*
2 *tablespoons lukewarm water*
Pear brandy

1. Peel the pears, leaving the stem attached, and place in a large casserole. Add the vanilla stick, lemon and orange peel, 1 cup sugar and enough cold water to cover the pears. Bring to a boil. Place a piece of paper towel over the casserole, so that the tops of the pears are kept moist and do not discolor. Cover and simmer slowly for 5 minutes if the pears are well-ripened, and up to 35 minutes if they are green and hard. They should be tender to the point of a knife. Let cool slowly in the liquid overnight.

2. Remove the paper.

3. Drain the pears on paper towels.

4. Mix together the grated orange rind, egg yolks, the remaining ½ cup sugar, the vanilla extract and gelatin. Whisk until the mixture forms a ribbon.

5. Bring the milk to a boil and add the farina. Boil, stirring, for 2 minutes.

6. Add the egg yolk mixture and bring to a boil again. Remove from the heat, transfer to a clean bowl and cool, stirring occasionally to avoid a skin forming on top.

7. Mix the heavy cream with the confectioners' sugar. Whip to a soft peak. Do not overwhip or the custard will taste of butter, rather than of sweet cream.

8. When the farina mixture reaches room temperature, fold in the whipped cream, technique 42.

9. Rub a 6-cup mold very lightly with almond or peanut oil. Pour the mixture in, cover with plastic wrap and refrigerate overnight.

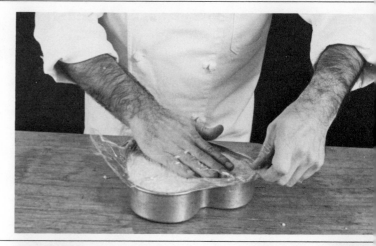

10. Run a knife around the *"gâteau."*

11. Invert on a large platter and cover for a few seconds with a towel wrung in hot water to help the unmolding.

12. Unmold.

13. If the sides or top are a little rough or coarse from the unmolding, smooth out with a spatula or knife.

14. Place 1 tablespoon of the apricot jam in each of 3 cups. Add a couple of drops of red, green and yellow food coloring to have three different colored jams. If you object to food coloring, you may use mint jelly (for green), currant jelly (for red) and apple jelly (for yellow). Prepare 4 small paper cornets, technique 33.

15. Melt the chocolate in a small bowl (see technique 169). Add 1½ teaspoons lukewarm water and mix. It will curdle; add more water (up to 2 tablespoons) a little at a time, and stir well until the mixture is smooth and shiny. Fill a paper cornet with chocolate and cut the tip off. Draw letters, flowers, leaves and the like according to your fancy.

16. Fill the 3 cornets with the different colored jams, and squeeze inside the chocolate outlines.

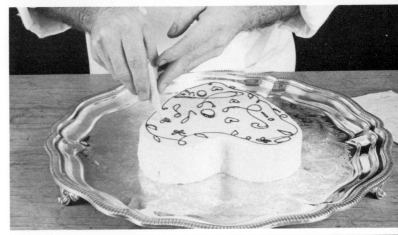

17. Place the pears around and coat with lukewarm apricot glaze (see technique 145, step 11) diluted with pear brandy. Serve with extra apricot glaze.

167. Bananes Flambées *(Flamed Bananas)*

1. Flamed bananas are an inexpensive and delicious dessert. For 6 servings, trim the ends of 6 large ripe (not over-ripe) bananas. With the point of a paring knife, make an incision down one side of each banana.

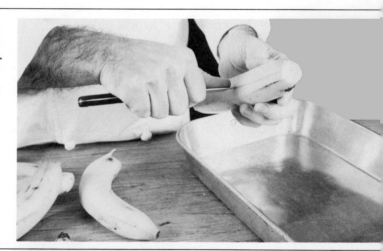

2. Place in a roasting pan or on a cookie sheet and bake in a 400-degree preheated oven for 15 minutes.

3. The skin will turn black and the bananas will become soft to the touch. Keep at room temperature until serving time.

4. At serving time, melt 1 stick (¼ pound) sweet butter and add ⅓ cup sugar, the juice of 1½ limes, the juice of 1 lemon and ¼ cup water. Cook on high heat for about 5 minutes, or until it turns to a nice caramel color. "Unwrap" the bananas into the sauce.

5. Using a spoon and fork, turn the bananas in the sauce. Add ⅓ cup good, dark rum (such as Négrita or Myer's), shake the pan and ignite.

6. Baste the bananas with the sauce until the flames subside.

7. Serve on warm plates, 1 banana per person with sauce.

168. Crêpes Suzettes

Though crêpes are best when they are fresh, they can be refrigerated (stacked and covered) and kept a few days. The basic crêpe can be used both for desserts and entrées. The best-known dessert crêpe is the crêpe suzette, flavored with orange and flamed at serving time with cognac and orange liqueur. You will need a large handsome skillet and a powerful gas or electric burner. This recipe makes 2 dozen crêpes.

THE BATTER

1½ cups all-purpose flour
3 large eggs
1 teaspoon sugar
¾ teaspoon salt
1½ cups milk
⅔ stick sweet butter, melted
½ cup cold water

THE SAUCE

2 sticks (½ pound) sweet butter, softened
8 tablespoons sugar
Grated rind of 2 oranges or 4 tangerines, technique 17
Juice of 1 orange or 2 tangerines
Cognac and Grand Marnier

1. To make the batter, place the flour, eggs, sugar, salt and half of the milk in a bowl. Whisk until the mixture is smooth. By adding just enough liquid to work the dough into a thick batter, you eliminate the possibility of lumps. Add the remaining ingredients and stir well. The consistency should be that of a light syrup.

2. Use a small cast-iron crêpe pan, or a teflon-lined pan, 5 to 6 inches in diameter. Heat your skillet on a medium to high flame. Do not grease the skillet. The melted butter in the batter will suffice to prevent the crêpes from sticking. (The first few may stick until the pan "gets into the mood.") Hold the pan slightly tilted and pour about 3 tablespoons of batter on the high side.

3. Quickly tilt the pan so that the batter has a chance to coat the whole bottom before hardening. Shake the pan to force the batter all over. The thinner the coating, the better the crêpes.

4. Another method is to pour a lot of batter in the hot skillet so that it fills the bottom and

5. then pour the excess batter back into the bowl. This also gives a thin crêpe, but

6. the "lip" has to be trimmed off for each crêpe.

7. Cook the crêpes on medium heat for approximately 50 seconds. Then bang the skillet a few times on a potholder or a folded towel to release the crêpe.

8. Flip the crêpe over or turn it with a spatula and cook approximately 30 seconds on the other side. You will notice that the side which was browned first is nicer than the other. When stacking them, place the nicer side underneath so that it shows on the outside after the crêpe is folded.

9. To make the sauce, place the butter, sugar, grated rind and juice in a food processor or blender. Blend until smooth. Transfer to a bowl.

10. At serving time, melt 4 to 6 tablespoons of the sauce in the skillet (about 1 tablespoon per crêpe).

11. When sizzling hot, place 4 to 6 crêpes flat in the sauce. Using a fork and a spoon, turn the crêpes in the sauce. When coated, fold each one into fourths (the nice side showing) and arrange in the skillet as you go along.

12. Pour 1½ to 2 tablespoons of both cognac and Grand Marnier on top of the crêpes.

13. Ignite with a match and, keeping your head back, stir the crêpes in the flaming sauce.

14. Serve the crêpes on warm plates, 2 or 3 per person, with some sauce. Repeat to make all the crêpes in several batches. Add more cognac and Grand Marnier to each batch.

169. Cigarettes en Chocolat
(Chocolate Cigarettes)

CHOCOLATE IS VERY TRICKY to work with. Bitter chocolate curdles easily when combined with another ingredient; sweet chocolate (or semisweet) is often too light and too sweet. I usually use baking chocolate in 1-ounce squares and mix half bitter and half sweet or semisweet. The proportions may be varied to suit your own taste.

Take your time when you melt chocolate. Chocolate burns easily, stiffening and becoming granular and bitter when burned. The best method, I believe, is to place the chocolate in a glass or stainless-steel container and leave it overnight in a regular oven with the pilot on. Stir to get it smooth. You may also place the container of chocolate in a pot of boiling water. The water should be as high as the chocolate. Cover and let melt for 10 to 15 minutes. Then stir until smooth.

Chocolate cigarettes, as well as chocolate strips and flowers, are often used in decoration. They require a bit of practice to make, but the ingredients can be reused as many times as necessary until the technique is perfected.

1. You need to work on a flat, hard surface such as marble, stainless steel or glass. Pour 6 ounces of melted chocolate on the marble surface.

2. Spread with a long, narrow spatula, going back and forth until the top of the chocolate becomes cloudy. It should be thin, but not too thin, at least ⅛ inch thick.

3. Take a large, strong knife. Holding it on an angle, start cutting into the chocolate, applying pressure down and forward on the blade of the knife. The pressure is strong enough to bend the blade slightly.

4. The chocolate rolls on itself as you move the knife down. The consistency is very important. Chocolate which is too soft will gather in a mush; chocolate which is too hard will flake and crumble under the blade. Scrape it from the marble, melt it again and try until it works. Practice makes perfect.

170. Cheveux d'Ange *(Angel Hair)*

Angel hair is very decorative and though making it is a messy business, it can turn an ordinary dessert into a glorious affair. It is akin to the spun sugar cotton candy is made from. Although it can be made with sugar and water, we use corn syrup instead of the water because it prevents the sugar from crystallizing during and after cooking, making it more "flexible" and easier to use.

1. Combine 1 cup sugar and ¾ cup corn syrup in a saucepan. Mix well and place on medium heat. Do not stir the mixture anymore. After it boils, cook 12 to 14 minutes on medium to low heat until the sugar turns into a very light ivory color (about 335 degrees on a candy thermometer). If there is any crystallized sugar on the sides of the pan, cover the saucepan for 30 seconds to 1 minute during the cooking. The steam produced will melt the sugar crystals.

2. Remove the sugar from the heat and grate approximately 2 teaspoons pure beeswax candle into the saucepan (optional). The pieces will melt right away and mix with the sugar. Angel hair has a tendency to stick together, especially during hot summer days. The wax will coat the sugar threads, making them "dry," smooth and easier to store and use. The pure beeswax is from the honeycomb and is a natural, edible product.

3. Let the syrup cool off a few minutes. You may place the saucepan in a bowl of cold water to accelerate the process. Using 2 forks side by side, lift some of the syrup. It should be thick.

4. Cover the floor with newspaper. Place a wooden spatula on the table so it extends over the edge of the table. Dip both forks into the syrup and wave it over the spatula, high enough and broad enough so that the threads are long, thin and have time to solidify in the air. You may have to use a stepstool to get higher.

5. Slide it away from the wooden spatula and use or store in a tightly covered container.

General Conversions

WEIGHT

American	British	Metric
1 ounce	1 ounce	28.4 grams
1 pound	1 pound	454 grams

VOLUME

American	British	Metric
1 U.S. teaspoon	1 U.K. level teaspoon	5 milliliters
1 U.S. tablespoon (3 teaspoons)	1 U.K. dessertspoon	15 milliliters
1 U.S. cup (16 tablespoons)	⅚ breakfast cup (8 fluid ounces)	236 milliliters (about ¼ liter)
1 U.S. quart (4 cups)	⅚ Imperial quart	1 scant liter
1 U.S. gallon (4 quarts)	⅚ Imperial gallon	3¾ liters

LENGTH

American	British	Metric
1 inch	1 inch	2½ centimeters (25 millimeters)
12 inches (1 foot)	12 inches (1 foot)	30 centimeters

Note: All conversions are approximate. They have been rounded off to the nearest convenient measure.

Oven Temperatures

Farenheit	Centigrade	British Regulo Setting	French Setting
212°F	100°C		1
225°F	107°C	¼	2
250°F	121°C	½	3
275°F	135°C	1	3
300°F	149°C	2	4
325°F	163°C	3	4
350°F	177°C	4	4
375°F	191°C	5	5
400°F	204°C	6	5
425°F	218°C	7	6
450°F	232°C	8	6
475°F	246°C	8	6
500°F	260°C	9	7
525°F	274°C	9	8
550°F	288°C	9	9

Selected Measurements

American (spoons and cups)	British (ounces and pounds)	Metric
BREAD CRUMBS		
1 cup	2 ounces	60 grams
BUTTER		
1 teaspoon	⅙ ounce	5 grams
1 tablespoon	½ ounce	15 grams
½ cup (1 stick)	4 ounces	115 grams
1 cup (2 sticks)	8 ounces	230 grams
2 cups (4 sticks)	1 pound	454 grams
CHEESE (*grated*)		
1 cup	3½ ounces	100 grams
FLOUR (*all-purpose, unsifted*)		
1 teaspoon	⅛ ounce	3 grams
1 tablespoon	⅓ ounce	9 grams
1 cup	4¼ ounces	120 grams
3⅔ cups	1 pound	454 grams
HERBS (*fresh, chopped*)		
1 tablespoon	½ ounce	15 grams
MEATS (*cooked and finely chopped*)		
1 cup	8 ounces	225 grams

NUTS *(chopped)*

1 cup	5½ ounces	155 grams

ONIONS *(raw—chopped, sliced, or minced)*

1 tablespoon	⅓ ounce	9 grams
1 cup	5 ounces	140 grams

PEAS *(fresh)*

1 pound unshelled = 1 cup shelled	1 pound, unshelled	454 grams, unshelled

RICE *(raw)*

1 cup	7½ ounces	215 grams

SPINACH *(fresh, cooked)*

1¼ pounds, raw = 1 cup, cooked (squeezed dry, chopped)	1¼ pounds, raw	550 grams, raw

SUGAR *(regular granulated or superfine granulated)*

1 teaspoon	⅙ ounce	5 grams
1 tablespoon	½ ounce	15 grams
1 cup	6½ ounces	185 grams

confectioners' (powdered, unsifted)

1 teaspoon	⅛ ounce icing sugar	4 grams
1 tablespoon	⅓ ounce icing sugar	9 grams
1 cup	¾ ounces icing sugar	100 grams

TOMATOES *(fresh)*

¾–1 pound, whole = 1 cup, peeled and seeded	¾–1 pound, whole	340 grams

VEGETABLES *(raw—chopped fine, such as carrots and celery)*

1 cup	8 ounces	225 grams

A Note to the User: All conversions are approximate. The weights have been rounded off to the nearest useful measure for the purposes of the recipes in this volume. Weights and measures of specific ingredients may vary with altitude, humidity, variations in method of preparation, etc.

Index